Highbrows, Hillbillies & Hellfire

Highbrows
Hillbillies
& Hellfire

Public Entertainment in Atlanta
1880–1930

⤳ STEVE GOODSON ⤶

THE UNIVERSITY OF GEORGIA PRESS
Athens & London

© 2002 by the University of Georgia Press
Athens, Georgia 30602
All rights reserved
Designed by Walton Harris
Set in 11/14 Bulmer by G&S Typesetters, Inc.
Printed and bound by Maple-Vail

The paper in this book meets the guidelines for
permanence and durability of the Committee on
Production Guidelines for Book Longevity of the
Council on Library Resources.

Printed in the United States of America
02 03 04 05 06 c 5 4 3 2 1

Library of Congress Cataloging-in-Publication Data

Goodson, Steve.
    Highbrows, hillbillies, and hellfire : public entertainment
in Atlanta, 1880–1930 / Steve Goodson.
        p. cm.
    Includes bibliographical references and index.
    ISBN 0-8203-2319-5 (alk. paper)
    1. Performing arts—Georgia—Atlanta—History—20th
century.   2. Performing arts—Georgia—Atlanta—History—
19th century.   3. Amusements—Georgia—Atlanta—History—
20th century.   4. Amusements—Georgia—Atlanta—History—
19th century.   5. Atlanta (Ga.)—Race relations.   I. Title
    PN2277.A8 G66 2002
    791′.09758′231—dc21   2001034725

British Library Cataloging-in-Publication Data available

For Martha

⤙ CONTENTS ⤚

⊰ ACKNOWLEDGMENTS ⊱

This book is the culmination of nine years of work, beginning with its incarnation as my dissertation at Emory University. I welcome this opportunity to express my gratitude to all of those who have helped me along the way.

First I would like to thank the institutions and organizations that provided funding, enabling me to research and complete my dissertation. Thanks to Emory University for a Woodruff Fellowship and a Mellon Southern Studies Fellowship, to the Colonial Dames of the State of Georgia for a one-year dissertation fellowship, and to the Emory University Women's Club for another one-year dissertation fellowship.

Thanks also to the staffs of the Woodruff Library at Emory, the Ingram Library at the State University of West Georgia, and the Atlanta History Center Library and Archives. Thanks to the editors of the journal *Atlanta History* for publishing an earlier version of chapter 3 as "'This Mighty Influence for Good or for Evil': The Movies in Atlanta, 1895–1920."

I would never have made it this far without the instruction, encouragement, and inspiration I received from the faculty of Emory's history department. In particular I would like to thank Jim Roark, Kristin Mann, and Doug Unfug. Above all thanks to the members of my dissertation committee—Dan Carter, Jonathan Prude, and Allen Tullos—for giving my work such close and intelligent readings. My special gratitude extends to my adviser, Dan T. Carter, for the example of his warm and generous spirit and for his continued assistance to me not only during my years at Emory but up to the present day.

My undergraduate professors at Auburn University at Montgomery introduced me to a new world and started me on the path that has led to this book. I wish to express my unending gratitude to them for showing a shy carpenter how worthwhile and fulfilling an academic life can be and for convincing him that he was up to its demands. In particular my thanks go out to Robert Evans, John Fair, Michael Fitzsimmons, Paul Pruitt, David Walker, Pat Hill, and the late Sanford Benis.

Thank you to the many friends who have sustained and encouraged me since I began this project. I especially want to thank Mary Margaret Johnston-Miller, James Miller, Mark Schantz, Nancy Barr, Steven Hornsby, Martha Sledge, Jenny Sartori, John Rodrigue, Tom Chaffin, Theresa Ast, Jacki Stanke, James and Belle Tuten, Diane Mutti, Colleen McMahon, Susan Colgate, Phyllis McClarnand, Lisa Grezon, Phil Block, Dede and Brian Chase, Carol Wade, and Andy Dickens. Special thanks to Ruth Dickens, Jennifer West, and Ernie Freeberg for going beyond the call of friendship to read and critique my dissertation. This book is much the better for their efforts. Thanks as well to my buddies on the St. Margaret's softball team, who have kept me laughing and taught me how to accept frequent defeat with good humor.

I am fortunate to teach in such a warm and supportive department here at the State University of West Georgia. I am grateful to my department chairs—Steve Taylor, Richard Chapman, and John Ferling—for their encouragement and their efforts to provide me with sufficient time over the past five years to complete this project. Thanks to all of my other colleagues as well, especially Elaine Mackinnon, Cita Cook, Ann McCleary, Aran Mackinnon, and Ron Love, for their friendship and support. And thanks to the students who have made teaching such a pleasure here, especially Kim Kelly, Mandy Denney, Laura Smith, Jason Hammett, Charles Crafton, Arden Williams, Suzanne Holland, Kelly Gilstrap Randall, Stephanie Lanier, and Joe Meeler.

Georgina Hickey and David Godshalk served as readers of this manuscript for the University of Georgia Press, and I am deeply indebted to them for their insights and suggestions. They more than anyone helped me turn a dissertation into a publishable book. Thanks also to Press editor Malcolm Call, who has worked diligently to shepherd the manuscript along the long road to publication, and to managing editor Jennifer Comeau and copy editor Jeanée Ledoux for their fine work.

Thank you to my in-laws, Jack and Lyn Glynn, for their continued support over the years. Thanks as well to my sister-in-law Nancy Glynn Blum for her rigorous devotion to e-mail and for the innumerable pats on the back that she has unstintingly doled out over the years.

Thanks to my inimitable brother, Gary, just for being Gary, and to his wife, Kim, and son, Joe, for brightening our trips back home. Above all thanks to my parents, Howard and Gloria Goodson. Neither attended college, but both encouraged me to go as far as I could in terms of education, and I would not have survived graduate school without them. Much of what is good in me is rooted in their example, and for that I am grateful.

My son, Sam, has consistently provided joy amidst the occasional storms of the past nine years. The ideal son—he likes history, good books, sports, joking around, and old music—he has deeply enriched my life and helped to make me a better person.

Finally, my wife, Martha. She has put up with me, largely uncomplainingly, for thirteen years now, and with this project for almost as long. She has been unfailingly encouraging and supportive and for some reason never loses faith in me. She deserves a great deal of the credit for whatever I manage to achieve, and so I devote this book, with love, to her.

Highbrows, Hillbillies & Hellfire

⇥ Introduction ⇤

S outh of the North, yet North of the South, lies the City of a Hundred Hills, peering out from the shadows of the past into the promise of the future."[1] So wrote Atlanta University professor W. E. B. Du Bois in the early years of the twentieth century, as Atlanta's population surged toward one hundred thousand and its leaders worked tirelessly to make their city the foremost metropolis of the New South. Du Bois was not alone in noting the curiously ambivalent position that the "Gate City of the South" occupied in the years between the Civil War and the Great Depression. During this period Atlanta's promoters sought to move their region toward a reconciliation with the North and toward an embrace of the industrial capitalism that had triumphed in 1865. But Atlanta also played a prominent role in the glorification of the "Lost Cause," and white Atlantans ferociously defended southern racial conventions. Thus, whether exalting the Gate City as "the Chicago of the South" or satirizing it as a "vest pocket edition of New York,"[2] commentators recognized that Atlanta represented something new, a Deep South city aspiring to the vitality and swagger of its northern counterparts while clinging tenaciously to old ways and priorities, a city with one eye on the future and the other ever on the past.

Atlanta's divided temper was in part a reflection of the city's varied and continually changing population. New South capitalists shared the streets with textile workers who had fled the collapsing rural economy of the late nineteenth century. Shopkeepers, clerks, peddlers, artisans, and factory hands—all of the typical residents of a growing nineteenth-century city—plied their trades during the week, and many of them filled Atlanta's numerous church pews on Sundays. Freedmen began trekking to the Gate City immediately following emancipation, and blacks continued to seek a better life in Atlanta in the ensuing decades. Some blacks secured employment in the railroad yards or as domestics in the homes of white Atlantans, while many others found little beyond a squalid struggle for existence in the city's slums. At the same time, Atlanta became a mecca of black scholarship and enterprise, providing a haven for a proud class of African American educators and businessmen. From the ostentatious homes along Peachtree Street to the earthy din of Decatur Street, Atlanta was a city of contrasts, between boosterism and insecurity, between racial hatred and racial progress, between evangelical propriety and secular abandon.[3]

Atlanta was an unplanned child of the railroads, and the city's centrality as a commercial crossroads brought near ruin at the hands of William T. Sherman's troops in 1864. The city quickly rebounded, however, and residents ever after likened the Gate City to a phoenix rising from its ashes. Hardly had the war ended before Atlanta, meeting place of five railroads, regained its status as a crucial gateway linking North, South, and West and commenced its speedy climb toward preeminence as the most important city in the Southeast.[4]

Atlanta's rise to prominence began in earnest in the 1880s. This was the decade in which Henry W. Grady transformed the *Atlanta Constitution* into a major American newspaper and earned a correspondingly national reputation for himself as an eloquently persuasive spokesman for the New South Movement. It was during this period as well that Atlanta held the first of its industrial expositions and witnessed the opening of its first textile mill. Attracted by multiplying possibilities for employment or driven by sheer desperation, migrants poured into the city, beginning a population boom that would only accelerate with the years.

The local entertainment business developed in stride with the city, contributing to and reflecting Atlanta's growth, image, and sense of itself. The Gate City's mere existence in a region so overwhelmingly rural helped to lure traveling entertainers to the South, and by the 1880s Atlanta was becoming a southern cultural center. Laurent DeGive's Opera House on Marietta Street served as a linchpin of the southern theatrical circuit and gave Atlantans the opportunity to see many of the leading actors, minstrels, and musicians of the day. The Opera House also hosted Atlanta's earliest classical music festivals, aimed at bringing the prestige associated with highbrow European culture to the city, state, and region.

Atlanta continued its economic and demographic ascent in the 1890s. The keystone of the decade was the Cotton States and International Exposition, held at Piedmont Park in the fall of 1895. The culmination of efforts by Atlanta's leaders to showcase the South's resources and economic potential to prospective northern investors, the exposition attracted upward of a million people to the Gate City. Some of them heard the historic opening-day address by Booker T. Washington, in which the Tuskegee educator proposed his "Atlanta Compromise"—offering black acceptance of segregation in return for economic opportunity—to a region riven by heightening racial animosities. Thousands of editors and reporters from around the world published tens of thousands of articles about the exposition, gaining for Atlanta the publicity that the directors had hoped for and taking the sting out of the fact that the exposition actually ended up losing money.[5]

Commercial culture, meanwhile, sought to keep pace with the Gate City's increasing importance and visibility. The resplendent Grand Opera House opened its doors in 1893, providing a more sumptuous setting for the traveling dramatic companies of the day than had the old Marietta Street theater. In addition, given a boost by the exposition and its crowds, vaudeville, burlesque, and even motion pictures sought a foothold in the Gate City, though with decidedly mixed results. Atlanta was growing, but in many respects its reach still far exceeded its grasp, and entertainment that was catching on in the great cities of the North would need a while longer to take root in this still relatively small town.

The first years of the twentieth century, however, constituted a dramatic turning point for Atlanta, as its population growth rocketed upward and economic development accelerated, providing residents with graphic lessons in both the costs and the benefits of rapid urbanization.[6] Expansion outraced infrastructure; coal smoke frequently choked the city; and simmering racial, sexual, ideological, and economic tensions exploded in a bloody riot in September 1906, when whites driven to hysteria by exaggerated reports of black attacks on white women raged through the streets, indiscriminately beating and killing African Americans who crossed their path.[7]

As Atlanta, for better or worse, became a true city, amusements that had faltered earlier—like vaudeville and, especially, movies—firmly established themselves, while the once-dominant "legitimate" stage (a revealingly biased term that excluded such theatrical forms as vaudeville and burlesque) declined. At the end of the decade, a successful campaign brought New

York's Metropolitan Opera Company to town for the first of what would become annual visits, generating boundless civic pride and a sense of cultural validation for the city's elite.

Such "big-city" achievements, however, could not paper over the fact that Atlanta continued to suffer from acute growing pains. The furor that ended in the sordid 1915 lynching of Leo Frank, a Jewish factory owner from the North accused of murdering a young female employee, revealed the widespread public bewilderment and anger that accompanied profound social and economic change, as did the Ku Klux Klan's fiery rebirth atop Stone Mountain a few months later.[8] Deepening concerns over Atlanta's "cosmopolitan" ways repeatedly touched the city's burgeoning entertainment business, as in battles over censorship and Sunday movies and in criticism of cheaper amusements in general.

The entertainment industry more than weathered these crises; by the 1920s the movies in particular had vanquished all opposition, marking their triumph with motion picture palaces that rose in Atlanta just as in the big northern cities. Meanwhile Atlanta's "commercial-civic elite" persuaded national corporations to establish branch offices in the Gate City; downtown streets became clogged with the traffic that would remain an unremitting headache for the remainder of the century and beyond; and the population neared three hundred thousand as the city finally attained, in 1930, the official "metropolitan" status that many had long coveted for it.[9] Beneath the hubbub, largely unnoticed by the movers and shakers and tireless boosters, black and white working-class migrants brought their musical talents to their new home, making Atlanta a thriving hub of indigenous southern culture.

Many of the challenges that Atlanta faced during this half century of growth also confronted the nation as a whole. Between 1880 and 1930, the United States became more urban than rural for the first time in its history, with immigration and internal population shifts fostering intense racial and ethnic enmities. Enormous industrial and financial combinations increasingly dominated the nation's commercial life as local and regional markets gave way to an ever more interconnected national economy founded on mass production and advertising. The new era brought an emphasis on consumption over production and helped to create a new mass culture that would eventually work to homogenize American life. At the same time, a dizzying series of technological breakthroughs drove breathtaking change in the tempo and quality of day-to-day existence. All of these developments sparked passionate disagreement over the moral implications of such rapid and epochal change.

Thus, Atlanta, with its self-conscious regional and national significance, rapid and problematic growth, uncomfortably diverse population, multiplying ties to the national market, frequent battles over public morality, and lively entertainment history, offers an ideal focus for a study of how the profound national transformations of the late nineteenth and early twentieth centuries played out in a southern context.

Such an exploration is all the more important because U.S. cultural historians of the period have so routinely overlooked the South. As for the rest of the country, scholarship has shown how by the late nineteenth century the vast extension of the railway system and the corresponding development of a national market had sparked an enormous expansion and centralization of the entertainment business. The theater offers a telling example. Early in the nineteenth century there was in most cities of any size at least one theater hosting a resident stock company. But as the construction of railroads eased travel throughout the country, these local stock companies were first disrupted by traveling "stars," to whom the company actors were expected to play second fiddle, and were later displaced altogether by touring dramatic companies sent forth from New York City to offer one play or a small repertoire in theater after theater, town after town. At the same time, control of these companies and frequently of the theaters in which they performed was gathered in fewer and fewer hands, until the great firm of Klaw and Erlanger ruled the American theater in a monopoly paralleling those in other U.S. industries.

As the entertainment industry grew and centralized, the audience for commercial amusements in the United States fragmented. Historian Lawrence Levine has argued that American culture was fundamentally unified into the early nineteenth century. Audiences of all classes attended the same theaters to witness the same shows, shows that blended a wide array of "high" and "low" cultural elements, from Shakespearean soliloquies to juggling acts. The audiences of the day were vocal, reacting enthusiastically to what they liked and responding aggressively, even violently, to what displeased them. By mid century, Levine asserts, this cultural unity was breaking down as local elites, anxious to set themselves apart from the growing legions of immigrants and workers, began establishing their own exclusive theaters in which "elevated" works could be "tastefully" performed for decorously "appreciative" audiences. And by the turn of the century, in Levine's view, the artificial but increasingly taken-for-granted division between "high" and "low" culture and between the types of audiences deemed appropriate to each was complete. Classical and operatic music, along with the more "refined" dramatic works, once enjoyed by all classes of Americans in the same noisy theaters, were now regarded as the province of the educated few. And even in theaters catering to more ordinary Americans, managers increasingly imposed strict new standards of conduct, insisting that audiences quietly accept what was presented to them.[10]

However valid Levine's argument might be for the rest of the country, it runs into problems when applied to the South. The social, economic, and political contexts in which southerners sought or resisted commercial entertainment differed sharply from those in the North. The South did not experience the massive influx of immigrants, with their competing mores and religions, which created cultural friction in northern cities. For the South, racial, not ethnic, division was the defining problem of the era, and evangelical Protestantism remained supreme throughout most of the region. In addition, the South was an essentially rural region uneasily confronting the social and cultural stresses inherent in urbanization, industrialization, and modernization. Many Atlantans therefore approached commercial entertainment with a profound ambivalence, at times longing for the latest amusements, at other times dreading or rejecting them, and sometimes managing to hold these contradictory notions all at once.

Furthermore, some southerners put culture to different uses than did their northeastern counterparts. Elites everywhere, as Levine suggests, employed high culture as an aid in creating class solidarity and exclusivity, and Atlanta's rising New South plutocracy eagerly followed their example. But as a distinctively southern elite, leading Atlantans also struggled mightily (and very insecurely) to use an ostentatious "appreciation" of European-derived culture as a means of escaping the South's reputation for backward provincialism and as a tool for winning the respect and acceptance of their more established peers in New York and Boston, both for themselves and for their city.

For all of these reasons, issues such as the moral content of amusements and the division between "highbrow" and "lowbrow" culture played out differently below the Mason-Dixon line. Clearly, in culture, just as in politics, economics, and social mores, the South has its own tale to tell. And precisely because it grasped for "progress" and "cosmopolitanism" with one hand while vigorously pushing away with the other, Atlanta offers an ideal focal point, something of a contested middle ground, in which to see this story develop. Commercial entertainment, in particular, a controversial site of conflicting values, a welcomed or disdained harbinger of modernity, presents a superb window through which to view the story.

Thematically, I have approached this subject with two fundamental questions in mind. First, and most simply, what happened? What is the story of public amusements in New South Atlanta? In addressing this question, I will trace the local history of a succession of entertainment genres. In doing so, I hope to add a new chapter to the history of entertainment in the United States, detailing the particular hazards, opportunities, and consequences involved in bringing cultural products manufactured in the North to a relatively poor and underpopulated region with its own proudly distinctive traditions and predispositions.

A second and deeply interrelated question is, what does entertainment history illuminate about Atlanta (and the South) more generally? What do the city's experiences with commercial entertainment show us about local society? About class, race, and gender relations? About the region's economy and the commercialization of culture? About Atlanta's evolving place in the South and in the nation? About the city's own view of itself, of its values, of its mission? Sometimes these two major themes—what Atlanta reveals about American entertainment and what American entertainment reveals about Atlanta and the South—are considered separately; frequently the same evidence addresses both. But taken together they form the organizing principles of the book.

Topically, this study focuses on such amusements as theater, vaudeville, burlesque, dime museums, motion pictures, classical music, grand opera, blues, and hillbilly music, entertainments linked in being staged and scripted, in a broadly conceived sense of these terms. This list is of course somewhat arbitrary. The circus, for example, fits these criteria and drew ardent crowds in Atlanta during this period. There were also amusements of a more participatory nature—dance halls, amusement parks, and fairs— that had great appeal, especially among the city's working classes.[11] Finally, there were sports, which were becoming increasingly popular in Atlanta as elsewhere during this period, and which, as a growing literature reveals, can provide an abundance of information regarding social, economic, and cultural history.[12] But for all of the scholarly possibilities such areas represent, there are definite limitations as well. For one thing, Atlanta's newspapers simply do not provide enough information about some entertainments to make fruitful study of them possible. And in any case, sports and explicitly participatory amusements such as dance are distinctive enough to justify their exclusion from a study such as this one. A professional baseball game and a vaudeville show share certain basic qualities in common, but there are many other attributes that set them apart. A ball game is, after all, just that— a game. It is physically competitive and spontaneous in ways that a staged play, a concert, or a monologue is not. The roles of the spectators and the performers in a playhouse differ from those at a ballpark, and there is a degree of intentionality that sets apart the values expressed on stage or in song from those unconsciously embodied in a sporting contest. Likewise, as scholars have shown, dance halls pulsated with social and cultural significance. Again, however, this entertainment is different in kind from those I will be examining. Participants on the dance floor more or less created their own amusement. They were not professionals who put "entertainment" for sale to a paying and evaluating audience.

The values expressed in the theater and the reactions evoked in the audience are often revealingly discussed in newspaper accounts. So not only are the various staged entertainments that I discuss part of an important yet neglected regional history, but Atlanta's newspaper coverage offers a rich array of insights into the attitudes of the Gate City's residents. Such coverage is crucial because my work relies heavily on these newspapers, in particular the *Constitution,* the *Journal,* the *Georgian,* and the *Independent.* In some ways Atlanta's newspapers played different roles and had different agendas. The *Independent,* an African American weekly, promoted the idiosyncratic views of its unpredictable editor, Ben Davis, and provoked heated disagreement within Atlanta's black community. The *Constitution,* a morning paper founded in 1868, could justifiably claim to be the region's leading newspaper; it possessed a national readership and wielded vast influence within the South. The *Journal,* an afternoon daily, first appeared in 1883. More innovative than its elder competitor—as in its early creation of a woman's department, for example—the *Journal* continually sought local predominance by focusing on local concerns, leaving more national aspirations to the *Constitution.* The *Georgian* began rolling off of the presses and competing with the *Journal* for afternoon readership in 1906 and in 1912 became a part of William Randolph Hearst's national newspaper empire. The three white papers frequently battled politically and differed at times in tone and emphasis. The *Georgian,* for instance, exemplified the crusading yellow journalism of its day and purported to represent the interests of "the people." Typically, however, political differences were more personal than fundamental, reflecting the intense factionalism of a one-party region. Accordingly, while editors Henry W. Grady or Clark Howell might use the pages of the *Constitution* to fight for political advantage over rivals such as the *Journal*'s Hoke Smith, on the basic tenets of New South ideology the papers remained strongly in accord. And they all worked fervently, day in and day out, to promote their city and their region.[13] There is thus little to distinguish the white papers' coverage of commercial culture; the same boosterism, the same dedication to white supremacy, the same social and moral preoccupations characterize all three.

However indistinguishable in editorial policy, there is little doubt that Atlanta's dailies played a pivotal, occasionally even an incendiary, role in local affairs. In drumming up support for expositions and opera visits, in igniting the madness that swept the city during the riot of 1906, in stoking the bigoted hatred of Leo Frank, and in countless other ways, the newspapers—sometimes individually, often in concert—made themselves heard, swaying the emotions and molding the opinions of their readers.[14] On a more mundane level, Atlanta's papers, like their counterparts elsewhere during this period, offered templates for appropriate behavior in the nation's emerging urban, consumer society, a particularly important function in the South, where the population was so new to industrial and big-city life.

The pitfalls of using newspapers as sources are obvious and well known. Their coverage is incomplete and is tainted with the biases of reporters and editors. Read and used carefully, however, newspapers can provide an irreplaceable wealth of information about a city and its people. This is especially true of the newspapers of this era, which devoted a great deal of column space to local incidents and personalities. Moreover, the biases of the city's journalists are frequently every bit as valuable as the "news" itself in reconstructing the preoccupations, assumptions, and worldview of the age.

Structurally, I approach the material in a roughly chronological fashion, dealing with each genre in the order in which it came to prominence. Chapter 1 treats the legitimate theater in Atlanta and follows the career of Laurent DeGive, the Belgian immigrant who became Atlanta's foremost entertainment entrepreneur. The story of theater in the Gate City helps to highlight much that was socially, economically, and culturally distinctive about late-nineteenth-century Atlanta and the South.

Chapter 2 deals with the wave of cheaper amusements—dime museums, vaudeville, and burlesque—that hit Atlanta around the turn of the century. Here we are able to explore the ways in which commercial culture changed in Atlanta over time as Atlanta itself changed.

Chapter 3 looks at the rise of motion pictures, which made a rocky debut in Atlanta during the Cotton States and International Exposition of 1895. The Gate City's experience with the movies reveals a city grappling with the rise of mass culture and with its own identity as it enters the twentieth century. In battles such as those over Sunday motion pictures, we see a city struggling to mediate between an older and a newer vision of the South.

Chapter 4 details the history of classical and operatic music in Atlanta from the 1880s into the 1920s and examines the relationship between the Atlanta elite and "high" culture. Here we see the clearest example of the strategic manipulation of culture by one social class.

The fifth chapter explores the Jim Crow context of black cultural developments and aspirations in the Gate City. As in the previous chapter, we see efforts to employ culture as a tool or a weapon, either to demean another group of people or to exalt one's own. The white determination to "keep blacks in their place" is thus counterposed with middle-class black efforts to use high culture as a simultaneous means of racial uplift and class distinction.

The final chapter focuses on examples of working-class culture and entertainment in Atlanta, from fiddling conventions to blues recording sessions. Here, among the laboring classes, black and white—and not during the lavish festivities of Opera Week, when the New York Metropolitan Company came to town—the Gate City's true cultural contributions to the nation and the world took form. Ironically, the boosters and social leaders who had for so long attempted to purchase or manufacture some sort of cultural relevance for Atlanta were, at best, oblivious to the developments that actually gave their city enduring cultural significance. By the 1920s, beneath the elite's notice, and largely beneath its contempt, the gate that had long swung inward to welcome commercial culture into Atlanta was beginning to swing decidedly in the other direction.

I hope that upon finishing this book, the reader will agree with me that Atlanta has a rich history that deserves recounting, but that in many respects has only begun to be told. And in resurrecting the story of entertainment in the Gate City, there is no better place to start than with the theater, the mainstay of late-nineteenth-century commercial entertainment. Colorful, exciting—human, in a deeply satisfying way—the Gate City's theatrical heritage has been almost completely forgotten.

⇥ 1 ⇤

The Theater in Atlanta

In the fall of 1894, the Women's Christian Temperance Union of Atlanta launched a campaign against "lewd advertising" for shows appearing at DeGive's Opera House. The uproar began in late October, when Martin Dooly, who earned his living as the city's "billposter," plastered playbills around town advertising the production *A Black Sheep*. These posters, featuring the likeness of an actress in bright, full-body blue tights against a lurid red background, had already caused controversy in Chattanooga, and the Atlanta WCTU sought to prevent the display of such material in the Gate City.[1] The temperance women of Atlanta quickly found powerful male allies. Rev. J. B. Hawthorne of the First Baptist Church took up the cry, and an assembly of local Methodist ministers composed a resolution condemning theatrical show bills for "corrupting the youth of our country": "If theatrical companies intend to debauch all those who look upon their corrupting scenes inside the playhouses, we object to an attempt to debauch those who never go to theaters by displaying their sensuality on a public bill board," the ministers declared. They urged the local police commission to enforce the city code and prevent the posting within the city limits of "notoriously indecent show bills" such as those for *A Black Sheep* and *The Spider and the Fly*.[2]

The conflict came to a head a few days later, after Dooly posted new playbills advertising actress Lillian Lewis's coming production of *Antony and Cleopatra*. Someone, offended by the posters, lodged a complaint at police headquarters. Aware that trouble was brewing, Dooly—following a hasty conference with Opera House owner Laurent DeGive—sent his employees scurrying about town to cover the offending playbills with strips of paper carrying the dates of the upcoming performances. These efforts, however, proved futile. City police arrested Dooly, then released him upon orders to appear in the police recorder's court on November 8.[3]

The controversy divided public opinion and disconcerted city officials, who felt relief over the prospect of having the issue of show-bill morality settled by a judge in a court of law. Dooly expressed befuddlement over his plight. "Fanny Davenport played Cleopatra here two years ago and no complaint was made," he lamented. "As this is a Shakespearean play I certainly did not think any one would complain of the advertising paper." The besieged billposter insisted that he had "no desire to break the law or offend the people of the city. If they will tell me where to draw the line I will try to accommodate them."[4]

According to Rev. Hawthorne, this was precisely the problem: no one was willing to draw such a line. In his view, responsibility for ridding the city of obscene plays and shameless actresses lay not with the city's government, but with its citizenry. "We have already laws against" immoral theatrical productions and indecent posters, he sternly informed his congregation, "but they are not enforced." Why? "Because the moral sentiment of the people is too weak to demand it." For if "Atlanta's civil authorities had felt the pressure of a strong virtuous public sentiment those peripatetic harlots and their managers would not have escaped from this city unwhipped of justice."[5] The unfortunate Dooly provided a convenient focus for local anger: not only did his work bring the "horrors" of the stage to the streets of the Gate City, but, as an Atlantan himself, he personified the laxity of "moral sentiment" that so concerned Hawthorne.

The trial, held before Judge Andy Calhoun, attracted a lively courtroom crowd and wound up pitting newspapermen such as Clark Howell, called as "experts" on the influence of the print media on public morals, against three spokesmen for the city's evangelical ministers—W. O. Butler, J. W. Heidt, and H. H. Parks. The case turned upon those issues that most animated local clergymen in their crusade against the stage: the general morality of the theater, the distinction between art and pornography, and the consequences for the community of the public display of sexually suggestive images.

Defendant Dooly opened the trial by unfurling a large copy of the poster in question—after Judge Calhoun had shooed all minors from the room—and attorneys then questioned a series of witnesses about their personal reactions to the poster and about the influence that such playbills might have on the public. The responses were pointed and contradictory. After arguing that the theater as an institution should be abolished, Rev. Butler went on to say that posters such as those for *Antony and Cleopatra* were bound to spark "lewd and lascivious" thoughts in the minds of the city's youth. Clark Howell disagreed. When asked for his assessment of the playbill hanging before the court, he flatly stated, "I see nothing indecent in it." The *Constitution*'s notoriously shy Joel Chandler Harris unwittingly provided comic relief as he blushed his way through testimony regarding the effects that images of women in blue tights might have on young people generally and on him personally. The most dramatic moment of the trial came when DeGive took the stand. Not only did DeGive defend the artistic worth of the disputed posters, but he also used the opportunity to speak out publicly, for perhaps the only time in his career, against claims that the theater was immoral and that it corrupted all who associated with it. Referring with pride to his own children, he insisted, "For twenty-five years they have been almost raised about the theater. I defy any one, even these ministers here, to say that they are not just as modest and decent and virtuous as any one."[6]

In the end, Judge Calhoun determined that the city code had not been violated, and he accordingly dismissed the charges against Dooly. The *Constitution* drolly spelled out the significance of the trial for its readers, noting that hereafter "The lolling form of the voluptuous Cleopatra may recline in her rose-colored barge unmarred by superfluous date lines, and Antony may flaunt his abbreviated toga wherever the breeze may blow."[7] But Rev. Butler, vanquished for the moment, hoped that something positive might yet come of the ministers' efforts, that "the recent discussion of the matter will develop a sentiment antagonistic to 'leg dramas,' and that when the cloud of dust kicked up has settled . . . the moral atmosphere of our city will be purer and . . . the experts will be able to distinguish between good and bad."[8]

This incident represents in microcosm many of the concerns and tendencies that would characterize Atlanta over the next several decades as powerful social and economic forces transformed the city. Here is the divided public opinion: the fears harbored by many Atlantans that their city was being morally polluted from beyond, the uncertainty felt by some citizens over just what was and was not immoral, and the conviction held by others that the material seen as offensive by some was actually harmless, if not culturally enriching. Here are middle-class white women leading the initial charge against the perceived evil, then giving way to authoritative male spokesmen. Here are the newspapermen, interpreting the conflict for the public, milking the event for its amusement value, and confidently offering opinions on the matter. And, finally, here is ultimate judgment being rendered by a public official (inevitably, at this time, a white male) as the defeated parties vow that they will live to fight another day. Similar scenarios occurred time and again in the Gate City—an amusement would be viewed by some as a challenge to received moral standards, an attack would be mounted (and would usually fail), and then the city would move on, growing larger and more worldly all the while.

The controversy also indicates the centrality that the theater held in such debates and in Atlanta's cultural life generally. DeGive's Opera House—and later his other, more magnificent theater, the Grand—contributed greatly to Atlanta's evolving sense of itself as the premier city of the New South. The stream of railroad-borne theatrical troupes, musicians, and opera companies that strolled across Atlanta's stages entertained the city's citizens and visitors while helping to build Atlanta's reputation as the cultural capital of the Deep South. At the same time, the theaters gave Atlantans the opportunity to evaluate the cultural and social trends of the industrializing world to which many—but by no means all—of them wished to commit their city. And thanks to Atlanta's size, its position of regional leadership, and the extensive influence of its newspapers, the preoccupations and experiences of the Gate City had a disproportionately large influence on the cultural development of the South as a region.

A survey of Atlanta's theatrical past reveals much that was culturally, socially, and economically distinctive about the South during the late nineteenth and early twentieth centuries. The business of running a theater in the South entailed obstacles and demands different from those in the North. A southern manager such as Laurent DeGive had to confront a variety of economic difficulties, all the while facing a vocal clergy that condemned the theater as an institution. Equally challenging, he had to please an audience that brought different expectations and behaviors to the theater than did its northern counterparts. It is remarkable that a man of DeGive's background could succeed so well for so long in so trying an atmosphere.

By the time he weathered the poster controversy, DeGive had been a dominant figure in Atlanta's cultural life for almost twenty-five years. His origins, however, were far removed from the city and region in which he made his fortune. Born and educated in Belgium, DeGive studied law there and settled into the prosperous life of an attorney. But then, hoping that a change of climate would ease his nagging ill health, he volunteered in 1860 to accompany a shipload of Belgian goods to Georgia as part of an effort to establish direct commercial ties between Europe and the U.S. South. Although DeGive did not speak English at the time, the Belgian government appointed him Consul to Atlanta and asked him to explore the prospects for Belgian trade. As it turned out, DeGive would return to the land of his birth but once during the long remainder of his life. And while he never became an American citizen, he did become one of the most successful and important residents of the up-and-coming city he chose to call home, as well as one of the most prominent theater owners in the post–Civil War South. In his obituary, the *Georgian* lauded DeGive as "one of Atlanta's pioneers" and "the father of the Southern stage." The paper paid tribute to his early faith in the city and to his undying "belief in the South's ability to support music and the drama."[9]

A career as a theatrical entrepreneur, however, was the farthest thing from DeGive's mind during his first years in Atlanta. He invested his money in cotton, tobacco, and real estate; dealt with family tragedy (three of his children died within a period of a few months back in Europe); and fled Atlanta to live with a fellow Belgian in Augusta when Sherman began shelling the city in 1864. It was only in the economically pinched period following the war that DeGive found himself with an unexpected opportunity to enter the theatrical business.

At this time DeGive loaned money to an Atlanta attorney, receiving in turn a mortgage on a piece of centrally located property at the northeast corner of Forsyth and Marietta Streets. When the attorney defaulted on the loan, DeGive foreclosed on the land and in 1866 sold it to a Masonic fraternity that began constructing a large meeting hall on the site. Long before the project was completed, however, a financial panic bankrupted the

Masons and left their workmen unpaid. DeGive reacquired the property, including the shell of a building, in 1869 for $21,000. A friend noted that Atlanta's principal playhouse, Davis Hall, had recently burned and suggested that DeGive complete the structure and make a theater of it. At first skeptical that any place of amusement could succeed in so small and cash-strapped a city as Atlanta (the population at the time was under twenty-two thousand), DeGive ultimately took the advice.[10]

The result was the opening, on January 24, 1870, of DeGive's Opera House. Atlanta had long hosted stage performances, usually at makeshift sites, but the Opera House easily eclipsed these earlier theatrical venues.[11] By young Atlanta's standards, it was an imposing structure. DeGive's playhouse was three stories high with a granite front, tall iron columns, and a spacious second-floor balcony on the outside. Elaborately decorated private boxes and the other trappings of a modern theater graced the inside. The *Constitution* revealed local pride—and hinted at local insecurities—in describing the theater as "One of the finest, handsomest, most coquettish in the Southern States" and in praising its "delicate, fresh, blooming" fresco; scenery painted by a New York artist; arched ceiling; damask-cushioned seats; and gas pipes ("laid on the plan of the large European theaters") that supported a lighting system that "in an instant" could change day to night or night to day. Its large seating capacity—which the newspapers boasted was "greater than any other opera house south of Richmond and outside of New Orleans"—was expected to make the theater a crucial stop on the southeastern theatrical circuit, and fed hopes that "the best performers of the United States and those of renowned artists that come from Europe . . . will appear as performers among us."[12] (Not everyone in Atlanta was as impressed by DeGive or his theater. At the end of DeGive's premier season, one newspaper editor remarked, "We want a good theatre in Atlanta. . . . The one on Marietta is not large or beautiful, but plain and respectable. Let some man of cultivation, then . . . build a splendid temple to the Muses in this city. The 'star' troupes of the country will not then give Atlanta the go bye."[13])

Its size and its location in the heart of the city instantly made the theater central not only to Atlanta's cultural life, but to its civic and social life as well. The Opera House was a natural site for spontaneous public gatherings, as on the evening of October 12, 1870, after word of Robert E. Lee's death reached Atlanta. In 1882, while the new state capitol was under

Interior of DeGive's Opera House. (Courtesy of the Atlanta History Center)

construction, Governor Alfred Colquitt addressed the state legislature in the theater and Governor Alexander Stephens was inaugurated there. And on through the 1890s the Opera House was the scene of a variety of political rallies and conventions dealing with issues such as prohibition and women's suffrage.

Of course, DeGive's theater functioned first of all, from the night it opened until the day that workers razed it fifty years later, as a place of amusement. Or rather, from Laurent DeGive's perspective, as a place of business, a business fraught with pitfalls and challenges.

As the theater managers of the day liked to point out, they were first of all businessmen. "We don't manage theaters for fun, and the companies don't play for fun," insisted Jacob Tannenbaum of Mobile. Their theaters were investments and were expected to pay dividends. But the many demands and difficulties involved in running a profitable theater in the South tested the acumen and tried the patience of the most astute managers. In an article published just prior to DeGive's death, the *Georgian* noted that the Belgian "has always maintained that he made little profit from his theatrical enterprises, but he has built up a large fortune thru real estate investments." [14]

The problems began with the South's geography and demographics. Theatrical companies traveled the country by rail, so railroad fares were an important consideration for any troupe. In the South, where cities were fewer and much farther between, the "jumps" that had to be made from city to city were far longer than those in the North, which meant greater expenses for any manager who desired to travel below the Mason-Dixon line. [15] To make matters worse, railroads generally charged higher rates in the South, making it even more costly to transport acting companies from city to city. Hard-pressed managers passed on their expenses in the form of higher admission fees, causing resentment on the part of theater patrons. Angrily responding in 1881 to criticism of the ticket prices he had demanded in Atlanta, the manager of the Hess Acme Opera Company explained that his company included forty-five people, that he had to pay up to twice as much in railroad fare in the South as elsewhere, and that anyone who wanted to see a company such as his at lower rates would "have to find some more philanthropic manager than myself to furnish it." [16]

The extreme precariousness of the South's economy in the late nineteenth century confronted any business with formidable obstacles but caused particular difficulty for amusements such as the theater, which depended on the existence of surplus income that could be spent on leisure. The higher the ticket prices, the smaller the pool of potential theatergoers that DeGive and his peers could draw upon. As the frequent criticism indicated, however, a night at DeGive's playhouse did not come cheaply. DeGive aggressively defended his pricing policies, arguing that the regular admission rate was set by the southern circuit of theater owners of which he was a member and that particularly famous stars and unusually large companies stipulated in their contracts that they could ask for "advanced" (higher) prices for their performances.[17]

In 1880, the least expensive seat that could be had for a typical Opera House performance cost \$.50, with the better seats going for \$1.00. As the decade wore on and DeGive added a second gallery, prices on the lower end of the scale fell to \$.25, but the best seats still sold for \$1.00. Prices remained remarkably steady until after the turn of the century, when the cost of the best seats rose to \$1.50. Admission for more glamorous or prestigious performances could run even higher. When legendary concert singer Adelina Patti appeared at the Grand in 1904, the poorest gallery seat cost \$2.00, and front-row seats ran \$5.00 apiece, prices that would have been unimaginably high for the vast majority of southerners.[18]

During periods of particularly acute economic crisis, theater companies had even greater trouble booking acts and attracting audiences in the South. The *New York Dramatic Mirror* noted in 1892 that an initially promising southern theatrical season had been ruined by a plunge in cotton prices, which crippled the region's economy and caused some managers to cancel their southern dates.[19] And as the economic depression of the 1890s deepened, the situation grew steadily worse. By October of 1896 the *Atlanta Journal* was reporting that northeastern theatrical managers were "afraid to venture south on account of the hard times, combined with the big railroad jumps and heavy fares. . . . The consequence is that fewer attractions are touring the south than ever before at this season of the year."[20]

If a perpetually lean economy made life difficult for southern theater owners, it was equally hard on those traveling companies that did hazard southern tours. The newspapers of the period are strewn with references to troupes that went under on the road. A little over a month into the season of 1884–85, the *Journal* observed that nearly fifty companies had already been stranded on tour.[21] Frequently a troupe's collapse meant financial loss for the theaters that the company had contracted to visit. When, for instance, the Tagliapietra Opera Company folded in 1881, DeGive was left to pay for the advertising already supplied for their Atlanta appearance and to buy a return ticket to New York for the troupe's "penniless agent."[22]

The risks and difficulties associated with touring the South meant that many of the better companies avoided the region altogether, opting to remain in more prosperous and populous areas of the country. Consequently, the troupes willing to gamble on southern tours were often distinctly inferior in quality. The managers of these companies naturally did everything in their power to give the opposite impression, zealously promoting their productions as aesthetic gems that had been enthusiastically received in New York City, the theatrical capital of the nation. A long run in New York—even if a play had to be staged at a loss to obtain it—could translate into success on the road, so managers worked overtime to convince potential ticket buyers of the big city's hearty approval of their offerings.[23] A typical ad in the *Constitution* appealed to the cosmopolitan pretensions of theatergoers by urging, "All New York is still laughing. Go and join!" Another contained blurbs from no less than seven New York newspapers.[24] In further efforts to woo audiences, "advance men" came to town ahead of each company, providing posters to plaster across the city (such as those that got Dooly into trouble) and paying local newspapers to carry "puffs"—unlabeled advertisements—extolling the unequaled merits of their troupe's work.

Occasionally, the play would live up to the advance billing, but all too often it did not. Even productions that might actually have received warm receptions in New York City frequently toured the country in scaled-down versions played by second- or third-rate actors. Such practices perennially provoked the ire of local theater critics. DeGive's Opera House was nearly three years old when a local columnist dismissed a musical drama as "trash": "We feel outraged at the effrontery which could bring . . . fourth-rate actors and actresses to this city, and attempt to palm them off as people worth seeing."[25] Atlanta's critics felt that big-city managers treated southerners as yokels who were incapable of recognizing deficient drama. This presumption was particularly galling to the residents of Atlanta, a city whose boosterish pretensions only partially cloaked an abiding sense of provincial inferiority. The *Constitution*'s Josiah Ohl, responding to rumors that a manager was prolonging the run of a critically lampooned production in

New York in the belief that the accrued prestige would sell the play else-where, sneered, "Try it, brother! You may be one of those who think every-thing outside of New York Jayville, but you'll find out that a New York run obtained by anything but real merit doesn't go." A *Journal* critic, disgusted by the woefully inadequate presentation of a vaunted play, characterized the attitude of managers sending plays south as "We are playing to hayseeds and anything goes." [26]

Indeed, inflated claims and exaggerated advertising could go only so far in capturing patronage. The *New York Dramatic Mirror* reported in 1891 that the appearance in Atlanta of the *Out of Sight* company had attracted one of the season's largest audiences on its opening night, but that it "hardly paid expenses" thereafter. The paper explained that while the first-night crowd had been taken in by the bogus claims of the company's advance man, the city could not be fooled twice.[27] The deceptive tactics of the advance agents ultimately disillusioned theatergoers all over the country, making it increasingly difficult to attract paying audiences to the theater, especially after the turn of the century, when alternative forms of amuse-ment began to appear. In fact, one reason that the "legitimate" theater suc-cumbed so easily to the onslaught of motion pictures was the existence of accumulated resentment on the part of audiences toward those who had for years misleadingly promoted inferior plays.[28]

DeGive repeatedly faced another issue that fanned public animosity and held down attendance: the denunciation of the theater and its devotees by the clergy. Atlanta was not alone in this. Attacks on the theater and other amusements increased all over the country toward the end of the nineteenth century as part of a clerical war against the advancing "worldliness" that many saw accompanying the vast social and economic transformations of the era. From 1877, for example, the *Discipline* of the Methodist Episcopal Church held that a member could face censure or expulsion for attending the theater, a ban that was not repealed until 1924.[29]

The South, however, was an especially evangelical region, and in Atlanta DeGive encountered a vocal, well-organized, and assertive group of minis-ters intent on defending the city and its residents from the defilement threat-ened by the theater and other amusements.[30] No less than their local coun-terparts in journalism and industry, Atlanta's clergymen believed that the Gate City occupied a crucial position of leadership within the South, that it was a "city set upon a hill."[31] Both the number and percentage of Atlantans who belonged to churches increased tremendously in the decades following the Civil War, leading the Baptist reverend William W. Landrum to boast in 1898 that the city was "foremost in the state, the nation, and the world in its commitment to evangelical Christianity."[32] At the same time, its spiritual leaders believed, Atlanta faced special hazards. The very growth in church membership that filled ministers with pride brought weakness as well as strength, as the new congregants were frequently less committed to the church and its doctrines than an earlier generation of churchgoers had been.[33] Evangelicals saw cause for concern beyond church walls as well. Even ministers who had initially supported the goals of the New South movement felt that a dangerous slide in morality had accompanied the urbanization and industrialization that underpinned and symbolized economic growth.[34] Thus, even as Rev. Landrum praised Atlanta's embrace of Christianity, he warned that the growing city, with its "immigration, civil strife, illiteracy, intemperance, political corruption," and congested population, provided an environment that was in many respects hostile to religion.[35] Like other leading Atlantans of this period (and beyond), the city's ministers exhibited an aggressive self-confidence curiously counterbalanced by a gnawing insecurity that would continually place them on the defensive. Depending on the context, these ministers could see themselves either as leaders of victorious holy legions or as voices in the wilderness, howling against the deafness of the multitudes.

For many evangelicals, the theater, with its brazen commercialization of vice and sensuality, epitomized the materialism that they blamed for what they deemed a startling erosion of faith and ethical standards. A visiting clergyman echoed local feeling when he argued that the theater substituted mere "artificiality" for the "finer feelings": "If you wish to be infected with vice, to burn for excitement, excite low appetites, knock down the effect of home and religious training, go to the theater." The theater was even more dangerous than were more overtly sinful haunts, precisely because the unsuspecting Christian in search of amusement was less likely to take its perils seriously or to repent of the "sins of worldliness" that he or she absorbed there. Indeed, the mere existence of the theater indicated a blindness on the part of the community, the same blindness that perpetuated the existence of other social evils. As one Atlanta minister bluntly explained while denouncing the theater, "As long as the people are morally stupid—as long as

they have a feeble appreciation of the distinctions which God makes between right and wrong, there will be class legislation, despotic monopo-
lies, political rings, bribery and ballot box stuffing. A righteous civilization
can be established and maintained only by a people who love and honor
righteousness." [36]

Three men in particular—Methodist evangelist Sam Jones, Rev. J. B.
Hawthorne, and Rev. Len G. Broughton of the Tabernacle Baptist Church—
caustically denounced the theater and the individual productions that appeared in the Gate City. The frequency and ferocity of these men's attacks
highlight the importance of the theater not only as a place of entertainment
but as a symbol of the changes wrought by modernization.

Jones enjoyed enormous popularity in Atlanta. He wrote a regular column for the *Journal,* and Atlantans flocked to see him when he spoke: a
Jones revival in March of 1896 drew hundreds of thousands of participants
from the city and surrounding areas.[37] So the evangelist's plainspoken attacks on the stage and other worldly evils carried great weight with a large
number of Atlantans. He wrote emphatically in one of his columns, "I believe the devil is in the average theater of this country."[38] Ironically, Jones
was an extremely theatrical evangelist who believed that in order to compete
effectively with worldly amusements he had to borrow some of their tactics.[39] One of the chief weapons in his arsenal was a broad and biting sense
of humor, which he was more than happy to train upon the theater, as when
he reported the reply of a man at a turkey dinner who was asked how he
would like to be served: "Fix me up like the ladies at the entertainment last
night were fixed up—a good deal of breast and very little dressing." For
those who might have missed the point, Jones added that this story said "a
good deal about something besides turkey and stuffing."[40]

Hawthorne adopted an angrier tone when speaking of amusements. He
occasionally devoted his Sunday sermons to diatribes against the offerings
of the local theaters and against the people of Atlanta for allowing them to
continue. When *The Devil's Auction* appeared at the Opera House in 1886,
Hawthorne called for the suppression of the play and questioned the morality of a city that would allow such garbage to be staged: "I grieve to say
that not merely the young but the old bald heads crowded to see the obscene spectacle. I repeat that in a city that tolerates, patronizes and applauds
such things there is something rotten beneath the surface." He returned to
the same theme in 1894, when Atlanta theaters hosted two productions that

the reverend deemed to be of unsurpassed "indecency and vileness." He asked, "What must be the moral condition of a community that will quietly tolerate such damnable iniquity? What epithet is bitter enough for the husband and father who will take his wife and daughters to a place where abandoned wretches make an exhibition of their unblushing shame?" Alluding to the good/evil dichotomy so many ministers saw in the Gate City, Hawthorne concluded in a crescendo of despair: "Oh Atlanta, Atlanta! Thou who art exalted unto heaven shall be brought down to hell!"[41]

Broughton too viewed the theater as "a moral cesspool. It is conceived in sin, shapen in iniquity and acted in disgrace."[42] His disgust for the theater and for all associated with it brought him more than once into public controversy with famed contemporaries. When *The Clansman* made its first Atlanta appearance in 1905, Broughton verbally assailed Thomas Dixon, the play's author. Allowing that he and Dixon had been boyhood friends and had attended Wake Forest together, the reverend nevertheless attacked Dixon for having abandoned the ministry for the stage. "The theatre is as rotten as hell," Broughton insisted. "There is not a moral theatre in the world and when Tom Dixon left the pulpit for the stage platform he stepped from the upper to the lower regions."[43] A little more than a year later, when Carrie Nation appeared at the El Dorado Theater between acts of the temperance standard *Ten Nights in a Barroom,* Broughton clashed with her as well. He had originally agreed to Nation's request that she be allowed to speak at his church, but when he learned that she was appearing in the local theater, he abruptly changed his mind, leading Nation to characterize him as "a great and good man," but "simply ignorant."[44]

The Evangelical Ministers' Association (EMA), an organization devoted to ministerial cooperation and civic morality, provided a more organized form of opposition to the theater. The EMA rarely protested specific plays, concentrating instead on offensive theatrical business practices. Well into the motion-picture era, for example, the EMA fought any attempt on the part of commercial amusements to open on Sundays and thereby to "desecrate" the Sabbath.[45] The EMA demonstrated its influence in December of 1900 when, at the organization's insistence, Atlanta's police commission prohibited the scheduled Sunday-evening appearance of the Edouard Strauss Orchestra of Vienna, in spite of a petition, reportedly signed by more than one thousand Atlantans, favoring the concert.[46]

The EMA also took an active part in the ongoing crusade to purge Atlanta of "indecent" playbills. In 1899, its members attempted to persuade city authorities to suppress the exhibition of posters featuring what one minister described as women who were "unclothed" in that they were clad "only in tights." The EMA argued that such playbills inevitably had a "demoralizing effect upon the young people of the city." At this time the association claimed to represent some twenty-five thousand white Atlanta churchgoers, along with five or six thousand blacks whose ministers supposedly backed the EMA's efforts. Despite this numerical strength, however, the EMA was to prove no more successful in its efforts than the anti-poster reformers of 1894 had been. When a delegation of ministers visited Mayor James G. Woodward with complaints, the mayor, while agreeing to discuss the matter with the police chief, insisted that it was extremely difficult to draw a line distinguishing the artistic from the obscene. Those who ran the police department agreed with him. As police commission chairman William Patterson stated in refusing to act against the posters, "Hundreds of the best people in Atlanta attend the theatres here and witness the representations of which the pictures are an advertisement. . . . which they most certainly would not do" if they regarded the posters or the plays as indecent.[47] This defeat had a chastening effect on the EMA; when the association next attacked "immoral" advertising posters, in 1906, the *Journal* reported that the ministers specifically exempted theatrical playbills from the campaign, "for while the association did not explicitly approve theatres, it was thought unnecessary to court opposition from that source."[48]

As its failures and setbacks suggest, the views of the EMA did not reflect those of many leading Atlantans. At times, far from persuading people to abandon the theater, clerical denunciations of immorality actually increased audiences for controversial plays. This had happened in 1894 during the poster controversy, and in 1903 thirty-five thousand people turned out over the course of a week to see *Ben-Hur* at the Grand—far more than saw the play in any other southern city—even as Rev. Broughton and a visiting evangelist at the Tabernacle Baptist Church vilified the production as "sacrilege" and urged Christian Atlantans to "stay away from it."[49] Six years later, *Georgian* columnist J. D. Gortatowsky scathingly upbraided the hypocrisy of men and women who blamed theater managers for "the so-called degeneracy of the stage," yet who "fairly fought each other" to get seats at the Grand to see a much-denounced production of *The Blue Mouse*. Why had the mayor, "the high brows . . . the boasted creme de la creme . . . the aristocracy" come to see such a play? "For the same reason they would have coughed up the price of enough to supply a poor family with coal for a week just to see Punch and Judy if gossip had it that Judy was going to present a new and pulpit-condemned version of the can-can."[50] The *Georgian*'s cartoonist joined the attack with a front-page drawing showing a congregation responding with fervor to a minister's denunciation of a play, then trampling over the same minister at the box office as he and they scrambled to purchase tickets.[51] Clearly, much of the clergymen's fury toward the theater sprang from their grim sense of themselves as leaders without followers. Little wonder that by this time at least one Methodist minister in Atlanta had begun to challenge the wisdom of the church's attacks, asking whether such actions might actually be driving more people out of the church than out of the theater while further corrupting the stage by depriving it of a Christian audience.[52]

For a variety of reasons, then—high admission prices, the difficulty of attracting consistently good shows to the South, the persistence of hard economic times in the region, and the revulsion that many evangelicals felt for the stage—life could be difficult for a southern theater manager.[53] But in spite of all the hardships, Laurent DeGive managed to survive and even to prosper. In order to do so, DeGive had to understand his audience and provide them with the types of entertainment that they wanted to see.

In general, Atlanta's theatergoers might be described as resolutely "middlebrow." Historians have recently argued that by the latter half of the nineteenth century, American audiences had begun sharply dividing along lines of taste and "refinement." Whereas once citizens of all classes had attended the same productions at the same theaters—making each playhouse a miniature reflection of society—urban elites now began self-consciously frequenting theaters that catered to their tastes by providing more elegant and "elevated" productions than were generally found in the older popular playhouses, and by enforcing rigid codes of audience dress and behavior that discouraged working-class attendance. At the same time, certain types of entertainment that had previously attracted audiences from all classes— Shakespearean drama and Italian opera, for example—came increasingly to be seen as suitable only for an economically and culturally elite audience that was capable of truly "appreciating" such fare. By the turn of the century, the argument goes, the clear-cut (if artificial) dichotomy between "high" and "low" culture taken for granted today had been more or less established and accepted throughout the United States.[54]

At first glance, Atlanta seems to have taken part in these national trends. Well-to-do Atlantans certainly liked to *think* of themselves—and of their city—as being particularly "tasteful" and "cultivated." The *Georgian* boasted editorially in 1909, for instance, when famed thespian Robert Mantell—allegedly attracted by the "Atlanta Spirit"—scheduled a full week of Shakespearean productions in Atlanta. This was quite a feat, the newspaper assured its readers, given that "few cities of Atlanta's size on the continent have ever claimed him for half this length of time." On the other hand, Atlanta supposedly had its share of "lowbrow" playgoers as well. Theater reviews often described action-packed melodramas as going over particularly well with the "gods of the gallery," who could be quite vocal in their appreciation of the goings-on on stage, and who could be even more vocal in their disapproval. Such differences in taste sometimes sparked conflict, especially as some local patrons claimed to loathe precisely the kinds of entertainment that the gallery relished. Such was the case with the author of an 1892 letter to the *Constitution,* who expressed contempt for the "horse-play farces and miserable balderdash . . . presented on the boards in Atlanta nine nights out of every ten," and who longed for the day when "the miserable trash which now fattens on gallery audiences to the disgust of all intelligent people . . . may be forced to seek more congenial climes."[55]

Some Atlantans hoped that the opening of the lavishly appointed Grand Opera House in more fashionable north Atlanta would ease such aesthetic tensions, that the theatrical "wheat" could now play the Grand while the "chaff" could be relegated to the Marietta Street house.[56] To some extent, this occurred, as the old Opera House, soon renamed the Columbia (and still later, the Bijou), began showing "popular-price" melodrama, and as the Grand staged all of the "first-class" attractions that could be routed through Atlanta. But in truth the division between the theaters was never that clear. For one thing, the Grand could not have survived by appealing solely to the financially better off and presumably more "refined" portion of Atlanta's population. Thus, while the Grand had the third greatest audience capacity of any theater in the United States, the bulk of its twenty-seven hundred seats were in the galleries. And whatever the Grand's cultural pretensions,

The Grand Opera House, 1895. (Courtesy of the Atlanta History Center)

the people who filled these galleries could be just as "coarse" and unruly as those who had frequented the upper tiers of the old opera house, as was made depressingly evident to the *Journal*'s theatrical correspondent on the Grand's opening night, February 10, 1893. After noting the "gorgeous and artistic beauty" of the new theater and asserting that "in point of brilliance, size and culture no such audience has ever been assembled in a southern theatre and but few in any playhouse on this continent," the reporter went on to complain about the behavior of the gallery dwellers, "who made noises that disgusted everyone present." As he described it, "In the affecting scenes in the various acts, as the lips of the actors met, the echo of smacks from the gallery were [*sic*] numerous and startling. Every one perched there would smack his lips, and not only embarrassed the actors but always spoiled the scenes."[57]

If there was little to distinguish the conduct of the Grand's audiences from those of the old Marietta Street house, the productions presented at the two theaters were not always that different either. The Grand hosted many of the leading actors and most famed productions of the day but also routinely staged plays of more dubious reputation and quality. It was, after all, the Grand's presentation of Charles Hoyt's *A Black Sheep* that drew the ire of J. B. Hawthorne and helped to spark the playbill controversy of 1894.[58] Even the more exalted attractions that played the Grand were usually not the aesthetic and intellectual triumphs that their managers purported them to be. In Atlanta as elsewhere, the most popular plays of this period typically drew crowds through the elaborateness of their sets or the beauty of their stars rather than through any inherent dramatic worth.[59]

The plays presented at the Columbia were not necessarily of poor quality. It is true that the theater specialized in ten–twenty–thirty–cent melodrama, but this was a dramatic form capable of speaking deeply to the needs of many Americans during a period of tremendous social and economic upheaval.[60] Nor were audiences at the Columbia and Bijou hostile to or unappreciative of more classical fare, as Shakespearean standards held the stage there on several occasions.[61]

Moreover, as a few disgusted critics made clear, when a production considered to possess genuine dramatic merit did appear at the Grand, more likely than not it failed to draw a good house. The Atlanta correspondent for the *New York Dramatic Mirror* put it very simply when he observed that the "legitimate drama, as a rule, fails to draw here."[62] The editor of the *Atlanta Journal* expressed himself more disdainfully, complaining in 1898 that three plays just presented at the Grand by English actor E. S. Willard and "his splendid company" had "played to a much smaller business than the average farce comedy company, which has nothing to distinguish it save perhaps an excessive display of lingerie and vulgarity." He concluded, "that which is ennobling and inspiring, that which is well and artistically done on the stage today, is not appreciated."[63] Apparently manager DeGive, who should have known Atlanta audiences better than anyone, shared this view, as on one occasion he reportedly urged famed actor Sol Smith Russell to forgo plans to stage Sheridan's *The Rivals* in favor of something with more mass appeal.[64]

The Atlantans of this day—like many other Americans nationwide—responded most enthusiastically not to Sheridan or Shakespeare but to elaborate stage settings, technical wizardry, and celebrated stars.[65] In an era of breakneck technological change, it is not surprising that audiences would like to see striking special effects made possible by new innovations. This sort of appeal is evident in an ad for *The Fast Mail,* a play that boasted "10 Sets of Special Scenery. Flight of the Fast Mail. Niagara Falls by Moonlight with Boiling Mist. Practical Working Engine and 14 Freight Cars with Illuminated Caboose. The Dago Dive. Realistic River Scene and Steamboat Explosion and Other Startling Effects"—all of which was to be presented at the "Usual Prices."[66] Even disappointments illustrate heightened expectations in this age of wonders. The reviewer of a 1907 play about auto racing, for example, complained that the production did not live up to its billing. "First dash out of the box the picture machine in the gallery burst a tire and kerflummuxed." Then came the touted "real racing car race" on stage: "It was a frost. Awful spluttering behind the scenes, dreadful popping like a gatlin [*sic*] gun, and up goes the curtain. Two low, rakish craft, alleged to be racing cars, roll gently in on a track, with little speed and great explosiveness. A curtain in the background gives a few convulsive movements in the reverse direction. The race is over."[67]

Even more exciting to Atlantans than special effects were the stars of national or international stature who passed through the Gate City. Actors and actresses of great renown drew crowds in Atlanta regardless of the productions in which they starred, and frequently overcame the dampening effect that hard economic times usually had on theater attendance.[68] The biggest stars of the day could even cause Atlantans to forget, temporarily at least, their usual distaste for "legitimate" drama. Edwin Booth packed the Opera House when he played Hamlet in 1882 and pulled in similarly large crowds six years later when he toured the South performing Shakespeare with Lawrence Barrett.[69] Likewise the *Mirror* reported in 1887 that the famed acting team of Robson and Crane, appearing at the Opera House in Shakespearean comedy, had drawn "the largest audience that have assembled [here] in five years"—probably a reference to Booth's 1882 performance.[70]

Whatever the triumphs of Booth and Barrett or Robson and Crane, however, Atlantans reserved their most fervent applause for the great female stars. Adelina Patti drew an $8,500 house to the Grand in 1894, with the *Mirror* reporting that her audience was "the most brilliant ever assembled in Georgia."[71] For years Patti's audience set the size standard by which all other Atlanta crowds were judged.

But the greatest sensation created by an actress in Atlanta occurred the first time that Sarah Bernhardt came to town. The Young Men's Library Association eagerly raised a three thousand–dollar guarantee to persuade Bernhardt to make a stop in the Gate City during her 1881 American tour.[72] When tickets went on sale at DeGive's Opera House for her performance in *Camille,* the waiting crowd snapped up within a few hours nearly enough two- and three-dollar tickets to cover the YMLA's guarantee. Some men had spent the night in the Opera House to ensure themselves good seats. Surrounding towns and cities also sent delegations to purchase tickets; the great demand meant that scalpers—a perennial problem in Atlanta—were able to command up to ten dollars a seat.[73] The coming of Bernhardt received extensive newspaper coverage, with the *Constitution* magnanimously forgiving the actress for having begun her life in "gilded sin" as a prostitute.[74]

When the much anticipated day of Bernhardt's appearance finally arrived, a large crowd gathered to greet her train, only to find the curtains drawn on the windows of the actress's private car. More frustration was to follow. Although the Opera House was "packed from pit to gallery" for her appearance, Bernhardt "failed to do herself justice" due to a severe cold, and most of the audience went home disappointed. The performance did pay off in another way, however. A few months later the *Constitution,* always on the lookout for comparisons favoring the Gate City, cited a *New York Herald* report claiming that Atlanta had provided Bernhardt's most profitable house outside of New York City. "Considering the fact that she played Philadelphia, Boston, Chicago, Cincinnati, New Orleans and other great cities," the newspaper crowed, "this is quite a compliment."[75]

In truth, Atlantans may have grown giddier over the prospect of seeing Sarah Bernhardt than did residents of northern cities, if only because in the South stellar attractions were fewer and farther between. Despite boosterish claims by the local newspapers, however, there is little to indicate that Atlanta's theatergoers were in any sense more "cultivated," "tasteful," or "sophisticated" than were audiences in other cities.

If the general nature and quality of the shows that attracted them is any indication, then, the wealthier and better-dressed Atlantans who frequented the pit and the boxes of the Grand were not much more aesthetically "cultivated" than were the poorer folk who jeered from the gallery or crowded into the Columbia—the distinction that contemporaries drew between the two audiences was exaggerated. Patrons of the Grand simply paid higher admission prices to enjoy the air of sumptuousness and "refined elegance" that the new theater strove to provide. So whatever had happened elsewhere in the country by the late nineteenth century, there was little overt conflict in the Gate City's theaters between exponents of "high" and "low" culture. To the contrary: Any division occasioned in Atlanta audiences by the opening of the Grand was based less on aesthetic standards, real or supposed, than on the social pretensions of an insecure yet socially ambitious class of well-to-do patrons.[76] As we shall see, these pretensions would reach fullest flower with the arrival on the Atlanta scene of the Metropolitan Opera Company of New York in the early twentieth century.

Laurent DeGive's worries did not end once he had booked a production that he thought his customers would enjoy. There remained the ominous question of how an Atlanta audience would behave when it turned out to see a play. Disruptive crowds had provided headaches for managers from the earliest days of American theater, but historians argue that the issue had been resolved by the late nineteenth century. In the Northeast, the ascension of Victorian standards of self-control, increasing attendance of the theater by formerly hostile Protestants, and the growing presence of "respectable" women in the audiences had gone far toward quieting once-volatile theater crowds.[77] Once again, however, the South presents a different story. As opening night at the Grand showed, unruly audiences continued to cause problems in the Gate City long after theater patrons had calmed down elsewhere. As late as 1911, the *Constitution* reported that additional police officers had to be sent into the gallery of the Atlanta Theater—the city's leading playhouse—to impose order after the audience grew too uproarious in response to the racier elements of the play *The Red Rose.*[78]

By the time DeGive opened his first theater, Atlanta already had a history of fractious playhouse crowds. A *Journal* reporter reminisced in 1883 about the audiences that frequented the old Athenaeum, which had reigned above a livery stable as the city's only theater until consumed by Sherman's flames in 1864. He recalled that "the gallery gods in those days were a power in the land. . . . They laughed, hissed, hooted, swore, carried on conversations with the actors," and "made love to the actresses." A favorite tactic of the gallery dwellers then had been to reach over the railing and tilt the candles used for lighting, "so as to cause the melted tallow to trickle down upon the necks and shoulders of the parquette people." The behavior of the Athenaeum crowds ultimately persuaded an anti-theater mayor and council to order the playhouse shut down a few months before it burned. The Athenaeum nicely reflected the atmosphere of 1860s Atlanta, which the *New York Times* had described as a "go-ahead town, where enterprise, license, and lawlessness form a blissful and inseparable trinity."[79]

The city and its playgoers mellowed a bit in the ensuing decades, but Atlanta's theaters still attracted some tough customers.[80] With many of Atlanta's presumably more sedate but pious citizens still fiercely opposed to the theater, and with a small proportion of "proper" women in its audiences, these "customers"—who had their own more traditional notions of what constituted "decorum"—found an atmosphere in which they could thrive. Local theater columnists frequently referred to the boisterous behavior of such patrons, who often defied the policemen assigned to the theaters to prevent disturbances.[81] The *Journal's* dramatic critic, for example, fumed, "Atlanta has the reputation of gathering the most heartless and the rudest audiences in the United States." Aiming his comments at the "denizens of the galleries," he claimed that he had attended theaters in all of the country's largest cities and therefore had grounds on which to state that "an Atlanta crowd . . . seems more like a herd of ruffians than people trying to amuse themselves in a rational way."[82] The manager of a production that was disrupted in Atlanta by an uproarious crowd—and the uproar was not confined to the gallery—agreed. "We have played in western frontier towns, where people go to the theater with pistols and bowie knives

Ushers at the formal opening of the Grand Opera House, February 1893. Seated at right is amateur actor Scott Thornton. (Courtesy of the Atlanta History Center)

stuck in their belts," he complained, "but I never, in my life, saw such a misbehaved crowd as that last night. They began their guying before the curtain went up, and, at times, acted like they had never been inside a theater before."[83]

The appearances of Scott Thornton in the 1890s provide particularly good examples of the potential for disorder that always existed within Atlanta theaters. A young (and apparently unbalanced) local amateur, Thornton held an unshakable belief in his own acting abilities, yet he achieved renown—not just in Atlanta but throughout Georgia—as a laughable figure whose productions were routinely broken up by riotous audiences.[84]

Thornton's 1896 presentation of *Richelieu* at the Columbia Theater was typical. All went relatively well early on, with the audience limiting itself to verbal sallies upon Thornton and his troupe. But then, near the end of the fourth act, "Our Scott"—as he was called with mock pride by the local newspapers—was abruptly struck in the chest by a banana launched from the gallery. With this incitement, the crowd lost all restraint, quickly inundating the stage with eggs, rotten fruit, "long strings of red sausages," and a shower of silver coins. In an attempt to stem the onslaught someone dropped the curtain, but then moments later it was suddenly raised again—supposedly by mistake—to reveal, where the quarters and dimes had landed, "an indiscriminate mass of humanity, made up of negro curtain raisers, pages in close-fitting tights, dukes, soldiers and lords of high degree, all scrambling for the money." Further, the "police were power-less" to restore order, as "from every part of the house came a deluge of every conceivable object, organic and inorganic, under the sun." Someone in the gallery launched a "cuspidor that crashed upon the stage near the head of a prostrate actor. A chair was thrown from one of the boxes. . . . The orchestra took flight. Every man in the audience was on his feet. The lights were turned out for a while. The end of a great production had come." The police arrested several members of a boisterous mob that gath-ered outside the theater to "receive" Thornton but that dispersed after word spread that the aggrieved thespian had slipped away down a rear flight of stairs.[85]

Scott Thornton's debacles were relatively innocuous affairs—for every-one, perhaps, save Thornton himself—but Atlanta audiences could be more dangerous. In 1895, police and opera house workers narrowly averted a riot at a benefit put on for the Atlanta Artillery Company by the Baldwin-Rogers acting troupe. The trouble commenced following the first act of the play, when one of the performers summarily went on strike and made a passion-ate plea from the stage for the payment of back wages owed by Captain J. F. Kempton of the artillery company. Aroused both by the captain's refusal to refund their ticket money and by the righteousness of the actor's cause, the "gallery gods" assailed the box office, trapping the ticket seller inside. Deriding the commands of two policemen that it disband, the mob de-manded the return of its money and began threatening the lives of both the ticket seller and Captain Kempton. A quick-thinking opera house employee doused the house lights, and the confused crowd, informed that Kempton was outside, swarmed out of the theater, which was promptly locked against them. The captain, after promising the angry men who confronted him that their money would be refunded the next day, managed to escape with the help of his artillery company and the police.[86]

Atlanta audiences were rarely as disruptive as those that chased Scott Thornton or Captain Kempton from the theater. Managers normally concerned themselves with much more minor infractions, such as the persistent habit among Atlantans of noisily arriving for a performance in the middle of the first act. But as the stationing of policemen in the city's theaters indicated, the potential for crowd disorder was always present, and therefore a cause for concern among Atlanta's theater managers long after managers in other regions of the country had let down their guard.

The Gate City's theater audiences were in general more likely to hurl angry words than spittoons or sausages, but they clearly held strong opinions regarding what transpired before them on stage. Atlantans were particularly sensitive about certain of the topics explored in the drama of the day. Above all, the determination of the city's whites to maintain racial supremacy pervaded every aspect of Atlanta's theatrical experience.

Race relations deteriorated sharply throughout the South during the late nineteenth and early twentieth centuries. State and local governments formalized a rigid system of segregation through Jim Crow laws while racial violence consumed the region.[87] The *Journal* and the *Constitution* gave regular and detailed coverage to the acts of vigilantism that occurred with increasing frequency all over the South and particularly in Georgia, which led the nation in lynchings between 1889 and 1928.[88] Although these newspapers editorially abhorred such extralegal violence, they helped create an atmosphere that favored such brutality by continually portraying African Americans as morally inferior and threatening to whites. The *Constitution,* for instance, carried a long-running column called "At the Police Matinee," whose author presented exaggerated descriptions—accompanied by cartoons portraying blacks as chimpanzees—of the proceedings of the police recorder's court, drawing humor from the supposed ignorance and criminal predispositions of black defendants.[89] And competition among the Atlanta dailies to out-sensationalize one another with regard to rumored rapes of white women by black men played a large role in sparking the bloody Atlanta race riot of 1906.[90]

Atlanta's theaters were inevitably subject to the same climate of racial hostility that poisoned all aspects of the city's life. Racial concerns not only determined where patrons sat when they entered local theaters, but helped to dictate as well how audiences assessed the performers and the productions that appeared before them.

Languishing for the most part at the bottom of the Gate City's economic heap, African Americans as a group were the least likely to possess the leisure time and spare change necessary to attend the theater. Those with the means, however, were allowed entry to Atlanta theaters—in contrast to some southern theaters that did not admit blacks at all—but, as was the case throughout the country, blacks were strictly separated from the white portion of the audience.[91] Usually they were allotted a portion of the upper gallery, with the rules occasionally being waived—when a given performance was expected to attract an especially large black audience—to allow them the full gallery and sometimes the balcony (lower gallery) as well.

Even these restrictive arrangements were too liberal for some Atlanta whites. The *Journal*'s theatrical correspondent was appalled by the scenes he witnessed at a minstrel show that featured African American as well as white entertainers. The black turnout was enormous, he claimed, and "The man who took a lady through the sweaty, odoriferous crowd last night, and afterwards was unable to enjoy the performance by their riotous behavior inside, will hardly ever venture to see another entertainment in Atlanta in which negroes participate." He complained that no fewer than fifteen policemen had been needed to manage the crowd. "Both within and without the theatre the wildest and most disgraceful disorder prevailed. . . . It was a long time before the decent element of the house could hear what was going on." He angrily concluded by suggesting that local theaters should in the future be entirely "turned over to the colored people" on nights when black companies were scheduled to appear.[92]

Some white Atlantans were as skittish about the prospect of blacks appearing with whites on stage as they were about the possibility of racial intermingling in the audience. The author of the review just quoted admitted that the mixed-race minstrel troupe put on a performance that was "excellent in every particular," but he nevertheless confessed the disgust he had felt when the opening curtain had gone up, and "here, in full view of a southern audience . . . sat, cheek by jowl, blacks and whites!" It was simply too much to bear, and he urged that henceforth productions of this nature be limited to the North, where they would not insult regional traditions and sensibilities.[93]

Even critics who were more open to the idea of blacks performing with whites defended the notion with a large measure of racial condescension. One observer questioned why southerners should "feel offense or degradation when they see funny negroes on the stage any more than when they see trained bears and monkeys. Both are seen for amusement, and cannot possibly have any other sort of influence over the audience."[94]

In 1895, Sissieretta Jones, a concert singer known professionally as "the Black Patti," made her first appearance in Atlanta. Jones had begun her career as the leading soprano of the Tennessee Jubilee singers and had gone on to sing before royalty and even to serenade the president of the United States.[95] At the time of her initial visit to the Gate City, however, she was touring with an all-white company, and this offended many white Atlantans. Despite her artistic credentials, no hotel in the city would accommodate her, and she was forced to stay at the home of a black minister. The newspapers questioned whether whites would turn out to see her. In this instance the *Journal* recommended that its readers judge the singer on her merits. While insisting that no white southerner would ever stoop to perform in a mixed-race company, the paper went on to say that Jones was "a very humble and interesting negress, who knows her place and keeps in it" and to argue that "Genius is not a matter of race, color or previous condition of servitude. It's just genius. . . . Does she not deserve credit for rising so far above the poor average of her race's capacities[?]" But in the end such atypical broad-mindedness did not prove convincing to many of the city's whites. When Jones appeared at the Grand on the evening of January 24, "There were about a hundred and fifty people in the parquet, a hundred in the balcony, and a [h]orde as numberless as the sands of the sea shore in the uppermost gallery," which had been turned over for the occasion to the theater's black patrons.[96]

Closely related to this obsession with racial propriety was white Atlanta's prickliness regarding portrayals of the South in plays produced in the Northeast. Stereotypes abounded in these works, and many southerners found them irritating. In a statement that could easily be adapted to present-day characterizations of southerners by the national media, a local columnist once confessed to a "wild flight of fancy" in which he imagined "a stage Southerner who doesn't say 'you all' in the singular, and who actually lives and grows fat without the aid of a mint julep." (The writer also criticized stage stereotypes of other groups but of course had nothing to say about the most demeaning stereotypes of all, those of African Americans.) Of

greater concern were dramas dealing with southern history and race relations. In 1893, the editor of the *Atlanta Journal* seconded an editorial that
had appeared in the *Richmond Times* denouncing the rage for "war plays"
that distorted southern life. Echoing the clergymen who saw corruption
beneath the theater's glittering surface, he insisted that such plays were more
"insidious than even northern school histories, because their falsehoods are
concealed by the glamor of stage scenery, and lights and pleasing music."
The *Heart of Maryland* was a case in point, inspiring in 1898 another in-
censed *Journal* editorial claiming that the production was "false in its history and miserable in its art—or its lack of art." Preposterously, the play
had two Confederate soldiers—a colonel and a "youth of noble birth"—
betray the South, a situation that the *Journal*'s editor insisted was quite
simply inconceivable. "Another absurd thing" was the portrayal of Confederate soldiers as fearful of Union general Joseph Hooker, when in reality the
Confederates "were not afraid of any man on earth." [97]

No play so raised the hackles of southerners as did *Uncle Tom's Cabin*.
Although probably performed more often than any work in the history of
American theater, *Uncle Tom* was not a hit below the Mason-Dixon line,
even in the postwar years when most productions of the play muted the
criticism of slavery that had outraged southerners before the war.[98] Henry W.
Grady caught a performance of the play while visiting New York City in
1881 and reviewed it for the *Constitution*. Even Grady, a confirmed white
supremacist, was struck by the "vivid" power of the production, but he was
also appalled—as he had expected to be—by what he saw as the work's
grotesque falsification of southern history. "There was no hint on the
stage," he lamented, "of the real ante bellum life of the south that made the
old plantation darkey the happiest laborer on all the earth." In Grady's view
Uncle Tom's Cabin contemptibly obscured the fact that the real heroes of
the Old South had been the men and women who had been "saddled" with
the slaves yet had bravely shouldered the burden to give "the poor creature[s] for a century a happiness and contentment to which the servants of
New England were utter strangers, and which we fear the negro will never
see again." [99]

A few months after Grady saw the play in New York, the Chicago Ideal
Uncle Tom Company—featuring, according to their newspaper ad, "A Full
Troupe of Genuine Colored Jubilee Singers! A Pack of Thoroughbred

Bloodhounds!" and Marks, the "Educated Donkey"—made a disastrous tour through Georgia.[100] The company played to very poor business in Augusta, while in Griffin theatergoers tossed eggs at the actors and vandals tore the company's scenery and baggage. When the house that greeted the troupe in Covington consisted solely of "two small boys," the beleaguered company canceled the production there and moved on.[101] The play actually drew a large crowd for one of its shows at DeGive's Opera House, but the audience was supposedly "disappointed" by what a local newspaper termed the company's "exceedingly wearisome" work. Not everyone shared this assessment, however: the reviewer referred with obvious irritation to the "negroes in the galleries, who seemed to have an idea that it was their show from the interest they took in the performance."[102]

Thirty-four years would pass before another company dared present *Uncle Tom's Cabin* in Atlanta, and this troupe encountered much more resistance. When the local chapter of the United Daughters of the Confederacy learned that manager Walter Baldwin planned to bring his version of the play to the Gate City in February of 1915, the organization sent representatives to see Mayor James Woodward and Homer George, the manager of the Atlanta Theater. Arguing that the production of *Uncle Tom* "would be inimical to the growing spirit of unity and peace which is desired between the two sections of our country by all Christian people," the UDC insisted that the play be substantially revised. When the mayor went along with the women's requests, Baldwin and George reluctantly agreed to make any necessary changes, pleading only—according to newspaper accounts—that Uncle Tom himself be allowed to remain in the cast and that "we would like to have Simon Legree kept in, too, because he's the guy that draws big galleries." The UDC found even the play's title offensive—it "carried suggestions that are filled with injustice and misrepresentation towards the south and her people"—and so when the expurgated production finally limped into Atlanta, it was under the name *Old Plantation Days*.[103]

Of course, some plays during this period of national reconciliation were more to the tastes of white southerners. When, for instance, the 1903 production of *A Texas Steer* began with a reference to Theodore Roosevelt's dining with Booker T. Washington—"A nigger to see me," asks a Texas congressman, "who says he is my personal friend and comrade; you must 'a made a mistake. This is not the white house"—the Atlanta audience responded with applause that "rumbled and roared throughout the interior of the Bijou theatre . . . like barrels of crockery rattling down a cellar stairway. The racket was simple [sic] ferocious, but it was to the point." [104]

More problematic was the 1905 appearance of Thomas Dixon's *The Clansman*. White southerners complacently accepted the play as historically accurate, but some leading whites feared that the production might dangerously inflame racial tensions. They apparently had reason to worry: before arriving in Atlanta, *The Clansman* had visited Macon, where the play had so enraged some in the audience that they had threatened the actor playing the role of the black lieutenant. As the *Journal* reported it, "Curses were hurled forth" along with "desperate yells of 'Lynch him!' 'Burn him!'" [105]

Several leading Atlantans denounced Dixon and his work. Rev. Len Broughton, in addition to excoriating Dixon for being associated with the theater in the first place, assailed *The Clansman* for stirring up explosive emotions, branding the work a "disgrace to southern manhood and womanhood. To claim that it is necessary today for him to go girating [sic] about over the south, stirring up such passions of hell, to keep the races apart and thus prevent . . . an impending amalgamation of the whites and blacks . . . is a slander of the white people of the south." When asked by the *Journal* for her opinion of the play, author and suffragist Rebecca Latimer Felton likewise began with a searing attack on the theater as an institution. As for *The Clansman*, she asserted that her credentials as a critic of this particular play were impeccable, as she had during her public career "defended southern men who felt obliged to take the law in their own hands, when white girls and women were ravished by bestial lust and fiendish violence." But Felton went on to insist, "I do not propose to inflame my own mind and enrage my own soul by going to a theatre to have sham rape violence portrayed," concluding that there was no excuse "to send a show through the length and breadth of this country that will feed a terrible flame into a consuming conflagration simply to advertise a book and draw money from the pockets of men, women and children." [106]

In the end, these criticisms may have seemed overblown given what actually occurred when the play reached Atlanta. Standing-room-only crowds and "tremendous" applause greeted *The Clansman* at the Grand Opera House. Racial hostility charged the theater's atmosphere, and the police roughly handled some blacks in the gallery, but from the point of view of white Atlantans the production played out its run largely without incident. The long-term influence of the play, however, may have been more destructive: less than a year after *The Clansman* first showed in Atlanta, the Gate City experienced the deadliest incident of racial violence in its history, the great riot of 1906.[107]

In the wake of this bloodbath, two white Atlantans, perhaps inspired by Dixon, wrote their own play, *The Exodus,* which purported to offer a peaceful solution to the "Negro Problem." The authors, Joseph D. Glass and John Miller Gregory, proposed in their drama that the answer to the nation's racial dilemma lay in "an exodus of the American negroes from their homes to a great American state composed of territory now within Texas, New Mexico, Arizona and Utah," where "the negroes will live and govern themselves and be alone." Although there is no evidence that plans to stage the play in Atlanta ever came to fruition, the work did attract the interest of the newspapers, as well as the attention of prominent southerners such as South Carolina's race-baiting U.S. senator, "Pitchfork" Ben Tillman, who took issue with the play's message, denying the ability of blacks "to do anything when left to themselves. He must be led or driven by a white man." Georgia congressman Thomas Hardwick was more approving of the play, agreeing that "the solution suggested by [the] play will probably be the true, just and final settlement of [the issue]." [108]

Whatever their own preferred "solution" to the "race problem," white Atlantans demonstrated in a variety of ways—whether as writers, critics, or spectators—their common conviction that African Americans were an inferior race that would never attain equality with whites and that was more to be feared and restrained than encouraged. White supremacy was to be aggressively defended against any threat or misguided criticism. These attitudes surfaced forcefully again and again, one reliable constant in an era of dramatic change. Laurent DeGive, a foreigner by birth, had to adopt—or at least adapt to—these views to succeed in the South.

Issues of gender and sexuality similarly engaged the attention of Atlanta's theatergoers. Like racial preoccupations, gender considerations helped determine where a patron sat when he or she arrived at the theater, how acceptable a given performer might be, and how a particular production was

to be appraised. Restrictions based on gender were never as legally formalized nor as adamantly enforced as were racial constraints, but they profoundly influenced Atlanta's theatrical life nonetheless.

Take seating arrangements, for example: women were not strictly confined to one area of the theater, as blacks were, but no "respectable" woman
would think of sitting in the upper galleries, where African Americans and
the rowdier whites congregated. It was furthermore assumed that no self-
respecting woman would go to the theater in the evening without a male
escort. As late as 1909 the *Journal* poked fun at five women who attended
a performance at the Orpheum Theater with nary a male companion:
"Friends of theirs in the audience explained to others . . . in whispers that
the girls had banded themselves together under the name of 'Suffragettes,'
their aim and determination being to attend the theatre, without the assistance of mere man, as often as they pleased." Matinees, on the other hand,
were considered the preserve of women and children, so males generally
felt timid about attending afternoon performances.[109]

"Respectable" white women also avoided certain types of shows, especially those deemed at all "suggestive." When an act known as the London
Gaiety Girls appeared at DeGive's Opera House in 1891, the *Constitution*
reported that while "Both galleries were packed" and the parquet and dress
circle were "fuller than usual," "there was not a lady in the house." And as
DeGive well knew, all-male audiences were the most dangerous audiences.
Indeed, men were especially likely to misbehave during just those sexually
bold productions that proper females shunned. After such a performance in
1890, a witness attributed a playhouse disturbance to the fact that the few
"ladies" who had shown up for the play had left in disgust long before it
ended. Consequently, "the boys felt no restraint. It was a lively crowd, and
they made things lively."[110]

Atlantans expected female performers, like women in the audience, to
exhibit higher moral standards than did their male counterparts. In 1905 a
local editor complained about actresses who did not consider themselves
"the real thing" until they had "forsaken the simple heroines, who marry in
the last act and live happily ever afterward, to flaunt stage immorality before
a depraved public taste in the role of some gilded courtesan or king's favorite." Southerners held natives of the region to particularly high moral standards. A *Constitution* theatrical correspondent urged southern girls not
to perform light opera or burlesque because of the "craze for tights" and

"for a thousand other reasons." The columnist praised southern women for their tendency to choose more respectable theatrical genres, noting that this was "a good sign" that spoke "volumes for the modesty" of southern womanhood.[111]

As to just what constituted a "suggestive" or "immoral" production, local critics and audiences disagreed, just as they differed over the alleged obscenity of advertising posters. On the one hand, by the turn of the century advertisements and theater reviews routinely stressed the physical allure of female performers, often to the exclusion of anything else. A 1905 ad for the Bijou Theater, for example, was typical of countless others in promising its patrons "Pretty Girls—Catchy Music." And *Journal* theater critic Stuart Maclean concluded a rapturous description of actress Anna Held and her retinue by asking his readers, "Don't you just love girls, anyway? You never saw so many good-lookers at one time in your life."[112]

On the other hand, some columnists were quick to condemn plays in which female characters—who were expected to personify the Victorian moral strictures that supposedly undergirded civilization—violated conventional sexual norms.[113] Like the ministers who heaped opprobrium on the theater in general, these critics worried about the effects that sexually "indecent" plays might have on the city's young people—and, again, particularly on its "impressionable" young women. The reviewer of an 1895 production that told a tale of twin sisters—one good, the other of decidedly looser morals—bitterly criticized the play for the influence that he was certain it had had on impressionable female minds: "Every young woman who knew nothing of the seamy, of the half world, of the wretchedness of the fallen, learned it last night at the Grand. . . . Seeds were planted in guileless breasts, that were guileless from ignorance." Likewise, in a letter to the *Georgian,* an Atlanta woman warned, "A mother should guard her young daughter from immodest theatrical spectacles as carefully as she would shield her from the plague."[114]

Some Atlantans found the notion of women attending the theater at all to be troubling, regardless of the quality of the play. In 1909, Rev. John E. White complained of a "matinee habit" among Atlanta's young people that he deemed especially harmful to the city's daughters. This theater craze was "no friend to the womanhood and motherhood of tomorrow," White argued, since it diminished feminine interest in "education and worship and domesticity" while producing a harmful "flush of fever in the veins of maidenhood at exactly the period of life when character is building foundations, and when the home should be doing its best for the child."[115] Charged with anchoring community morality in their roles as housewives and mothers, women were seen as an essential resource that must be shielded from vile influences.

For most observers, however, the pressing problem was not the composition of the audience, but the moral quality of the productions that Atlantans had the opportunity to see. In 1899 Smith Clayton of the *Journal* began a vehement one-man war against the play *Zaza,* which was scheduled to appear at the Grand. *Zaza* told the story of a French music-hall singer who carried on an affair with a married man and, like similar plays of the period, managed to work both sides of the moral fence, presenting titillating images of wayward sexual behavior counterbalanced by an ending that emphasized redemption. Despite the play's denouement, Clayton scoffed at the argument that *Zaza* was in fact a "sermon" in disguise and decried it as "the vilest play that has yet disgraced the American boards," pointing out that even the jaded New York newspapers had assailed the work as the "very worst production which has so far degraded the stage of the metropolis—a stage which for years has reeked with immoral suggestiveness, from top to bottom and through and through." Unfortunately for Clayton, such attacks only increased attendance, as *Zaza* drew large houses in Atlanta. The *Journal* found some consolation, however, in the fact that "There was a noticeable absence of young girls at both performances and they are the ones most liable to suffer bad effect from seeing such a play."[116]

Still, the large turnout for such a fiercely criticized production suggests that at least a portion of Atlanta's theatergoing population was much less concerned than was Clayton with the propriety of plays dealing with extramarital romance. Such divisions help to explain the relative uncertainty of gender restrictions as compared to those of a racial nature. White Atlanta was united in its belief that blacks were inferior and were to be treated as such; this was an element of the region's past that local whites were absolutely determined to maintain. Gender roles, on the other hand, were beginning to change somewhat by the early twentieth century, even in the Deep South. More women were entering the workforce, taking stances on public issues, even asking for the vote. So while substantial numbers of Atlantans, led by the city's clergymen, denounced all breaches of traditional sexual propriety, others were not so sure, providing just the evidence of encroaching worldliness that frightened the devout and lent stridency to their calls for a return to old-fashioned righteousness.

So, however intense the jeremiads, many Atlantans were clearly not listening. They were willing to tolerate a wider scope of feminine behavior—at least on stage—and they accepted a double standard that saw nothing wrong with a healthy male appreciation for the "good-lookers" in the chorus line. These Atlantans may have expected their wives, mothers, and sisters to adhere to a rigid code of behavior, but, as their attendance at one condemned play after another demonstrated, they were not about to pass up the chance to see others behave differently, particularly when it was all make-believe anyway, and when transgressors were suitably punished in the end. DeGive realized this and knew that he had much more leeway in booking plays of a sensitive sexual nature than he ever had when dealing with race.

Of course, this was only true to the extent that DeGive controlled his own bookings. For although he had the power to pick and choose productions during his first twenty-five years in the business, 1895 brought fateful changes. DeGive would learn that the theater was indeed a business in which sentiment and loyalty played no part.

In many respects, the fall of 1895 represented the high point of Atlanta's theatrical history. With the city's population swollen by the hundreds of thousands of visitors who came to attend the Cotton States and International Exposition held in Piedmont Park, the local theaters had a field day. Laurent DeGive's Grand Opera House vied with southern theater magnate Henry Greenwall's newly opened Lyceum Theater for patrons of the legitimate drama, the Columbia presented popular-priced fare, and three vaudeville houses sprang up over the course of the exposition to offer Atlanta a taste of this rising form of entertainment. An unprecedented variety of bills appeared at the Gate City's playhouses while the exposition was in town. During the last week of November, for example, theatergoers could choose from among Shakespeare at the Lyceum, John Philip Sousa at the Grand, and McCart's Dog and Monkey Comedians at the City Trocadero vaudeville house.[117] Atlantans and their guests flocked to such attractions. One local newspaper estimated that on the evening of October 28 a combined audience of ten thousand people had visited either the city's theaters or the Buffalo Bill Wild West show on the exposition grounds.[118] The Gate City seemed at last to have attained the big-league status that locals had always longed for, as visiting companies could now play full one-week stands, just as they did in the larger cities of the North. By the end of the year Atlanta's theater columnists were euphoric. "Every American star of any magnitude in the theatrical firmament has shown [*sic*] upon Atlanta during the present season," exulted the *Journal,* which proclaimed that, thanks to its exposition, Atlanta had "by one tremendous stride leaped into the airs of metropolitanism." [119]

"Metropolitanism," the status craved by many and abhorred by others, seemed at last to have arrived. But Atlanta's glory was to be fleeting. With the end of the Piedmont Exposition, the visitors went home, and the city found itself unable to support so many theaters. Equally important, with the season of 1895–96, Laurent DeGive lost the power to determine what played in his theater and when. For from this date the booking of the Grand Opera House fell into the hands of Klaw and Erlanger, the powerful New York firm that was then consolidating its control of the nation's theatrical life. Thus, the same fall that witnessed some of Atlanta's greatest triumphs ushered in as well the end of the city's theatrical independence and the beginning of the end of Atlanta's theatrical distinctiveness. Indeed, the events of 1895 would help augur the eventual demise of the theater as the country's dominant form of commercial entertainment.

In the summer of 1894 DeGive had found himself in the midst of a war being waged between Klaw and Erlanger and their principal southern rival, Henry Greenwall of New Orleans. Both sides sought to dominate theatrical booking in the South by winning control of the region's principal touring routes. Because of its size and Atlanta's strategic location, control of the Grand Opera House was crucial to this strategy, so DeGive was ultimately forced to choose between one side and the other. [120] Believing that the firm could supply him with more attractions, DeGive in the end threw in his lot with Klaw and Erlanger, signing a contract providing the New Yorkers with exclusive booking rights for the Grand beginning in the fall of 1895. [121]

For his part, Greenwall carried through on a threat to build an Atlanta playhouse to compete with the Grand. He completely overhauled the Edgewood Avenue Theater, which had quickly fallen on hard times after opening in 1891 as a rival to DeGive's Opera House. Greenwall rechristened his playhouse the New Lyceum and opened for business on April 29, 1895. Once the exposition crowds left the city, however, the resurrected theater suffered the same fate as had its older incarnation, and for the same principal reason: as DeGive had long held, Atlanta simply could not adequately support two first-run houses. The theater staggered along under a series of managers and featuring varying types of shows until 1901, when it burned to the ground.[122]

Klaw and Erlanger quickly vanquished Greenwall not only in Atlanta, but throughout the South, and by 1896 the victors were eager to expand their dominance beyond their secure regional base. In August of that year Klaw and Erlanger combined forces with the partnerships of Hayman and Frohman and Nixon and Zimmerman to create what became known as the theatrical "Syndicate," or the "Trust." The Syndicate worked to acquire control of theatrical booking throughout the nation, just as others in this great age of economic consolidation achieved domination of the oil or steel industries. And the Syndicate was phenomenally successful: at its peak around the turn of the century, it exclusively booked at least seven hundred theaters, or virtually every first-rate playhouse in the United States.[123]

At first the Syndicate offered definite advantages to the theaters under its sway. It supplied them with all the attractions that they needed over the course of a season, it controlled so many combination companies that it could offer virtually all the season's New York successes, and it promised to reduce ruinous local competition by providing for only the number of theaters that a city could support.[124] But there were also clear disadvantages, which grew more onerous with time. Under Syndicate control, managers had no say over what plays came to their theaters or when; they had to take what was sent them, good, bad, or indifferent. And when opposition to the Trust arose, the Syndicate strictly prohibited the theaters it ruled from staging plays controlled by rival groups. "In short," as a chronicler has put it, "the attractions and theatres of the country were puppets, and the Syndicate, through the masterful hand of Abraham Lincoln Erlanger, pulled the strings."[125]

DeGive ran his theater under these conditions for fifteen long years, to mixed local reaction. Some Atlantans defended the Syndicate, arguing that Klaw and Erlanger provided a better run of attractions than had come South previously.[126] But others were sharply critical. The *Constitution* raised ob-

The *Journal* (May 11, 1910) applauds the attack on the Theatrical Trust. (Courtesy of UGA Photographic Services)

jections familiar to Gate City playgoers in 1898 when it accused the Trust of discriminating against the South. The paper charged that, under the Syndicate, "the big attractions are held in the north as long as possible and the south has to wait for them until they have had their 'run' in the larger cities." Furthermore, the Trust continued the practice of sending inferior companies to the South and of misrepresenting them: "If a play has made a hit in the metropolis largely by virtue of the company presenting it, it is sent on the road with a cheapened company, the claim always being made that it is presented by the 'original' cast."[127] Whatever the complaints, however, and whatever DeGive's own feelings, the power of the Syndicate was such that theater managers could do little for the time being.

It was only with the rise of the Shubert brothers in opposition to the Syndicate and following the disastrous season of 1908–9—when theaters nationwide were starved for attractions because of the Syndicate blacklist against Shubert productions—that effective opposition to the Trust emerged. At that time the Shuberts and their allies gained the support of theater owners all over the country through their call for the "open door," or the freedom for individual managers to book whomever they wished for their theaters, regardless of what firm handled the act. In May of 1910, hundreds of U.S. theater owners broke away from Syndicate control and formed the National Theatre Owners Association. A few days later the Association of Southern Theatre Managers ratified the break at a meeting at the Piedmont Hotel in Atlanta. With these actions the great theatrical war between the Syndicate and the "Independents" had begun.[128]

Laurent DeGive, however, did not live to witness this war. He had died, after a long illness, two months earlier, on March 17, at the age of eighty-two.[129] But he had lived long enough to see the conflict coming, and on July 19, 1909, he had taken up his pen in an attempt to divert it. Anguished over the "storm menacing our theatrical affairs," DeGive wrote at length to Klaw and Erlanger, imploring them to end the ban on Shubert productions that was angering the managers and playgoers of the South. He argued that it was no longer possible to keep the Shuberts out of the South, that they were going to stage their plays in Atlanta even if this meant construction of a new theater, and that a competing playhouse would mean "the deterioration of half at least of the value of my Grand without benefitting you one particle." The only way to prevent this was to allow the Shuberts to fill open dates at the Grand with the attractions that they wished to send South. DeGive concluded by noting that for fifteen years he and the New York firm had "lived and acted in perfect harmony and mutual satisfaction" and by assuring Klaw and Erlanger that he knew that he could rely on "your honor and your sense of justice, which would not permit you to sacrifice us, where there would be no possible benefit accruing to you, on account of a difficulty to which we are absolute strangers, and of which we do not even know the cause."[130]

MR. LAURENT DeGIVE, DEAN OF AMERICAN THEATRE OWNERS, DEAD

The death of Laurent DeGive receives front-page coverage in the *Atlanta Journal*, March 17, 1910. (Courtesy of UGA Photographic Services)

The Syndicate responded to this plea by promptly moving to secure control of the Forsyth Theater, then under construction, as a rival to the Grand in which Syndicate productions could be produced. DeGive, his sons, and Jake Wells—a rising theatrical entrepreneur from Virginia who was allied with them—managed to head off this effort, but the rift between the DeGives and Klaw and Erlanger was completed.[131] The Syndicate ultimately took over the Orpheum Theater, previously a vaudeville house, for its 1910-11 productions and in the fall of 1911 moved into the new Atlanta Theater on Edgewood Avenue. Meanwhile, the DeGives leased the Grand to the Shuberts, setting up a direct local confrontation between the two theatrical giants.[132]

In the end, the Shuberts gained the overall advantage in the struggle nationally, but in Atlanta the battle ended in something of an anticlimax, with Klaw and Erlanger coming out easily on top. After only two years of rising expenses and dwindling profits, the Shuberts abandoned Atlanta to the Syndicate, selling their lease on the Grand to Jake Wells, who turned the venerable theater into a vaudeville house.[133]

Klaw and Erlanger's triumph, however, was in many ways an empty one, for 1910 marked the beginning of the decline of theatrical touring in the United States. In large part this was a result of the theatrical war itself. Because of the conflict between the Shuberts and the Syndicate, cities such as Atlanta, which had supported one first-rate theater, now had two, without—as DeGive had predicted—enough patronage or decent attractions to fill them both. This led to falling profits for the theaters and to growing disgust on the part of patrons as the competing firms scrambled to fill their houses with whatever feeble productions they could hurriedly send out on the road. Combined with the emergence of motion pictures and vaudeville as alternative entertainments, the great theatrical conflict helped to close the period in which the legitimate theater had been the country's most popular form of commercial amusement.[134]

For forty years Laurent DeGive had presided over the dominant form of entertainment in one of the South's most important cities, and his death neatly coincided with the end of an era. DeGive had begun his career at a time when a manager's fortunes rose or fell based on his ability to "know" his audience, to sense its likes and dislikes, its predilections and prejudices.

The Belgian had the skills and sensitivity needed to accommodate unruly crowds and bitterly held racial prerogatives, to weather hard economic times and the withering abuse of evangelical ministers. But DeGive lived to see fundamental changes in the entertainment industry, changes that stripped local managers of their relative autonomy and placed power in the hands of distant businessmen. The legitimate theater fell from grace under the new system.

Of course, it would have fallen anyway sooner or later. For with American society changing so rapidly at this time, the future of amusement in Atlanta and throughout the nation lay with other entertainments, cheaper and more accessible to a mass public that increasingly had spare time and extra money to spend on recreation. By 1910 the theater may have been dying, but commercialized leisure—and the controversies associated with it—were not.

ᗠ2ᗢ

Cheaper Amusements

In 1948 the *Atlanta Historical Bulletin* published reminiscences by Walter McElreath, lawyer, politician, and founder of the Atlanta Historical Society. McElreath remembered the Gate City as he had first encountered it in the closing decades of the nineteenth century, fondly recalling the time when Atlanta's churches, its retailers and grocery stores, and the residences of its leading citizens were all clustered near the center of what was then a small and compact city. Life seemed to move at a slower, horse-drawn pace, and extraordinary individuals could seize the attention of the entire community in a manner that would be impossible later. "There were no radios and no motion pictures," he explained. "Everybody was at home and had nowhere to go. Any queer or amusing character was in those days an object of interest which would pass practically unnoticed in these days of hurrying traffic and multiplied diversions."

McElreath told the story of star-crossed actor Scott Thornton—whom he recalled as "the best example of near genius which Atlanta ever produced"—as an illustration of the simpler times and of the opportunities then available to unusual figures. But Atlanta had profoundly changed since the days when Thornton walked the stage. "Smoothly paved streets and swift automobiles have scattered the population over wide areas where intimate daily social contact is impossible. Luxury, undreamed of a generation ago, has been attained. Life is easier and longer, but is it happier or more humanly interesting?"[1]

Nostalgia obviously colors McElreath's recollections, as does his own social standing: Atlanta was never "just one great family of singularly vital people" bound together in a "close and intimate spirit." But he was correct in his central point: the Gate City did change dramatically in the first decades of the twentieth century. And as Atlanta changed, so did the city's amusement business, in a transformation that reflected national socioeconomic trends as well as Atlanta's own metamorphosis into what its inhabitants viewed, for better or for worse, as a "cosmopolitan" city.

While the legitimate theater was the predominant form of commercial entertainment in Atlanta between 1880 and 1910, it was by no means the only amusement in town. As the city's population surged from thirty-seven thousand in 1880 to more than two hundred thousand in 1920, great opportunities arose for those who could supply inexpensive entertainment with a broad popular appeal. And so many new amusements—such as dime museums, vaudeville, burlesque, and moving pictures—appeared in Atlanta during the heyday of the theater. All of these forms drew much of their original support from audiences that were less prosperous and less "respectable," as a rule, than those that frequented the pit of the Grand Opera House. Atlanta's turn-of-the-century increase in working-class employment meant a growing number of people with some spare money and leisure hours in which to spend it, whether at a vaudeville house, a dance hall, or a baseball game. This popular appeal, however, often aroused elite suspicions that placed some entertainments under moral and economic pressures to "refine" themselves. Vaudeville and, more spectacularly, movies, emerged from their dubious beginnings to find great success and even prestige in the Gate City. Burlesque, on the other hand, never overcame its initial aura of seediness and continued to provoke the wrath of city authorities.

At the same time that commercial entertainment profitably tapped new markets and leapt into social prominence, the amusement industry became increasingly systematized and centralized. The theater set the pattern during the nineteenth century as it evolved from a largely unconnected scattering of independent local stock companies into a tightly organized syndicate of playhouses and acting companies controlled by New York executives. The vaudeville and motion picture businesses were more centralized to begin with than the early theater had been, yet they underwent further consolidation in the early twentieth century as control by local and then regional entrepreneurs gave way to the great monopolizing power wielded by the big business centers of the North.

From the point of view of a provincial city such as Atlanta, these changes encompassed a number of tensions and contradictions while producing a complicated configuration of gains and losses. The example of Scott Thornton is, as McElreath suggested, a telling one. There is something appealing to the historian—as there must have been to Thornton's audiences—in the fact that the actor was a local resident, known personally to many of those who came to heckle him at his performances. "Our Scott" was a home-grown character at a time when, as McElreath points out, Atlanta was still small enough and its society organic enough to react more or less in unison to an offbeat individual. Thornton's public persona and histrionic reputation may have been in part the creation of the newspapers, but at least they were local newspapers. He was anything but a mass-produced commodity sent forth from New York City to captivate the hinterland.

But this quaintness had its drawbacks as well. Thornton drew so much attention and ridicule precisely because his actual talents did not equal his grandiose notions of himself. He was a colorful amateur with an amateur's shortcomings. And while (as Atlanta's drama critics liked to point out) many of the performers who toured the South professionally were likewise mediocre or worse, the best of the actors, singers, and musicians who visited the Gate City were very good indeed, with much more ability than a Scott Thornton could ever aspire to. And a mere decade after Thornton's death, with the arrival of the motion picture, Atlanta's situation as a consumer of cultural goods improved dramatically. Suddenly the same great artists—the Charlie Chaplins, Buster Keatons, and D. W. Griffiths—who worked their magic for audiences in New York City and Boston graced the screens of the Gate City as well. In a stroke Atlanta achieved a measure of cultural equality with the long-envied metropolises of the North.

Clearly, American commercial culture during this period was becoming increasingly homogenized, with the same "goods" that were produced in a few key cities being marketed to consumers all over the country. For their part, Atlantans reacted ambivalently to this great change. Many believed that the Gate City, because of its size and prominence, held a sacred obligation to protect the South's religious values, values that were threatened by the incursion of, say, sexually explicit stage productions or films that showed women acting in new and unapproved ways. But these same respectable citizens could frequently be found lined up at the ticket booth, eager to see what they viewed as the best that new forms of entertainment had to offer. In an attempt to mediate between the attraction and repulsion they felt, these men and women worked through organizations such as the local film censorship board, the Evangelical Ministers' Association, and the Better Films Committee of the 1920s to see that such entertainment entered Atlanta on Atlanta's terms. They fought something of a losing battle to achieve what they saw as the best of both worlds: a city that was at once morally insular and culturally open, defiantly provincial and proudly cosmopolitan. In the end, whatever the activists' goals or efforts, Atlanta inevitably changed, growing from the relatively self-contained "big town" of McElreath's youth, distinctively imbued with its own peculiarities and idiosyncrasies, to a sprawling metropolis largely indistinguishable in its tastes and activities from other cities of the same size around the country. Something fresh and exciting had been gained, but, undeniably, something richly and colorfully human had been lost.

Atlanta in 1880 was far from a beautiful city. The pleasant recollections of McElreath notwithstanding, his adopted hometown left a lot to be desired even by southern standards. The Gate City suffered from an inadequate sewer system, a shortage of water service, and the near nonexistence of paved streets. A visitor to the city in 1878 was "disappointed to find that it is not at all a pretty or nice town; very inferior in amenities to all the other Southern towns I have seen. It is, in fact, a new brick town built with no trees in the streets, but abundant mud."[2] Truer to Walter McElreath's memories, however, there was a smallness and—so far as entertainment was concerned—an openness to Atlanta that would disappear with time. During the 1880s charismatic individuals drifted onto the local scene, briefly seized the attention of the city, and then just as abruptly set out for the next town down the road.

Two men in particular—"Professor Leon," a tightrope walker, and "Yellowstone Kit," a medicine salesman—skillfully exploited the opportunities available to the low-priced entertainers of the day. Leon, whose real name was J. A. St. John, appeared in Atlanta in the summer of 1886, initially drawing attention with a bird exhibition that he set up near DeGive's Opera House.[3] When newspaper accounts subsequently broadcast his reputation as a tightrope walker, Leon undertook a series of high-wire spectacles that captured the imagination of the city. He attracted several hundred rapt observers with his debut, a walk from rooftop to rooftop across Peachtree Street.[4] Following this success, the professor literally set his sights higher.

In July, a crowd of one thousand excursionists followed him to North Georgia's Tallulah Gorge, where, under the auspices of the Young Men's Library Association, he reportedly walked five hundred yards across a wire stretched one hundred feet above the river below.[5]

His local star rising thanks to newspaper accounts of his exploits, Leon shifted his operations to Atlanta's Grant Park, where he placed his bird exhibit under canvas and regularly walked a wire pulled across the park's lake. By now his performances were drawing thousands of spectators, who taxed the capacity of the city's streetcar system.[6] But the climax was yet to come. The Singer Sewing Machine Company of Atlanta, eager to capitalize on Leon's celebrity for advertising purposes, sponsored a joint appearance by the popular daredevil and his wife. The spectacle began with a procession of wagons—each hauling a Singer sewing machine, and one labeled "What is home without a Singer?"—carrying the couple through the city en route to Grant Park, where the greatest crowd ever to gather there awaited them. Mrs. Leon seated herself before a sewing machine atop a small platform, which assistants hoisted into position some ninety feet above the lake, suspended from Leon's high wire. Mrs. Leon then put on an aerial sewing exhibition—a feat that, the *Journal* duly noted, had "never before" been "attempted by any living lady in the world." The display enchanted the audience: "Mrs. Leon made a beautiful picture suspended between earth and sky with the last rays of the afternoon sun falling full upon her, and tinging her face, hair and garments with red gold." Leon topped off the day by walking the rope above his wife, "his feet encased in brand-new street shoes, with heavy soles." Upon the couple's return to solid ground, the Singer Company presented Mrs. Leon with the machine that she had used, and the Professor gave a short speech on her behalf in which he avowed that the demonstration "was not an advertisement for the Singer Machine Company," while allowing that "the Singer was the best machine made."[7] This triumph—an early Atlanta example of the union of celebrity and mass marketing—notwithstanding, Leon soon disappeared from public view.

Yellowstone Kit's renown was similarly fleeting, but in its way more influential, as Kit apparently helped to end a brief Atlanta experiment with prohibition. Kit was a mysterious figure. The *Savannah Tribune*, an African American newspaper, described him as "a doctor . . . a preacher . . . a stump speaker . . . a puzzle." He was first of all a medicine salesman who hawked a "Japanese Herb Pad," which—for only one dollar—would cure "female weakness," kidney problems, or impotence.[8] In November of 1887 Kit brought to the Gate City a veritable carnival that the *Constitution* characterized as "a conglomeration of everything that was likely to amuse," combining elements of "a country fair, a husking or baking party," and "a go around."[9] Kit's festival attracted throngs from both races to the grounds at the corner of Hunter and Loyd Streets, where the men vied with one another in sprints and bag races and the women took part in cooking contests. His generosity in the way of prizes won for Kit a popularity that was particularly strong, according to the newspapers, among his black patrons.[10]

This is where the trouble arose, for Fulton County was at this time approaching an election that would determine whether or not a prohibition ordinance passed in 1885 would be repealed. Kit's supposed standing among the city's black voters—who held the balance of power between the warring white factions—was such that dignitaries from both the wet and dry camps assiduously courted him as the campaign wound into its final days.[11] When he came out in favor of abolishing the prohibition law, city authorities who opposed repeal summarily evicted him from the fairgrounds, but to little effect. He soon found a new lot and reportedly continued to sway voters as he made speeches for the antiprohibitionists.[12] And so, when the ordinance was indeed repealed, with the county's black population voting heavily for the wet side, the newspapers gave Kit a great measure of the credit.[13] Whatever his true importance to the election, Kit soon moved on and was largely forgotten.[14] Like Leon before him, he achieved great notoriety very rapidly, briefly wielded the influence that this gave him, and then moved on to ply his talents elsewhere. Both men engaged in a type of individually produced spectacle that would give way—as we shall see—to a routinized system of mass amusement in a transformation that paralleled Atlanta's transition from idiosyncratic small town to standardized big city.

As ephemeral as the fame of Leon and Kit were the dime museums that opened and closed in Atlanta during the late nineteenth century. Dime museums were popular across the country at this time, with big cities such as New York, Philadelphia, and Boston harboring large permanent museums, while smaller cities like Atlanta attracted more fly-by-night operations. The typical dime museum was a hastily converted storefront containing a small theater that alternately staged cheap vaudeville acts and exhibitions of "freaks" that a "lecturer" introduced to the gawking customers. These humble institutions might remain in a given location from a few days to several months before picking up and traveling on to the next town and the next curious audience.[15]

Perhaps the first real dime museum in the Gate City was George Johnson's Museum of Living Wonders, which opened under a tent downtown near the railroad station in 1869. Primarily a wild animal show, Johnson's establishment eventually branched out to include human oddities such as midgets, "wild" Australian children, and, for a few days, a man and woman billed as the world's tallest.[16] Over the years, at such transitory exhibitions, Atlantans with a few minutes on their hands could witness a bizarre array of human curiosities, including a boy touted as being half human and half groundhog; a young man blessed with the ability to make bagpipe noises with his mouth; Miss Leak, an armless woman who wrote and sewed with her feet; an "Albino child" put on display as a "wonderful freak of nature"; and Millie-Christine, the two-headed woman.[17] As elsewhere, most of the city's museums also presented other performers to augment the "freaks." When Zera Semon's Dime Parlor Show opened on Peachtree Street in 1885, the management promised to entertain its patrons with "acrobats, fire-eaters . . . trained birds, dogs . . . jugglers, glass-blowers," and so on. Another show that appeared under canvas on Calhoun Street in 1887 likewise presented trained horses, a "slack wire act," and a wrestling match.[18]

No matter what their original intentions, these museums never survived in the Gate City for very long. In late November of 1892, Dr. O. M. Crosby, described in the local papers as "a well-known circus man and sideshow proprietor," opened the Eden Musee at 16 Marietta Street. Crosby's museum boasted a number of colorful acts, including a contortionist, a snake charmer, an acting troupe known as the Lilliputians, and the museum's centerpiece: "Big Hattie" the fat woman, who supposedly weighed 718 pounds ("a monster mountain of animated nature—the largest human being the world has had any record of for the past two hundred years"). At first the Musee drew good-sized audiences, but within a month Crosby fled the city just ahead of an angry gaggle of tax collectors and creditors. A new managing team reopened the business under a different name, but this seems to have been a ruse, for a few days later the *Journal* reported that the managers, along with "the tattooed man, the snake charmer, the little people, 'Big' Hattie, the juggler, the tumbler, the fire-eater, the boy that plays the organ, and the 'What Is It?' have all left town and no one seems to know where they have gone to."[19]

Atlanta's dime museums sometimes suffered from more than mere financial problems. The often lurid entertainment that they provided and the largely working-class audience that they attracted occasionally brought the museums to the attention of city authorities. Managers attempted to combat the dubious reputations of dime museums through newspaper advertisements stressing the suitability of their shows for women and children.[20] But this was not always enough, particularly in the case of the anatomical museums, which represented the most sordid extreme of the business. These establishments enticed male patrons with promises of sexually explicit exhibits and then employed frightening models of diseased sexual organs to terrify the visitors into purchasing "remedies" for venereal disease from quack doctors.[21] In 1909 an Atlanta museum known as the "Hall of Science" met an untimely end when a local politician, his curiosity piqued by the "flaming posters" and the blaring phonograph out front, entered the male-only show to find himself "shocked by the waxworks revelations on the inside" and "outraged by the alleged artistic photographs displayed in slot machines," while "the dozen old wax heads of famous murderers, robbers and other criminals chilled his blood with the gruesome pictures which they conjured." The indignant official promptly reported the show to Mayor Robert Maddox, who, upon completing a personal inspection of the museum, declared it to be "indecent, disgusting and detrimental to the morals of youths who are allowed to witness it." The mayor ordered that the museum be closed immediately, despite the manager's protesting that "we've been coming here for three years . . . and we had no trouble until now. Our show is purely a scientific exhibition."[22]

By this time the dime museum was rapidly becoming a thing of the past anyway, supplanted by cheap vaudeville and the movies. But in its appeal to the poorer classes, in the variety of exciting and often sensational entertainment that it provided, and in the morally critical attention that it received, the dime museum previewed the days to come, when new amusements would promise, as had the dime museum, "a much better show" at ten cents than "people often pay a dollar to see."[23]

The dime museum served as a major influence—along with ten-twenty-thirty-cent melodrama and the minstrel show—on the development of vaudeville. Vaudeville's most important antecedent, however, was the concert saloon, which first appeared in New York City's Bowery section by the early 1850s. These saloons provided a mixture of variety entertainment and alcohol to audiences composed for the most part of working-class men. While this potent innovation attracted the attention of nineteenth-century moral reformers, the concert saloons also drew the interest of Tony Pastor, a New York City showman who was more responsible than anyone for transforming saloon entertainment into vaudeville. Pastor's triumph was in making the variety theater more appealing to middle-class men and women by removing it from its disreputable, liquor-sodden surroundings without completely sapping it of its working-class vitality. Pastor, in the words of one historian, "took vaudeville out of the Bowery without entirely taking the Bowery out of vaudeville." Businessmen B. F. Keith and Edward Albee carried on the refining process that Pastor had begun. Far more interested in money than in morality, Keith and Albee nevertheless realized from the day that they opened their first theater in 1893 that they could maximize profits only if middle-class women, at this time deemed walking imprimaturs of moral sanction, perceived vaudeville houses as suitable places of entertainment for their families. Keith and Albee succeeded in sanitizing vaudeville to the extent that it did indeed attract a wide middle-class audience—the partners' houses were known informally as the "Sunday School Circuit"—and in so doing they began the establishment of vaudeville as a national institution.[24]

The essence of vaudeville was variety. One act followed another in quick succession, leaving little time for boredom and supplying something for almost every taste. A typical early-twentieth-century Atlanta program included acrobats, a cycling act, singers and dancers, a short play, a comedy skit, and a group of "English Ballet Beauties."[25] Rapid pace, quick movement, and unpredictability within a predictable framework all made vaudeville a novel form of entertainment. And this novelty would take some getting used to in the South.

Atlanta experienced the same evolution from morally questionable to decorously respectable vaudeville houses that played out in the Northeast. In the late 1860s, the Gate City witnessed the opening and closing of several early "variety" theaters, many featuring bars. Criticized by the newspapers, and on at least one occasion shut down by the sheriff, these small venues offered their patrons an array of entertainment including song, dance, comedy skits, monologues, impressions, and "negro delineators." At least seven of these theaters existed between 1868 and 1870, demonstrating some short-lived popularity, especially among men. Their dubious atmosphere offended refined opinion, however—a local editor angrily charged that the nightly shows in the theaters "are characterized by profanity and vulgarity too broad for the eye and ear of man"—and no doubt left behind an aroma of immorality that helped make it difficult for more respectable forms of vaudeville to gain a hearing in the Gate City later.[26]

Atlanta owed its first encounter with "Pastorized" vaudeville to the Cotton States and International Exposition of 1895. Anticipating the opportunities that the exposition crowds would bring, local entrepreneurs scrambled to construct vaudeville theaters that could compete for the visitors' amusement dollars. W. H. and Sam Venable, who ran a local granite-contracting and street-paving business, entered the field first, throwing up a temporary structure at the southwest corner of Forsyth and Marietta Streets on the site of the old state capitol. Christened the City Trocadero, the Venables' theater opened in September 1895. The Trocadero was followed in November by the Casino, built on Broad Street by Will Healy, an Atlanta real estate man. And finally, after numerous delays, Harry Frank, described by the *Constitution* as a "ticket-scalping magnate," managed to complete his Imperial Theater, a twelve-hundred-seat house located on Decatur Street near Pryor.[27]

These theaters sought patronage through relatively low ticket prices and the promise of high-quality acts brought in from big northern cities.[28] At the same time, the managers of all three houses worked diligently to emulate Pastor, Keith, and Albee by assuring a skeptical public of the highly moral atmosphere of their establishments. The Trocadero was the most insistent in its claims of wholesomeness, with Manager Otto Weyl vowing from the beginning that no stage or audience misconduct would be tolerated in the new theater. In the *Constitution* he warned, "The Trocadero is to always remain a suitable place for ladies and the amusement of every member of the family. . . . The programme was especially arranged with a view to its adaptation to lady auditors and nothing tending to lower its high standard of respectability will be tolerated or condoned." A puff for the Trocadero in the *Journal* was even more blunt (if a bit wishful): "The Trocadero does not cater to hoi poloi [*sic*]." To the contrary, "there is not a place in the city more popular with the fashionable set than the Trocadero."[29]

Despite such efforts, each of the city's pioneering vaudeville houses faced disaster once the exposition crowds left the city. The Casino went under first when Manager J. W. Weiss, heavily in debt and drawing poor crowds, skipped town to avoid his creditors.[30] The Venables had wisely planned for the Trocadero to last only through the exposition, and it closed in early 1896, after a professional strong man who had appeared there during the fall failed to make a go of managing the house.[31] And the Imperial, opened too late even to take advantage of the exposition audiences, staggered on— through a rapid succession of managers—only by dropping all pretensions to respectability and converting into a burlesque house. Vaudeville's fast-paced, urban brand of entertainment, suffused with ethnic humor, must have seemed puzzling at best and at worst distasteful to the residents of Atlanta, still a small, if growing, southern city with a negligible population of European immigrants.[32] And even had the Gate City supplied larger audiences, local managers would have been hard put to keep their theaters afloat since they faced even greater difficulties in drawing good performers South than did Laurent DeGive.[33]

A second effort to interest Atlantans in vaudeville began in early 1901, when Jake Wells, a Virginian who owned vaudeville theaters in Norfolk and Richmond and who would succeed DeGive as the Gate City's premier amusement baron, attempted to make a success of the long-languishing New Lyceum Theater on Edgewood Avenue.[34] Vaudeville still had its local and vocal critics—Rev. Landrum of the First Baptist Church declared at about this time that there was "little difference between those who trod the vaudeville stage and those locked away in the penitentiary"—and Wells realized that even those Atlantans more open to vaudeville would have to be convinced that variety entertainment could be morally palatable. According to the *Journal*, "Atlanta will probably have to be educated up to polite vaudeville. Several monstrosities disguised as vaudeville companies have given the south a false idea of what it really is. Mr. Wells will have to fight and vanquish the idea and make it clear once [and] for all that there is vaudeville and vaudeville."[35]

Early indications were that Wells might succeed. When his brand of "polite" vaudeville opened at the Lyceum on January 14, 1901, the audience included highly respectable citizens such as Mayor Livingston Mims and Governor Allen Candler.[36] The theater continued to draw good crowds early on; ticket prices were more affordable than were those of the Grand,

and, as a newspaper reported, Atlantans were learning that "Vaudeville can be nice."[37]

Such success, however, was not to last. In November 1901—just days after installation above the New Lyceum of what management boasted was "the largest electric sign in the United States"—the theater burned when the sign collapsed during a matinee performance.[38] By this time Jake Wells had begun shifting his operations to DeGive's old Marietta Street theater, which he completely refurbished and renamed the Bijou. But vaudeville did not survive there for long either, as the Bijou eventually shifted to repertory company theater and then briefly to burlesque before returning to ten-cent vaudeville later in the decade.[39] A growing Atlanta may have shown its first signs of warming up to vaudeville by this time, but, from Jake Wells's perspective, it was still enormously difficult—given the dearth of southern cities able to support theaters—to make vaudeville a profitable proposition. Locals long accustomed to second-rate theater suspected that such logistical difficulties meant that only inferior performers would come to the South. On a streetcar headed home after actor Sidney Drew and his wife had headlined the opening of the New Lyceum, columnist Jacques Futrelle overheard two men discussing the show. "I thought Sidney Drew was a big actor," offered one. "Well, they are all going into vaudeville now," replied the other, bringing the puzzled response, "Possibly good vaudeville yes, but what makes Drew come down here to do it?"[40]

Vaudeville at last began to establish a long-term presence in Atlanta in late 1907, with the opening of the Orpheum Theater on Marietta Street.[41] By this time Atlanta was in the midst of its rapid transformation from "big town" to big city. Diarist Arthur Inman recalled the Atlanta of the first years of the twentieth century as a vibrant mixture of thronged streets, urban soot, and lingering rusticity:

> That was an up-and-coming little city, Atlanta, about 100,000 population. . . . I did not ever feel out of place as a boy in the turmoil of New York, being inured to its smaller copy. Well can I recall downtown Peachtree and Whitehall Streets linked by the viaduct over the railroad tracks. The sidewalks and stores were generally crowded daytimes with walkers—businessmen, countrymen with 'fascinators' around their necks, women shoppers, colored people—and the streets were filled with streetcars, carriages, country carts, drays. The tempo was faster than in Phila-

delphia. There were shops of all sorts. . . . There had been little time or taste, however stylishly the women (not always the men) dressed themselves, to develop handsome architecture. Most buildings were dark gray or red brick color. A bituminous coal shroud of smoke hung over the city. Peachtree Street alone, where most of Atlanta's who's who lived, bore any distinction, and it almost alone was paved with asphalt.[42]

As Inman's recollections suggest, the dawn of the twentieth century was a period of tremendous economic and physical change for Atlanta. Already a major railroad and distribution center as the century opened, the Gate City shipped out hundreds of thousands of bales of cotton every year and dominated a wholesale trading area that extended at least two hundred miles in all directions. In 1900 almost four hundred manufacturers called Atlanta home, generating products ranging from lumber to patent medicines, from clothing to furniture. Over the next thirty years, however, Atlanta's growth sharply accelerated as national and regional firms established branch offices there, as new waves of capital poured into the city, as office buildings sprang up one after another, as new jobs were created, and as the city expanded geographically. During this era of "economic awakening" Atlanta's population swelled remarkably, increasing 72 percent between 1900 and 1910, and 123 percent between 1900 and 1920, when it reached two hundred thousand, second only to New Orleans among southern cities.[43]

With this breakneck development and surging population came problems: a woefully incomplete and outmoded infrastructure, inadequate hospital and school facilities, deteriorating slums, and increasing crime, all symbolized, as Inman remembered, by an ugly pall of industrial smog that choked the city and sometimes turned day to night.[44] But along with the problems came big opportunities for amusement entrepreneurs, in the form of thousands of blue-collar and, especially, white-collar workers who had a bit of money to spend and a little leisure time in which to spend it.[45] As these men and women, like their northern peers, labored in an increasingly regimented and routinized economy, they found in inexpensive commercialized amusement an important avenue of freedom, independence, and enjoyment. The head of a New York settlement house spoke for Atlanta as well as the rest of the nation when he observed that "leisure has come to millions in the past few years. It has come with shorter hours of labor and surplus wealth."[46] And while an evening at the Opera House might have been beyond the means of many, for more and more Atlantans a few hours in a vaudeville theater or a movie house were within reach. Enterprising businessmen in Atlanta as elsewhere were quick to take note of this fact. As one vaudeville promoter explained it, "There are clearly more people in the world who can only afford to pay ten cents for their theatrical amusements than there are who are capable of paying a dollar."[47]

Under these dynamic conditions, vaudeville made tremendous strides toward acceptance and solvency in the Gate City. The genre's effervescent recipe seemed to catch on with the type of audience that bustling Atlanta was increasingly able to provide. A *Journal* reviewer observed that vaudeville was popular "because it is a direct outgrowth of present-day life and needs, the need of spry, restful, constantly changing amusement for fagged-out brains and nerves." The management of the Orpheum's smaller contemporary, the Queen Theater, also claimed an appeal to harried big-city residents, such as "the tired and the languid, the business man and the lady-shopper with half an hour or so to spare."[48] Growing cities throughout the South increasingly supplied similarly agreeable bases for vaudeville and made it easier to route performers through the region.[49]

Vaudeville also worked to adapt itself to Atlanta and the South. More so than the legitimate theater, vaudeville was amenable to quietly effective local censorship: managers were free to remove from the program any act that they believed might be offensive to local tastes.[50] Thus manager Hugh Cardoza, in arguing with typical Atlanta verve that "Vaudeville in New York is not one whit better than vaudeville in Atlanta," could insist, "The only headline acts in New York that are not brought to Atlanta are the ones that the management knows the Atlanta audiences will not stand for."[51] The Orpheum presented the wholesome variety of vaudeville supplied by the Keith-Albee "Sunday School" circuit, reassuring mothers that they and their children might safely attend. Indeed, in an effort to make a visit to the theater even more comfortable for parents, the Orpheum went so far as to provide a nursery, "under the care of an old negro 'mammy'"[52]

Once established, vaudeville's popularity continued to increase through the teens and into the 1920s, as is evidenced by the success of Keith vaudeville, which moved from the Orpheum to the newly constructed Forsyth Theater in 1910, transferred to the larger Lyric Theater in 1917, and ultimately reigned at the million-dollar Georgia Theater, on Peachtree Street adjacent to the Henry Grady Hotel.[53]

There is a sense in which the Gate City and vaudeville had ultimately met one another halfway in a process indicative of the changes then sweeping the American entertainment industry, especially in the South. In 1895 a group of local entrepreneurs began exhibiting a brand of amusement whose original appeal had been to northern working-class audiences, particularly immigrants. These first efforts failed, but Atlanta grew rapidly and eventually came more to approximate—in size and urban tempo—the cities in which vaudeville had gained its initial popularity. The Gate City began to provide a more appreciative audience for the urbanized, rapid-fire entertainment that vaudeville excelled in presenting. In addition, through the continuing efforts of vaudeville producers, exhibitors, and performers, the genre gained an air of respectability that allowed middle-class men and women in Atlanta and elsewhere to feel comfortable about attending. And as vaudeville's popularity in the South increased, it attracted the interest and ultimately came under the sway of northern businessmen. Thus was consummated the complex cultural tradeoff typical of this period, as local idiosyncrasy and control gave way to a nationally homogenized and qualitatively superior product managed and supplied from distant points north.[54]

"Rev. Sam Jones, or some other reformer, has commented on the alleged fact that the recent Cotton States exposition left Atlanta very closely bordering on moral bankruptcy. Of course this is a great exaggeration, but it is true that some things are done in Atlanta now that no one would have dreamed of before the exposition. The flavor of the 'Midway' remains."[55] Thus began a review of the previous night's performance at the Imperial burlesque house. If "polite" vaudeville managed to overcome its initially suspect image among Atlantans and ultimately even attained a reputation of harmless respectability, the same can by no means be said of burlesque, which gained a foothold in the Gate City soon after the exposition helped pave the way by introducing Atlantans to the "coochee-coochee" dance.[56] With its heavy reliance on bawdy humor and minimally clad actresses, burlesque attracted more attention from Atlanta's police and courts than did any other brand of commercial entertainment. In the process it helped to shed light on the attitudes of the "better" class of Atlanta males toward women and sexuality.

Actually, as with variety performances, the Gate City had had some experience with burlesque years before the advent of the Cotton States Exposition. This new form of amusement had entered the United States in 1868 with the tour of Lydia Thompson and her British Blondes, and by 1870 American burlesque troupes were springing up in imitation.[57] As early as 1875 Laurent DeGive was sharply criticized for allowing a troupe of "Parisian can-can" dancers to offer a program of what a newspaper editor labeled "gross immorality."[58] In 1881 a company billing itself as "Miss Fanny Mays and her great troupe of BRITISH BLONDES! and Female Minstrels" appeared before a large and raucous crowd at the Opera House, only to be arrested and fined after the show became too racy and the audience too boisterous to suit local authorities.[59] Later the same year the Rentz-Santley Burlesque Company managed to get through their entire performance without police intervention but afterward fell into a brawl among themselves at the train station, which resulted in several arrests.[60]

Only in the wake of the exposition, however, did burlesque take up permanent residence in Atlanta. Within a few months of the departure of the exposition and its crowds, the Imperial had evolved into a theater in which an all-male clientele could settle in—comfortably free of the behavioral restraints that would have attended the presence of women in the audience—to enjoy a spicy program replete with off-color jokes and exposed female flesh.[61] Companies such as Flagg's Female Minstrels, the Climax Four, and the Bon Ton Burlesquers presented shows at the Imperial with provocative titles like "The Widow Gay," "Cupid in Paradise," the "U Touch Dance," and "Stolen Pleasures."[62] Imperial newspaper ads promised "shapely and pretty young women" and featured drawings of male faces leering at winged angels sporting low-cut full-body tights.[63]

Local newspapers treated the Imperial inconsistently, their tone alternating between masculine jocularity and righteous outrage. An example of the former is an 1898 *Journal* review of an Imperial show, the "most sensational feature" of which was "the disrobing act of Mlle. Bertha Dorian." "Mademoiselle may or may not be French," the columnist began, "but she is a very good looking young woman." Dorian stepped onto the stage "dressed in a very pretty costume of muslin or something or other—men are not judges of these things—with a broad-brimmed hat, as though ready for a stroll in a flower garden." Belying her appearance, she abruptly mounted a trapeze and swung toward the rafters. She then began to shed her clothing, which she pitched to "the Johnnies in the parquet," and at last stood "upon the bar clad in the usual pink tights of the trapeze performer. This disrobing act is all so much extra," the reviewer drolly concluded. "Her performance on the trapeze is up to the average."[64]

Other writers were more critical while nevertheless revealing that such entertainments drew crowds. One reviewed an Imperial burlesque show "of the most lurid type," consisting of Dorian's disrobing act and a skit entitled "The Bridal Chamber." "A description of either act," the columnist stated, "would be out of place in a family newspaper." It was "sufficient to say that each proved intensely interesting" to "the largest audience that ever assembled" within the theater's walls.[65] The *Journal's* reviewer described another Imperial program as the "most indecent exhibition given in Atlanta of late years. . . . Half a dozen men and as many women told old, vulgar 'gags' at the expense of each other, and sang suggestive songs. These 'gags' were of a nature to disgust all right-minded persons, yet few left the theatre." The correspondent somehow managed to enjoy a young woman's punching-bag demonstration but was later appalled when the same actress took part in the "edifying spectacle" of a male-female boxing match. "That the police did not put a stop to the performance is a wonder."[66]

As this statement suggests, Imperial management and performers worked under the constant threat of police interference. Newspapers occasionally reported that police officers had attended Imperial shows on the lookout for indecency, and one *Journal* review noted that the current salacious offering at the playhouse would doubtless draw large crowds, provided the police did not intervene. Usually, however, either because the actors bowdlerized the programs when they knew that policemen were present, or because the officers felt that the entertainment was not obscene enough to warrant legal action, the shows went on without interference.[67]

A notable exception occurred in January of 1900, when police arrested Imperial manager Fred Rider, dancer Vera Harvey, and comedian W. H. Truehart following an evening performance. The defendants appeared before Judge Nash Broyles in a case that a *Constitution* correspondent regarded as "possibly the liveliest that has ever been [heard] in the recorder's court." Rider was charged with running a disorderly house, and Harvey and Truehart with violating the section of the city code that prohibited the public presentation of "indecent or obscene dances or songs." A sensation-seeking audience packed the courtroom for the trial, lending a festive air to the proceedings. Officer Beavers attempted to describe to the court the "Bowery" dance that had sparked the arrests, but the *Constitution* writer found this account "too indecent to be printed." Other officers stated that the Imperial had long been the target of complaints by offended Atlantans, with one policeman stating that he himself had seen "young men and even boys going into the place. As for the show, it is about as indecent as it well could be and is a disgrace to any civilized community." Truehart insisted that he had presented the same act "before lady audiences" in "every city from Maine to St. Louis" without upsetting anyone, and Manager Rider threw in that he had seen the identical dance staged at the Grand and Columbia theaters in Atlanta.

To settle the issue, Judge Broyles agreed to Truehart's request that he and Harvey be allowed to demonstrate the dance. The eager crowd cleared a space for the impromptu performance, and the two defendants "waltzed around the courtroom" under the recorder's stern gaze. Afterward, Broyles asked Officer Beavers whether the dance as given matched the dance that was presented in the Imperial. "Yes," Beavers replied, "but with the trimmings off, and it is the trimmings that make it indecent."

With or without "trimmings," the dance sufficiently impressed Judge Broyles. He dismissed the case against Rider since the Imperial did not technically meet the city code's description of a disorderly house. He threw out the case against Harvey as well since she was "not fully identified as the one who was in the vile and indecent act." Truehart, however, was not so fortunate. Broyles fined him $100.75 and in the process delivered what the *Constitution* called "one of the most denunciatory excoriations ever pronounced by a judge in a court of justice."

Broyles began by defending the theater in general, stating, "Some plays are as good as sermons and no one enjoys them more than myself." But "when the stage becomes lowered from its high plane and becomes vile and polluted, nothing can do more harm in a community, nothing can so thoroughly disseminate its filth and slime among the people." As for Truehart, the judge asserted that "a man who would so lower himself as to publicly give . . . such an indecent exhibition as the evidence shows this to have been, is so morally rotten that even a self-respecting buzzard would be nauseated in his presence." But at least Truehart was male, rendering such behavior comprehensible. Broyles was at a loss in condemning Harvey's actions: "As to a woman who would do such a thing, I have no words in my vocabulary to express my contempt for such an unsexed creature."[68] Clearly, in Broyles's view, men could behave vulgarly and remain men; a woman who conducted herself in so unwholesome a manner was defined as an abhorrent "creature" beyond the bounds not only of her sex but of her species.

However negative the opinions of many Atlantans, the Imperial continued, under a series of different names and managers, to stage racy shows with varying degrees of success.[69] Whatever the name or manager, though, the theater's reputation remained constant. Sometimes this alone was enough to frighten off potential performers. A 1906 *Journal* article related the dire situation of six Chicago chorus girls who had come to Atlanta on the understanding that they were to appear at J. B. Thompson's El Dorado Theater. When they learned that Thompson actually intended that they play his other theater, the Star, formerly the Imperial, they balked and as a result were left stranded in Atlanta. "Just to think," exclaimed one of the actresses, "just to think of us playing at the Star!"[70] A year later three more women came to Atlanta, this time from Cincinnati, to perform at the Star. But when they arrived and inspected the theater, they decided that they "did not like the appearance of things" and refused to go on stage, sparking a monetary dispute with manager Thompson, who demanded that they repay him for their railroad tickets.[71]

One of the final appearances that the Imperial, by now known as the Lyceum, made in the public eye occurred during the 1908 Atlanta mayoral campaign, which was bitterly fought over issues of personal morality. When candidate and former mayor James G. Woodward, under attack for episodes of public drunkenness, challenged his wealthy and eminently respectable opponent, Robert F. Maddox, to a debate in the Lyceum Theater, Maddox scornfully replied that he had "no intention of dragging" his cause "into the mire of the Old Star theatre on Decatur street . . . nor of engaging in joint debate with this man who is destitute of every sense of private and public decency."[72] For many Atlantans, the Star was the very embodiment of commercialized dissolution and depravity.

The burning of the Lyceum in 1909 left Atlanta without a regular burlesque house until 1913, when the Columbia Theater opened on Central Avenue, with the chief of police on hand to monitor the performance. The Columbia attracted a lively opening-night audience composed exclusively of males, who reportedly relished the "novelty of sitting coatless, smoking a cigarette or a stogie" while "endowed with perfect freedom to speak [their minds] upon any song, act or actor." The crowd cheered and freely shouted approval to the women in tights but were rebuked by a police officer when they became "over obstreperous" in their "disapproval of some of the 'gentlemen' performers." [73]

Within a couple of months of the Columbia's debut, Chief of Police James Beavers and Recorder Nash Broyles had begun a probe of the city's cheaper theaters, looking for evidence of "obscene jokes," underage actresses, and "over-brevity of costume." Edward Arthur of the Recorder's Court was appointed city theatrical censor with authority to order cuts in unseemly performances. [74] By April of 1914 Arthur had repeatedly brought Columbia actors and actresses before Judge Broyles, inciting City Councilman Jesse Lee, part owner of the theater, to complain about Arthur's "Sunday school attitude and methods" and to threaten legal action aimed at forcing the city to abolish Arthur's position. [75]

Over the next few years the Columbia continued to have trouble with the police. In 1916 officers raided the theater and arrested its manager, six actors, and eleven actresses. The motley troupe created "considerable comment" while being marched in costume down Decatur Street to the police court, where the recorder fined manager Jack Mashburn two hundred dollars for running an indecent show and fined two comedians one hundred dollars each for selling pornographic cards. As in the earlier Imperial case, however, the judge did not penalize the women involved. John Manget, the cotton broker and self-appointed moral guardian who had brought the original complaint against the theater, argued that the women "are not to blame. They are brought here by the managers, who tell them that Atlanta will stand for anything and order them to go the full limit." The court nonetheless threw the actresses out of work, as the recorder ordered that the Columbia be "closed and kept closed unless somebody wanted to use it for a Sunday school meeting." [76] This scenario recurred in 1917, when police hauled the manager of the reopened Columbia, along with eleven female dancers and their manager, before the recorder. After the lead actress performed the dance in question for the judge, he once again dismissed charges against the women while fining the male managers twenty-five dollars apiece. [77]

While the Columbia remained an inviting target for police intervention, more decorous mainstream theaters dabbled in burlesque with relative impunity. As early as 1909, the Bijou served briefly as a burlesque house. But after twelve to fifteen profitable weeks of "off-color" fare, managers Jake

Wells and Henry DeGive canceled further such productions, claiming that they did so in the name of "decency."[78] By 1914, however, Wells had apparently experienced a change of heart, as he again staged burlesque, this time at his Lyric Theater. Once more the effort was short lived, reportedly because the Lyric failed to draw sufficient crowds.[79]

Increasingly after the turn of the century, other brands of entertainment began eagerly appropriating the brazen sensuality that was burlesque's stock-in-trade, presenting it in ostensibly more respectable forms and settings.[80] By the late teens and 1920s, burlesque-style humor and revealingly clad actresses appeared with increasing frequency on the stages of Atlanta's leading theaters. In 1920, for example, Ward Greene reviewed *La La Lucille,* which was appearing at the Atlanta Theater. He characterized the play as a "gallery show" since the denizens of the theater's upper reaches had lustily cheered the production's dances—particularly the "shimmy"—and its humor. Greene asserted, "The naughtiness isn't in the dances—shimmies far more suggestive have been seen here several times this season—but in the lines, which aren't suggestive at all. They are quite definite, at times rankly so." Still, Greene allowed that the show was "genuinely funny."[81] Others were not as amused by the influence that this and similar productions had on Atlanta nightlife. A few months after the appearance of *La La Lucille,* Chief of Police Beavers authorized two policewomen to inform local theater and dance-hall owners that, in the words of the *Journal,* "the shimmy could not be shaken in Atlanta any more, and that any person caught shimmying would be subject to arrest on a charge of disorderly conduct." One of the policewomen insisted that the dance encouraged drinking, offering as evidence the title of a record she had heard, "You Cannot Make Your Shimmy Shake On Tea."[82]

The amused tone of this article and Greene's ultimately positive review of *La La Lucille* illustrate the hypocrisy that pervaded local newspaper coverage of theatrical sexuality in general and of burlesque in particular. The papers frequently assumed tones of righteous morality when editorially discussing such issues, as when the *Journal* congratulated Wells and DeGive for abandoning burlesque in 1909.[83] At the same time, however, the *Journal* often included titillating burlesque reviews that emphasized the physical allure of female performers. In his description of a Lyric burlesque show, columnist Britt Craig rhapsodized in the masculine lingo of the day over the production's dancers, especially the "blonde broilers on the extreme ends of the front row" and "the bathing girl": "Last night's bathing girl . . . was a 'bear'—or should I say 'bare!' . . . And the blonde broilers! . . . They are shapely, flaxen-haired and vivacious. It seems that the director of each . . . show has a weakness for little frivolous blondes on each end of his front row." As for the chorus, "Some are slim and some are lean . . . but, of course, the buxom show girls in the rear line are there, which offsets the elongated effect of the front division." Craig coyly concluded that the show was "worth the money." [84]

The history of burlesque in Atlanta reemphasizes what the various controversies in DeGive's theaters had revealed: the absence of any uniform set of community standards among an increasingly diverse urban population. What one spectator saw as a harmless and good-humored display of female beauty, another viewed as obscenely excessive and morally offensive. It periodically fell to the recorder to fix boundaries, to make decisions—based on a mixture of legal ordinance and his own perceptions—about what was acceptable to the community and what was not. Remaining consistent over the years were the attitudes of local journalists and officials toward women, who were viewed, on the one hand, as responsible for upholding a superior form of virtue—thus Broyles's horror over the actions of Vera Harvey— and, on the other, as helplessly malleable objects vulnerable to ruthless manipulation by male managers and promoters. Men were the autonomous figures with the prerogative to scrutinize and appraise female bodies, to lead young women into debauchery (or to protect them from such a fate), and to determine exactly when a woman had legally stepped over the ever-shifting line into indecency.[85] Also consistent over the years was the appeal to many Atlantans—and thus to their newspapers—of the sort of sexually charged plays and shows that horrified clerics and more conservative folk.

Burlesque never achieved anything approaching the success of vaudeville in the Gate City. The genre was too vulgar to be rendered respectable enough for broad public acceptance; indeed, burlesque probably appealed to its followers for precisely this reason. In contrast to vaudeville, the amusement itself was not made respectable, but rather elements of it were drawn—tamed and polished—into more respectable genres such as the mainstream theater.

The Cotton States and International Exposition, designed to showcase Atlanta and the South to the rest of the nation, had incidentally introduced the Gate City to new and exotic forms of entertainment. Vaudeville would only truly take root in Atlanta once the city began to approximate in reality the metropolis that in 1895 it had but brashly pretended to be. And burlesque would fight a running battle with city authorities for more than twenty years. Taken together, these amusements represented the promise and the threat that Atlanta faced as it rapidly grew and came more and more to be what its leaders had always claimed they wanted it to be: a major, cosmopolitan city respected by the urban titans of the Midwest and Northeast. Vaudeville held the allure of wholesome, family-oriented, big-city entertainment; burlesque seemed to many to embody the danger of collapsing morals and sexual debauchery. Vaudeville suggested that Atlanta could modernize on its own terms; burlesque implied that in gaining the world the Gate City might sacrifice its soul.

Before Atlantans could fully work out the ramifications of either of the new amusements, however, an even newer form of entertainment began to take hold. Although few had noticed it at the time, the exposition had also introduced Atlanta and the world to something far more lasting and significant than either vaudeville or burlesque, something that would sweep all before it in its startlingly rapid rise to the top of the entertainment world. This phenomenon was the motion picture.

⊰ 3 ⊱

Atlanta and the Movies

In September of 1895, inventors Thomas Armat and C. Francis Jenkins paid five hundred dollars for one of the last concessions granted by the Cotton States and International Exposition. On the eastern fringe of the midway, the partners built a one-thousand-dollar shed that would go down in history as the site of the world's first commercially operated movie exhibition using modern equipment. But whatever its significance for historians, the makeshift theater attracted little attention from those who actually attended the exposition. Although the *Journal* gave the movie house a small but positive review, and the partners employed a variety of promotional techniques, the expected crowds never came. Ultimately the disappointed entrepreneurs dropped the twenty-five-cent admission charge and simply encouraged tired fairgoers to come into the theater and rest, with the film thrown in as an added treat. When the show was over, a "spieler" would explain how expensive it had been for the exhibitors to set up shop at the exposition and would urge the spectators to drop quarters into a box on their way out.

Despite these efforts, the world's first movie house did not survive. Jenkins left the exposition after only a few days, and, following a fire that severely damaged the theater in mid October, Armat abandoned the enterprise as well, in his estimate two thousand dollars the poorer. As Atlanta city clerk Walter Taylor recalled the episode many years later, "I doubt if one person in a thousand who went on the Midway ever knew the movie theater was there. People don't go to a fair to sit down and look at pictures. . . . I remember I felt sorry for the boys when their theater burned down and their show was such a flop, but I never once thought that we

would be looking back on that unsuccessful little venture as the most significant thing on the Midway."[1]

Although few, as Taylor pointed out, could have imagined it at the time,
within two decades the movies would become by far the most popular form
of commercial entertainment in Atlanta. In this, Atlanta differed little from
cities and towns all over the country that quickly succumbed to the new
medium's novel appeal. But the movies arrived in the Gate City during
a particularly crucial period in Atlanta's history, as its population mush-
roomed and its people struggled to deal with the transformations and concerns that inevitably accompanied such rapid growth. To many Atlantans
the movies came to symbolize a new form of "cosmopolitanism," a worldliness and diversity that some welcomed but others believed should be rejected wholeheartedly. Conflicts and debates over the movies, then, were
more than merely arguments about images flickering on a screen; they were
at root disagreements over the future course of a growing city that seemed
to be approaching a decisive crossroads in its development. So whether the
focus of dispute happened to be the morality of the films themselves, the
atmosphere inside the theaters, or the times at which it was appropriate or
inappropriate to screen movies, underneath lay deep concern and disagreement over the path that Atlanta would choose for itself as it encountered
the many opportunities, demands, and dangers of the new century.[2]

Not everyone lost faith in the future of motion pictures following the quiet
debacle at the exposition. During the spring of 1896 a business group
headed by Thomas Edison began financing exhibitions across the country
featuring a variation of the Armat-Jenkins projector, now known as "Edison's vitascope."[3] In November, the vitascope reached Atlanta in association
with the Florence Hamilton repertoire company, which played DeGive's
Columbia Theater for a week at popular prices. Now rather than be persuaded to enter a ramshackle structure at the remote edge of a midway,
audiences could encounter film as an added attraction thrown in with an
inexpensive play at an established theater. In this context, the movies made
more of an impression. On the vitascope's first night in the city, the crowd
in the Columbia saw film of a "skirt dance" by an Atlanta girl who had
made good in New York, a scene of firemen rescuing children from a burning building, another sequence featuring "two Irishmen discussing politics
over their beer," and, finally, the famous "May Irwin Kiss," which showed

a man and woman exchanging a brief peck on the lips. This was Edison's most popular film of 1896, and it reportedly had to be encored several times for the Atlanta audience.[4]

Hard on the heels of the vitascope came its rival, the Eidoloscope, which made its Atlanta debut at the Lyceum Theater as part of Rosabel Morrison's production of *Carmen*. This time the film was actually incorporated into the play, in the form of a Mexican bullfight lasting over ten minutes.[5]

Other projecting systems, bearing names such as the "veriscope" and the "cinematograph," visited the Gate City in 1897 and 1898, presenting footage of exciting events such as the James Corbett–Robert Fitzsimmons heavyweight boxing championship and battleships purportedly "in action" during the Spanish-American War.[6] By the first years of the twentieth century it was becoming increasingly common for Atlanta theaters, like play and vaudeville houses throughout the country, to present films along with their main productions.[7]

The "nickelodeon" craze began sweeping urban America in 1905, and Atlanta was not long in taking part.[8] The Gate City's first movie house—the Peachtree Theatorium, housed in the Piedmont Hotel—opened unobtrusively for business in April 1906. Two months later Ezekiel Wall debuted the Electric Theater on Whitehall Street.[9] His son later recalled, "We nailed several chairs together, and used them for rows of seats." He described the Electric's projection booth as being "nothing more than a small uninclosed balcony" and claimed that "inquisitive folk would often climb over to see where the pictures were coming from. Others tried to get in back of the screen to see if real people were not behind it."[10] Wall's reminiscences suggest that these earliest theaters attracted, at least in part, an audience that had not been exposed to the films screened previously in Atlanta's larger and more expensive theaters, the same audience, in fact, that was also embracing other forms of cheaper entertainment.[11]

Although many of them would be short lived, by 1907 there were already some twenty "electric" theaters in Atlanta, clustered for the most part in the city's downtown business district on Peachtree and Whitehall Streets.[12] Nickelodeons proliferated so rapidly because they were relatively inexpensive to establish, information on how to open them was widely available, and the trade press helped to build expectations of quick and easy profits.[13] In its 1907 catalog, the Chicago Projecting Company promised that two hundred dollars would completely cover the costs of converting a store to a movie house, and by 1908, the Sears, Roebuck catalog was offering a do-it-yourself storefront theater kit that could be shipped anywhere, complete with "projectors, films, chairs, posters and rolls of tickets" and including "pressed-tin or terra-cotta" decorations for the nickelodeon's exterior. The catalog painted an enticing picture of the movie business, promising easy and certain success: "Almost any vacant store room can be made into a five-cent theater by removing the glass front and replacing it with a regular theater front," while "the low price of admission is an inducement which many people cannot resist."[14] Spurred by such encouragement, budding entrepreneurs and experienced businessmen alike threw together nickelodeons all over the country, using bright exterior lighting, colorful posters, bellowing barkers, and shrieking phonographs to lure patrons into the theaters' dim, undecorated interiors.[15]

Atlanta, like other cities, hosted a varied cast of motion picture pioneers. William Oldknow was one of the more successful. He had been a city councilman, president of the Atlanta Carriage Company, manager of an Atlanta motor company, and a poolroom owner before running a succession of movie houses, after which he moved on to become an executive in a movie equipment and film supply company. For Odis D. Posey, on the other hand, prosperity was more fleeting. His name first appears in the Atlanta *City Directory* of 1909, where he is listed as owner of the Elite Theater. He subsequently built another theater, the Posey, and formed the Posey Amusement Company. But by 1912 he was a mere "clerk" with the General Film Company.[16]

Other theater owners began movie houses as sidelights to their everyday careers. John and Gus Evins were running a furniture business when someone suggested that they convert a part of their store into a movie theater. Heeding the advice, they partitioned off an eighteen-by-eighty-foot space and opened it in December of 1908 as the Vaudette Theater. Successful here, they soon secured larger quarters near their store and, after traveling to New York and other cities to study movie-house design, built a new Vaudette, which premiered in September of 1911 with a seating capacity of eight hundred. At this point the brothers gave up the furniture business and devoted all of their energies to managing their theater.[17]

Atlanta's early movie houses competed with one another—and supplemented sometimes hard-to-get films—by offering live entertainment along with the pictures, a natural combination since movies had long been a fix-

ture at the end of vaudeville shows. One of Atlanta's earliest newspaper
movie advertisements, for Roll's Electric Theater, promised "Mr. Loyd
Kenney, Alabama's most Noted Tenor," would sing illustrated songs between reels. The Paris Theater in 1909 offered a tenor and a pianist performing daily, and the Queen Theater boasted in the same year that the
singing Brunswig Brothers were packing in audiences.[18]

In the beginning the motion picture business in Atlanta, as elsewhere,
was a rough-and-tumble affair. Theaters sprang up and disappeared, managers came and went, and everyone involved fought for the available films.
Pioneer Atlanta film man J. A. Rebb remembered that in the earliest days,
"when pictures arrived each morning at the offices of the Consolidated
[Film Company] first-run films were set aside on one end of a long table for
the Vaudette Theater, while second-run features were piled in a tangled
heap at the other end of the table. Then the . . . theater men engaged in a
mad scramble for material." The "managers hardly had a chance to look at
the titles of the pictures," Rebb recalled. "Those that came late got what
was left, and considered themselves lucky to find any pictures at all, for on
a few occasions there were not enough to go around."[19]

During the first years of Atlanta's moving-picture history, city authorities
expressed more interest in the safety features of the theaters than in the
content of the films that were shown. The possibility of fires was an early
concern, and in 1907 a special committee of the city council agreed upon
regulations that would help lessen the danger of theater conflagrations.[20]
Some officials also worried that the storefront theaters served as breeding
grounds for disease. After inspecting Atlanta's movie houses in 1909, the
head of the city board of health proposed measures to require better theater
ventilation. As the *Journal* vividly reported, with a clear measure of middle-
class disdain, "Some of the little theaters . . . are sanitary enough, and furnish enough unbreathed air to their patrons, but some of them are nothing
more than veritable boxes into which fresh air rarely enters and the impov-
erished air, laden with germs from expectorations on the floor and from
the breath of hundreds of catarrhal and otherwise diseased persons, is but
stirred about by the fans."[21]

Downtown businessmen sometimes complained about the noise that the
nickelodeons made. In 1907 R. F. Sheldon, local manager of the Mutual Life
Insurance Company of New York, brought to the city council's attention the
noise that blared from a theater across the street from his offices in the

English-American building. He argued that "unless something was done, he would have to move out of his offices, as the noises of the graphophone, the electric piano and the speiler [*sic*] made it impossible for him to attend to his work. He also objected generally to turning Peachtree and Whitehall streets, as he termed it, into midway amusement places."[22] That same year Southern Bell telephone operators had the manager of the Edisonia Electric Theater brought before the recorder for ceaselessly blasting music in the direction of their building.[23] Charles Glover went to court four years later to demand that the Ivy Theater be forced to relocate. As things stood, his real estate office was separated from the theater by only a thin wall, and Glover claimed that he was daily forced to listen to vaudeville acts and movies from ten in the morning till eleven at night.[24]

Nuisances or not, the early movie theaters claimed, as had legitimate theaters and vaudeville houses before them, to present their varied wares in a wholesome environment. A typical ad, for the Union Theater on North Broad Street, claimed that the house was a "Refined family theatre, showing high-class vaudeville; latest moving pictures and illustrated songs," with "Special attention given to ladies and children."[25] Individual movie-house managers also worked hard in other ways to win public approval. In 1907 J. P. Jones of the Terminal Electric Theater held a well-publicized free screening of "The Passion Play" for Atlanta-area orphans.[26] And George Crater turned the noise issue to pious use when he turned over his Elite Theater to the YMCA for Sunday afternoon services, the hope being that the house's "central location and the attraction of an electric piano playing religious music before the theater [would] draw hundreds who would not go down to Auburn-ave. and Pryor-st. to the Young Man's Christian Association building."[27]

Moreover, within a few years of the opening of Atlanta's first nickelodeons, a succession of increasingly large and comfortable theaters began to appear as the industry stabilized and as movie exhibitors sought to attract and maintain a more respectable middle-class audience.[28] As a 1911 puff in the *Georgian* noted, "the time has passed when people will give any extensive patronage to a motion picture theater which is no more than a hastily renovated store room." More and more theaters strove to provide "class and tone" for an "amusement-loving Atlanta public [that] appreciates artistic and pleasant surroundings and high class excellence in entertainment just as much in a five or ten-cent theater as in an opera house."[29] The Evins

Brothers' Vaudette was an example of this new breed of movie houses, as was its predecessor the Alcazar, "The Theater Beautiful," which opened on Peachtree Street in 1909. Owner R. C. Howard, of the Howard Safe and Vault Company, reportedly spent twenty thousand dollars turning a storeroom into this state-of-the-art movie house. The Alcazar boasted a five-thousand-dollar pipe organ and was capable of seating more than four hundred people on its main floor and balcony. Advertisements for the theater promised "Four exclusive Moving Picture Acts, 3 Illustrated Songs, Pipe Organ Solos and Orchestra Overture at every performance." Each program lasted one hour, and tickets sold for ten cents, with children under fourteen entering for a nickel.[30] Local movie men reminiscing for the *Journal* twenty years later recalled that the Alcazar represented a great advance in movie theater design. Older movie houses had never lost the look of roughly converted stores, but the Alcazar, with its paneled walls, attractive decorations, and expensive pipe organ, was something else again.[31] Atlantans flocked to the new theater. According to the *Journal,* the Alcazar attracted 19,573 patrons during the last week of April 1909, with 4,246 attending on Confederate Memorial Day alone. A few months later, 3,012 patrons spent a portion of their Labor Day at the popular movie house.[32]

An incident that occurred in 1910 shows how successful Atlanta's picture shows were becoming at capturing the audience that many of them desired. In February, the city council amended an ordinance in order to require women to remove their hats in the city's movie houses just as they already had to do in Atlanta's legitimate theaters. Alderman W. A. Hancock and Councilman Steve Johnston initiated the amendment after they had attended the movies only to have their views blocked by hats that they claimed were three feet across and two feet high. Mayor Maddox signed the law, but not without sparking some protest. According to the *Journal,* one woman angrily stated, "It is just such selfish laws that mould home-loving women into suffragettes." [33]

Two weeks later a special council committee recommended that the ordinance be once again amended, this time to require removal of hats only after 6:00 P.M. This move followed debate in which several movie men and their attorney complained that the law was hurting business. William Oldknow claimed that attendance at his two houses had declined by at least 30 percent since the hat ordinance had gone into effect, and the manager of the Majestic Theater said that his business had been cut in half. "Our patrons are composed largely of ladies who come to town shopping and visit the shows incidentally," argued the managers. "Their hair is not prepared as if for a matinee at a grand opera; they spend only a short while at our shows." These women become "indignant when requested to remove their hats and demand a refund of their ticket money." The managers' attorney called the ordinance "an exemplification of masculine selfishness. It is the divine feminine prerogative for women to war [*sic*] their hair and hats as they please and wherever they please. I'd rather see a woman in a pretty hat than any picture show in the world." Councilman Johnston was unmoved, insisting that movie patrons "want to be able to see what's on the screen. It is impossible to see the pictures through the hay racks worn by some of the ladies."[34]

Whatever else this conflict reveals, it shows that as early as 1910 the movies had attained a striking degree of respectability and popularity in Atlanta. City officials were not ashamed to admit that they attended the movies, and women—apparently quite reputable women—and children made up the bulk of the thousands of Atlantans who were passing through movie house doors every day, thus lending the much-sought-after feminine seal of approval to the motion picture as well. It had become unremarkable for an altogether proper woman to "consume" a reel or two of film as a restful break from more traditional consumption. Clearly, the movies were winning over the crucial middle-class audience.

On the other hand, many Atlantans continued to worry about the ramifications of easily obtainable commercial entertainment, especially in relation to the looming moral controversies of the day. The early twentieth century was a period of gnawing uneasiness and recurring crisis for Atlanta as the city experienced unbridled growth and the ills that accompanied it. The riot of 1906 had been an early manifestation of the deep social strains brought on by urbanization in a Deep South context, strains that only appeared to multiply in the 1910s. The Gate City seemed to be at a major crossroads; the traditional ways and mindset of an older South confronted the challenges and complexities of the modernizing industrial world. The profound misgivings that resulted often boiled to the surface in rancorous debates over the course the city was taking. Whether the issue at hand was prostitution, the proper use of the Sabbath, or the rebirth of the Ku Klux Klan, amusements frequently found themselves playing central, controversial, and usually unintended roles in the city's disputes.

As the movies grew in popularity, they in particular came under scrutiny. Many Progressive Era Atlantans, like their counterparts elsewhere, fretted over the effects that motion pictures might be having on their patrons, especially those viewers—such as the children and young women now pouring into Atlanta's theaters—whom the city's elite considered to be most vulnerable and impressionable. It was such concern in 1910 that led the *Constitution* to ask three "well-known" members of the Georgia and Atlanta Federations of Women's Clubs to inspect the city's movie theaters and to "report their observations as to the character of the pictures shown, from the standpoint of educational and moral value, and whether they were such as would exercise unwholesome influence upon the minds of those witnessing them, particularly of children."

Significantly, these women took pains to point out that they did not enter the project in a spirit of hostility toward the movies, but rather that they brought to their task a recognition of the vast educational potential of film. As they put it, "No modern invention can do more to interest, instruct, inspire, in the fullest sense to educate, than the moving picture, if properly censored." At the same time, however, as they added in boldface, "if carrying the wrong messages through that swift messenger to the eye, no other medium can do so much to sully and cheapen the standards of mind and soul."[35]

Upon entering the city's picture houses, the inspectors found examples of both the benefits and the dangers that they associated with the movies. They were heartily impressed by religious pictures that were showing at the Alamo and Elite theaters. One film in particular, *Moses Leading the Children of Israel Forth from Egypt,* won their approval by demonstrating the motion picture's powerful potential for good. The trio felt that this movie "would do more to print upon the mind of youth the drama of the plagues which brought about the proud Pharaoh's command: 'Let them go!' than years of verbal description could do."

The women also gave nods of approval to *The Clemency of Abraham Lincoln* as well as to less inspiring pictures that were nevertheless "entertaining" or "amusing," such as *The Fairies of Hallowe'en, Lassie's Birthday,* and *The Woodsman and the Ranchman.* One film in this category, *A Bargain in Hats,* nearly crossed the line into immorality by suggesting "a world in which at least suspicions of universal probity existed," but fortunately it managed to do so "very slightly and without offense."

The same could by no means be said of *A Sufferer from Insomnia,* which was playing at a theater that the women forbore to name, "in the hope that only by an accident could it have shown such a mass . . . of actual vulgarity." The inspectors were nonetheless disgusted by this movie house and its patrons, and at the film's close the offended censors had been "glad to escape into the fresh air without having been hurt or soiled by the crashing of old furniture, the falling of ashes, [or the] soiled clothes and more objectionable things upon some very unpleasant looking negroes."

Pressing onward, the women found "only one show which we were told did not court the presence of ladies. This was visited, however, and, from start to finish, it is objectionably obscene and profane, and should be abolished or made to mend its ways." Alas, "The crowds here were greater than at any other show."

Despite these exceptions, the report concluded, "In the main . . . the pictures presented in Atlanta [are] of a good class." The authors suggested that if only the city's theaters "would advertise more fully their educational or aesthetic specialties," patronage would increase enough to justify even more of this kind of programming. "Thus could this mighty influence for good or for evil be of more positive value, and become more profitable at one and the same time."[36] For the time being, it appeared, the city's movie theaters were conducting themselves in moral enough fashion that there was no need for closer city supervision.

If the growing presence of middle-class women and their children tended to give the movies a higher profile and an air of propriety, there were contradictory trends at work as well. As the inspectors' references to "soiled negroes" and shows not courting "ladies" suggest, for every large Vaudette, Alcazar, or Savoy theater that promoted its "class and tone," there were several smaller, cheaper theaters that appealed to predominantly working-class audiences and that increasingly alarmed city authorities. In particular, the small five-cent houses that combined movies and cheap vaudeville—the Bonita, the American, the National—attracted the critical attention of Atlanta's moral guardians.

From the start, of course, movie houses in Atlanta and elsewhere had drawn a large working-class audience. Low ticket prices made the theaters accessible to many workers, the movies required a much smaller investment of time than did the legitimate theater, and the audience was allowed to talk freely during the films, a practice more and more frowned upon in the opera houses. But these working-class folk had mingled in the early movie audiences with more affluent Atlantans in an atmosphere akin to that which had characterized the legitimate theater. After 1910, however, as movie houses began to distinguish themselves one from the other on the basis of the class of patrons each attracted, the cheaper theaters became more suspect in some people's eyes. The films shown, the acts staged, and the audiences drawn in all seemed dangerously free from the control of a concerned middle class and clergy desperate to rein in troubling social and cultural change.

Hostility toward the smaller movie/vaudeville houses sharpened in 1911 and especially in 1912 due to a deepening climate of concern over the "plight" of the city's young working women and the possible role that cheap theaters played in encouraging vice. In 1912, backed by the Evangelical Ministers' Association and the Men and Religion Forward Movement, which had branched into Atlanta the previous year, Chief of Police James Beavers launched a sensational offensive against prostitution and Atlanta's "Tenderloin" district.[37] Beavers and his men captured headlines as they closed brothels, sought to identify hotels that harbored prostitutes, and scoured the streets for loose women plying their trade outdoors.[38] Beavers and the newspapers also focused attention on the cheaper theaters and their possible connection to the flesh trade. As the *Constitution* editorialized, "There is no guesswork about the city ordinances as they apply to young girls appearing on the stages of moving picture shows in Atlanta. The law throws its shielding arms around the child-woman, and if the law is not being observed then the city should know the reason why." The editor concluded by warning, "Atlanta is growing so large that unless the streets and cheap theaters are scrupulously guarded, they may degenerate into recruiting places for vice."[39] As the editorial suggests, of particular concern was the issue of underage girls performing on stage, and perhaps being lured into lives of debauchery. The *Georgian* solemnly described the venues in which such tragedies played out:

> Pass down some of the uptown streets any afternoon. From the gaudily decorated front of these theaters you will hear the blare of a noisy or-

chestra or the thump of a piano and hear the shrill, raucous voices of a dozen girls. Pay your coin and step inside. There are the girls, dancing awkwardly, shrieking out a popular song without regard to time or melody. They are dressed in the cheapest of costumes, the shortest of skirts. They are daubed with grease paint, plastered with powder. The spectacle is more pitiful than amusing, but the audiences which throng these places are not critical.[40]

"More pitiful than amusing"—once again, as in burlesque, women were viewed as sympathetic characters led astray by exploitative males. From stages such as these it was supposedly but a small step for star-struck and deluded young women to lives of degradation and prostitution.[41]

The vice war eventually lost momentum, and, after passions had receded, presumably it was business as usual again in the small theaters and in the red-light district. There is no way of determining at this remove how accurate the charges against the cheaper houses might have been, how undergirded with evidence and innocent of class and gender bias. The episode does reveal, however, how potent issues involving class and gender were in Progressive Era Atlanta and how closely linked amusements were to debates over the Gate City's moral course.[42]

This intimate connection between amusements and apprehensions about change is also clearly central to Atlanta's most publicized dispute over the motion pictures. This time, the controversy did not concern the films themselves or the goings-on inside the theaters so much as it did the question of when it was and was not appropriate to screen films in the first place.

The conflict erupted in March of 1913, when local movie-house managers began to open their theaters on Sundays.[43] Disagreement over what constituted proper observance of the Sabbath had been simmering locally for a year or more, and the battle over the movies was foreshadowed in a brief skirmish over Sunday swimming in Atlanta's parks. The clergy and the city council opposed Sunday bathing, but Mayor Winn vetoed a council resolution banning the practice, apparently siding with park board president J. O. Cochran, who had argued that working men needed Sunday recreation. Cochran insisted, "This city has outgrown the Puritanical blue laws, and all the ordinances and resolutions of the council can not set back the wheels of progress."[44] Observers believed that the 1912 election of James G. Woodward to the mayor's office amounted to "a plea from the voters for a more liberal town," and this trend continued into 1913, as the *Georgian* editorially supported Sunday concerts by the Atlanta Musical Association "given at an hour that interferes with no service of a religious character, and upon a day furnishing hundreds of people with their only possible opportunity during the week to attend."[45] If these developments were not enough to convince theater owners that the public would welcome Sunday movies, they were surely inspired when Wesley Memorial Church began a series of Sunday religious screenings at which collections were taken.[46]

The Montgomery Theater took what its manager no doubt viewed as the logical next step by presenting the picture *From the Manger to the Cross* to a large Sunday audience, reportedly with the permission of Chief of Police Beavers, who attended the show.[47] Emboldened by this success, other theater men decided that they too would test the Sunday waters, announcing that on March 16 they would open their doors to the public, but with no admission charge and with all voluntary contributions going to charity. The shows would not begin until 2:00 P.M. so as not to conflict with church services, and the films offered would be carefully chosen for their educational or inspirational value. Thus the program for that first Sunday would include such features as *The Finch and Her Family, Egypt in the Time of Moses, A Trip to Wales,* and *Our Enemy, the Wasp.*[48]

If attendance figures are any indication, a substantial portion of Atlanta's population welcomed the introduction of Sunday films. Representatives of the ten or so theaters that opened that first Sunday claimed that over forty-four thousand patrons visited their houses, although since some people attended more than one show the actual number may have been substantially lower.[49] Nevertheless, a front-page photograph in the Monday morning edition of the *Constitution* shows a crowd of well-dressed men and boys lined up on the sidewalk outside the doors to the Alcazar Theater, and an article on the same page notes, "From the time the picture shows opened at 2 o'clock . . . the houses were practically crowded to their capacities." In addition, a reporter who followed Chief Beavers about as he inspected the movie houses claimed that the audiences were so large as to discourage Beavers from even attempting to enter most of the theaters.[50]

The movie houses opened again the following Sunday, offering a similar array of inoffensive films, including *Glimpses of Montana, Star of Bethlehem,* and *The Public and Private Care of Infants.* The managers announced in advance that all patron contributions would be used to help establish a home for tubercular children. Attendance fell off somewhat—management estimates placed the total at around thirty thousand—but the movie men attributed this to the Easter holiday and to the fact that the theaters had closed between 7:00 and 8:30 in deference to evening church services.[51]

Whatever their success, from the moment that the theater managers proclaimed their intention to show movies on the Sabbath, battle lines began forming within the community, with public officials coming down on both sides of the issue. The matter was complicated by an ongoing struggle involving the city council, the police commission, and Chief Beavers over control of the police department.[52] The opinions of city officials, therefore, were not always based solely on their views of Sunday movies in the abstract. In any case, journalists suspected that Beavers, despite his leniency in the case of *From the Manger to the Cross,* leaned against allowing regular Sunday pictures, and Assistant State Solicitor E. A. Stephens proclaimed that Sunday shows at which voluntary contributions were accepted would represent a "violation of the spirit and letter" of state law.[53] City attorney James L. Mayson thought otherwise—so long as the theaters charged no admission—as did Carlos Mason, chairman of the police board, who came out in favor of Sunday movies. Mayor James G. Woodward was vocally supportive of the idea as well, allowing that "If the shows are operated in a sane, sensible and first-class manner, and if the pictures are clean and wholesome I don't see why any one should object. I won't interfere. I think the people of Atlanta should have more amusements. We are no longer living in a crossroads village, but in a modern, cosmopolitan city."[54]

Woodward's comments are particularly significant in suggesting the larger implications of the controversy. Both supporters and opponents of Sunday films saw the dispute as part of a much greater debate over how Atlantans should respond to the powerful social and economic forces that were rapidly transforming their city. The mayor was correct in pointing out that Atlanta was no longer a "crossroads village," but Gate City residents differed as to what this fact implied. As Woodward indicated, at issue was "cosmopolitanism," a concept that had sparked disagreement among Atlantans for years. No one ever stopped to define the term, but all purported to know full well what it meant and what its implications would be for their city. To its proponents, the notion denoted an absence of those embarrassing qualities that they hoped Atlanta was overcoming as it grew and prospered: provincialism, backwardness, insularity—all of the weaknesses supposedly inherent in small, isolated towns. To its detractors, on the other hand, cosmopolitanism evoked a breakdown of revered traditions and moral values, a fatal openness to all that was socially, culturally, and ethically corrosive in a jaded and cynical world. In this view the Gate City was a fortress under siege, struggling to defend itself against a barbarian onslaught from without and against the treacherous actions of misguided citizens within.

Commercial entertainment played a central role in this continuing struggle over the city's future. Depending on how one felt about cosmopolitanism, amusements could be seen as either a welcome harbinger of civic maturity or a dreaded "opening wedge" for the kinds of abandoned materialism that local ministers harangued against. Indeed, entertainment provided a litmus test—arguably the best test, by contemporary standards—for measuring the city's level of cosmopolitanism. To the degree that Atlanta was open to the waves of amusements that washed against its gates, it could be seen as open to outside values and influences, however good or ill, however commercialized and packaged for sale. So when clergymen took a stand against Sunday motion pictures, they were concerned with more than preservation of the Sabbath. In their eyes they were fighting for the protection and preservation of Atlanta's soul.

Others, however, argued that the Gate City's civic health depended on innovations such as Sunday films. According to the *Constitution,* several "prominent men" who had attended the Sunday movies claimed that the pictures were valuable in allowing viewers to forget themselves for a while and escape the "scenes of the every day life of stress and strife in Atlanta that become commonplace and harrowing as the days go by." Some believed that in a city of Atlanta's size Sunday movies provided alternatives to less "wholesome" activities. Linton C. Hopkins, president of the Atlanta Associated Charities, asserted, "The majority of the people consider that as a matter of right they are entitled to recreation and amusement on Sunday, and I agree with them fully. If they are not afforded opportunity for innocent recreation, many of them are going to seek recreation not so innocent. Healthful amusements lessen crime." [55]

As this reference to criminal activity suggests, many middle-class commentators felt that the city's working men and women stood in special need of clean and "uplifting" diversion. Frank E. Block, for example, described by the *Constitution* as a "well-known manufacturer and employer of labor," told the paper that there was a "crying need" for the brand of Sunday entertainment that the movies offered. "I have seen hundreds of people who had no other time except Sunday afternoons for recreation, and who needed the recreation." He claimed, "There are in Atlanta today women working from early morning to night for $1 a day, six days out of a week. . . . [who] have families to support, and cannot even afford car fare, much less the price of a seat at a moving picture show." For the sake of these women and others like them, he hoped that the free Sunday pictures would continue. Carlos Mason added that the only religious instruction that many of Atlanta's working people received came from the newly instituted Sunday movies. He claimed that these unchurched audiences viewed the religious films as "a real treat."[56]

For their part, local movie men gladly played upon such sympathy for the city's laboring classes, claiming that the Sunday shows drew in hundreds of workers from area textile mill villages. One manager related that at his theater on Sunday "I had any number of boys and girls, pasty-faced kids who looked as if they came from the mills, who sidled up to the door as if they were afraid somebody would turn them down. They always got in, I assure you, and nobody enjoyed the show more than they did."[57] Thus Sunday movies supposedly lightened and brightened the lives of Atlanta's working folk while simultaneously easing the minds of the city's property owners.

Of course, it would never have occurred to a *Constitution* reporter to actually ask a working person what he or she thought of Sunday films. But for his part, local labor leader Jerome Jones vociferously opposed the idea. Writing in the Atlanta-based *Journal of Labor,* which he edited, Jones recounted how long and hard organized labor had struggled—particularly in states such as Georgia—to eliminate Sunday labor. And this "fight," Jones reminded his readers, had been carried on by the labor movement alone, "without . . . assistance from any class of men—saint or sinner, professional man or preacher." So he expressed some surprise over the fact that Atlantans who had at best sat on the sidelines during the struggle for a six-day work week were suddenly driven by concern for the recreational welfare of the city's working people. He suspected that the real motive driving middle-class Atlantans to push for Sunday movies was a desire to recommercialize the Sabbath and return to a seven-day work week. But, whatever these people's aims, "The fact is, the poor, wretched people whom it is supposed the Sunday amusement would help, will not be reached, for the very good reason they work too long hours, and for so pitiful a wage, that they would have neither time nor money to take advantage of the opportunity." On the other hand, if this energy devoted to the campaign for Sunday openings "would only be applied to assist the men and women of labor to secure an eight-hour workday and a higher wage rate, the question of our people having proper recreation and amusement would soon be solved," for given adequate leisure time, workers could "secure all the amusement necessary."[58]

The most adamant opposition to Sunday motion pictures came not from organized labor, however, but from the Atlanta clergy, men who as a group were deeply alarmed by the implications for Atlanta and the South of a more "open" Sabbath. Church leaders spoke out vehemently against the idea of Sunday movies and attempted to mobilize their congregations in the cause.[59] Much more striking than the churchmen's repudiation of Sunday movies— which after all was only to be expected—were the grounds on which they staked their opposition. Unlike the ministers of the late nineteenth century who had issued fiery condemnations of the theater and all who were associated with it, the clergymen who fought Sunday openings in Atlanta restricted their criticisms to the commercialization of the Sabbath. In public and in private these men were careful to make clear that they were not opposed to the motion pictures themselves, but only to the presentation of movies on Sundays for money.[60] For they were certain that whatever the protestations of the theater managers, profit, not charity, was the movie men's ultimate goal.[61] And the ministers feared that other businessmen would follow the lead of the theater managers. As the Evangelical Ministers' Association put it in resolutions drawn up for presentation to the movie men, "it is our conviction that the movement to open picture shows on Sunday, if permitted to succeed, will be but the opening wedge to a general freedom of Sabbath desecration, for which you must assume responsibility." Such statements, combined with the threat held out by some ministers that should Sunday openings continue, they would urge their congregations to boycott theaters during the other six days of the week, indicate that the motion picture had won wide acceptance among the churchgoing people of Atlanta and their leaders.[62]

On the evening of April 21, a remarkable meeting took place between a committee of five ministers representing the EMA and spokesmen for the theaters that were opening on Sundays. Each side presented its position on Sunday movies in the hope of finding some sort of solution to the controversy. Dr. John E. White, pastor of the Second Baptist Church and spokesman for the clergymen, went out of his way to insist that the ministers did "not wish to appear in the role of straight-laced [*sic*] Puritans. . . . We are admirers of and in sympathy with anything that makes life the happier." He conceded that he had personally visited the city's movie theaters and had found their offerings "good." Nevertheless, he continued, "We represent southern ideals and the safeguard of the southern moral standards which have been left to us by our southern forefathers. The south is today the leader in the conservative observance of the Sabbath, and we do not want to see this ancient custom departed from." It was particularly important, White argued, for the Gate City to uphold these cherished southern standards. "Atlanta cannot say to herself, 'I will do as I please,' because Atlanta occupies a position of influence, and any action she takes will send its immediate impression abroad. Atlanta is a city set upon a hill." Accordingly, he urged the movie men to discontinue their free Sunday showings, else their houses would lose the patronage of the one hundred thousand Atlantans that the EMA claimed to represent. And if the theater owners made so bold as to overtly break state and city law by charging Sunday admission, the EMA would see to it that they were prosecuted.

Frank Hammond, speaking for the movie men, responded that the theater managers felt that they were being discriminated against. Not only did Wesley Memorial Church show films on Sundays—a practice to which the EMA representatives maintained that they were opposed—but the Cyclorama portrayal of the Battle of Atlanta, "with all its scenes of carnage," was open to the paying public every Sunday as well. In addition, Hammond argued, boat rides were for sale every Sunday at Grant Park Lake, "Candy, soda water and cigars are sold on Sunday and without protest in open disregard of the law," and "Your own churches pay your choirs to sing as regularly as the Sundays come." And contradicting the EMA's claim of support from labor and Jewish leaders on this issue, Hammond insisted that Jerome Jones did not really speak for Atlanta's working people and that far from backing the EMA in this instance, the Jewish Educational Alliance held movie screenings of its own every Sunday night at which admission was charged.

Tempers began to run short when Hammond subsequently read aloud reports on Sunday moving pictures from New Orleans, Memphis, Houston, Montgomery, and Jacksonville, which, "when they expressed an opinion, were favorable to the Sunday shows." The ministers immediately called into question the moral character of these cities, especially New Orleans, which brought in turn a defense of the Crescent City from one of the movie men who had lived there. At this point a minister sprang to his feet and cut to the quick of the argument, denouncing the notion that Atlanta would inevitably take on the unsavory qualities of such cities as she grew more populous and demographically diverse. "We don't want a more cosmopolitan city of Atlanta. We don't want Atlanta to be a city like New York. She has grown to what she is without a cosmopolitan Sunday, and she can continue to grow without it. It is an asset." He added, in disgust, "Why in New York City my wife could not walk alone a block on Broadway after dark without being insulted." But "half a dozen voices" instantly responded, "She couldn't do it on the streets of Atlanta," either.

The movie men then sought to break the impasse by offering what they saw as a compromise: the theaters would continue to open on Sundays but would never operate during morning or evening church services. The ministers rejected this suggestion. The managers then proposed that the citizens of Atlanta be polled by postcard to determine their opinions on the issue. But the clergymen refused this idea as well, arguing—revealingly—that such polling would be "unfair" since "The people are not worked up to a fever heat on the subject." The ministers went on to predict that the picture men would not maintain the high moral tone of their Sunday films and pushed the managers into "virtually" admitting that, "while they were perfectly willing to give a fair amount of their profits on Sunday shows to charity, the ultimate object of their proposition was money in their pockets." The claim that the shows were a boon to charity was unfounded, anyway, the ministers insisted, for while "the moving picture men announced last Sunday an attendance of 40,000 with much show and boasting," they "were conspicuously reluctant in announcing that the receipts amounted to a little more than $500." In fact, Rev. White charged, the "forces of vice" were working behind the scenes to encourage Sunday movies "in the hope of making restitution for thousands of dollars lost since the war on vice was started."[63]

Clearly, the two sides held contrasting visions of Atlanta and the South. Having largely lost the long-fought battle over the general acceptability of commercial amusements, the ministers and their backers were determined to preserve some symbolic affirmation of lingering public commitment to evangelical Christianity. To them, Atlanta and its southern Sabbath represented a bastion of moral order in a nation rapidly giving way to spiritual bankruptcy. To allow commercial entertainment to intrude on silently sacred Sunday afternoons would be to begin the process by which the Gate City would degenerate to a level of immorality equivalent to that of New York or New Orleans.

To the movie men and those who supported them, however, Atlanta had moved beyond the outmoded strictures of a provincial past. In this view, increased commercialization represented not a threat but an opportunity for civic progress. The citizens of a growing metropolis like Atlanta were certainly entitled to enjoy harmless Sunday diversions free from the objections of old-fashioned preachers. So long as the films served "wholesome" purposes, they were good for the working class, children, and young women. The end justified the means: traditional conceptions of a southern Sabbath were less important in the end than a healthy adjustment to new economic and cultural realities. The city should be opened up, should be made, in a word, more cosmopolitan.

The movie debate therefore highlighted the central questions confronting the New South: What changes should be accepted? What traditions should be sustained? What values should be discarded? And, crucially, who was to make these decisions?

Neither this conference nor a smaller follow-up meeting the next day managed to settle anything. Rather, the deathblow to Sunday movies came when City Attorney Mayson ruled that theaters positively could not open if admission was charged. This scotched plans by the managers to open again on March 30 with an admission fee. They claimed that the money collected would go to victims of recent flooding in Ohio and Indiana, and Mayor Woodward had issued permits allowing such plans to go forth. Mayson's decision, however, put an end to this idea, apparently convincing the theater owners that they would not be able to reach their ultimate goal of running Sunday films for profit.[64] The city council, despite lobbying from the EMA and the Men and Religion Forward movement, subsequently tabled an ordinance that would have placed an outright ban on the presentation of Sunday motion pictures. The councilmen agreed that the measure would have too drastically curtailed the use of films by churches and that there was little need for the law in light of the managers' decision to close their theaters on the Sabbath.[65]

The Atlanta clergy had won the battle. Despite several skirmishes over the question in the following years, theaters generally continued to close on Sundays, at least until the Great Depression brought unprecedented demand for charitable funds and a compelling reason for Sunday movie openings at which donations could be taken.[66] But the ministers lost the war. For the cosmopolitanism that they so dreaded, the worldliness that they saw menacing their Deep South "city on a hill," slipped into the Gate City anyway, borne — at least in part — on reels of film, film that contained images of men and women who would further dilute the clergymen's influence as arbiters of culture and morality. As powerful a force as was evangelical Christianity, it could not prevent the ultimate triumph of commercial culture. As the logic of the free market and new definitions of time and leisure permeated the South, clergymen could only slow, not stop, the inexorable advance and acceptance of movies and other forms of entertainment that the ministers had once fiercely opposed. This did not mean, however, that ministers and city authorities gave up on efforts to monitor and control the filmed material that entered Atlanta. For just as the vice campaign of 1912 had set the stage for the Sunday showdown of 1913, so the battle over Sunday films paved the way for municipal censorship of motion pictures.

Perhaps because the occasional ad hoc investigation found most of the films showing in Atlanta to be innocuous at worst and at best genuinely elevating, city officials did not institute any more formal or permanent censoring body during the first few years of the movies' popularity.[67] Moreover, beginning in 1909 Atlanta's civic guardians could rely on the New York City-based National Board of Review — to which the major American production companies voluntarily submitted all of their films for approval — to ensure that the movies brought into the Gate City met standards of moral wholesomeness.[68]

By 1913, however, states and cities across the country had begun to grow dissatisfied with the National Board, which, after all, had no legal powers to suppress films or punish wayward exhibitors, and which in any case did not manage to review all of the pictures available to local theaters. Various localities eventually responded by setting up their own censorship boards. Pennsylvania enacted the first state censorship laws in 1912, with Ohio and Kansas following suit in 1913.[69]

Atlanta's Sunday-screenings controversy brought the city's first public calls for more formal censorship measures. Local Men and Religion Movement Forward leader Marion Jackson, in blasting Sunday movies, asserted that Atlanta "sorely needed" a censor to oversee films shown on weekdays. Rev. Len Broughton agreed, calling for a movie and vaudeville censor who could do something to change the fact that "the films shown in certain show houses on week days . . . are unbelievable in suggestiveness." [70] Even those who supported Sunday films sometimes pushed the idea of censorship. Margaret Laing, an officer of the juvenile court and an advocate of Sunday movies, called for censorship to limit the influence that immoral films could have on the city's youth. [71]

In May of 1913 the Atlanta city council answered such calls and joined the national trend by establishing a censorship committee, the members of which were to be chosen from among the trustees of the Carnegie Public Library. [72] The Atlanta board was typical of the Progressive Era in which it was formed. Secular-minded male business executives, real estate agents, and attorneys—not ministers—would wield moral authority on the committee, bringing what they considered to be rational and enlightened attitudes to the task of protecting Atlantans from the harmful tendencies of the motion picture. [73] The nation's movie exhibitors apparently agreed, to the extent that they viewed Atlanta as one of those cities (such as New Haven, Detroit, Kansas City, Milwaukee, and Nashville) that had created more or less reasonable censorship policies. [74]

Atlanta's film exchanges, which supplied movies to the city's theaters, also complied with the censorship law, routinely providing the board with a synopsis of each film slated for local release. The censors then read the opinions of the National Board of Censorship, when available (as of 1914 the national board was reportedly reviewing about 75 percent of those movies shown in Atlanta), and examined the synopses looking for evidence of material that might not be appropriate for Gate City audiences. When a synopsis aroused suspicion, the board privately viewed the film in question before approving it. The censors could then either forbid public screening of the picture altogether or, as was more frequently the case, simply order the removal of offensive footage. A newspaper article in August of 1916 noted that since the beginning of the year the three-man board had considered fifty-five hundred movie synopses and had "personally viewed 500 screen productions." Of this number, the board had banned twelve films outright and had ordered thousands of feet of film excised from other pictures that did end up showing in city theaters.

While they may have acted severely toward certain movies, the board members insisted that they were temperate and just in their rulings. Board Chairman W. L. Percy stated in 1915, "As far as we can we stand in the place of the people. We don't represent one class or one sex. We don't express our own prejudices or those of any group of people. We consider every picture from as broad and fair [a] viewpoint as we can." Thus, the *Journal* considered it fair to claim, "To all the trade Atlanta is known as the town that keeps the most open mind on pictures. Philadelphia and Cincinnati are straight-laced [*sic*] by comparison."

Whatever their claims, of course, Atlanta's censors did bring their own biases into play when assessing motion pictures. They were particularly concerned with the suppression of films featuring what they considered to be sexual misconduct, and of movies in which rewards came to those who performed evil deeds. As a writer for the *Journal* explained it, "Plays of the underworld, pieces in which women drink or smoke, sex plays and problem plays, productions featuring passionate love scenes—these are the releases which are closely watched by the Atlanta board of review of motion pictures." Summarizing board policy, secretary J. W. Peacock said that "the censor should see to it that the evil characters in the picture come to harm as a direct result of their evil doings and that the net effect of the picture is convincingly in favor of the good."

Such concerns were especially pressing, board members believed, in light of the large numbers of children who regularly visited Atlanta's movie houses. Censor Willis Everett told a reporter in 1914 that he did not "know of anything needed in Atlanta more than a campaign to educate parents to the necessity of their knowing what moving pictures their children see." He observed, "A large part of every picture play audience here is made up of children, and nine-tenths of them are unaccompanied by older people." This in spite of the fact that Everett himself would not have allowed his own children to see "more than half" of the 125 or so first-run movies that appeared in Atlanta each week.[75]

While Atlanta's Progressive Era film censors might appear to have been stereotypically narrow in some of their attitudes, this was not always the case. When, for instance, the National Board of Review in 1917 announced a ban on nudity in motion pictures, the *Constitution* solemnly editorialized in favor of the proscription, proclaiming it a "triumph for decency." But some people, including Chairman Percy, were not so certain that such regulation was necessary or appropriate. As Percy told a reporter, "The human form is the most beautiful of all nature's creations. . . . I have seen charming picture productions which made free use of the naked figure." He suggested that censors' efforts would be better spent in ridding "the movie industry of depraved producers, rather than handicapping its artistic mediums." [76]

Though moderate in some areas, on the issue of race Atlanta's censorship board was as rigidly uncompromising as were white Atlantans in other walks of life. Normally, race did not present a problem for local censors, since the moviemakers of the day rarely challenged notions of white supremacy. Occasionally, though, Atlanta's board felt compelled to act, as in 1915, when they prevented local presentation of *The Nigger*, a controversial picture filmed in part in Augusta. *The Nigger* told the fictional story of Philip Morrow, a young southern aristocrat who is persuaded to run for governor by Cliff Noyes, a political boss who is also a distiller of cheap whiskey marketed to a black clientele. Morrow wins the election, but then decides to push a prohibition bill that would destroy Noyes's business. Outraged, Noyes confronts the governor with evidence that he is partially of African American ancestry. Refusing to be blackmailed, Morrow signs the prohibition bill, resigns from office, and leaves his still-loyal white girlfriend to head north, where he plans to devote his life to uplifting the black race. Doubtless offended by the film's presentation of a South in which aristocrats might be tainted with black blood, white women could love mulattoes, corrupt bosses influenced politics, and blacks were oppressed and exploited, the censorship board attempted to suppress even a private screening of *The Nigger* for reporters and local movie men.[77]

In general, movie houses complied with the censorship board's requests, but some conflict was inevitable given that the primary aim of the censors was morality while that of the theater managers was profit. In 1913 the *Constitution* reported a cat-and-mouse dispute between a Whitehall Street movie house and the censorship board over the screening of a film entitled *The Vampire Dance*. As described in the newspaper, the movie told the story of a "country youth who went to town to make his fortune, made in the neighborhood of $500, wrote back to his sweetheart in the rural regions that he would soon marry her, and then fell in love with an adventuress, as is often the case in moving pictures—all leading up to the 'Vampire

Dance.'" The film had been showing for two days when "some arbiter of civic morals" alerted Willis Everett, who went to see the picture for himself. While he reportedly liked the "part of the picture that had to do with love, and the adventuress, and the hero losing his job and all that," the "Vampire Dance" itself was another matter, and the chairman "just naturally couldn't say that it fitted in the scheme of Atlanta's morality." Everett notified police headquarters, and Night Chief E. L. Jett ordered an officer to the theater to demand that the dance sequence be removed from the picture. When the manager obediently complied, however, angry patrons began to demand their money back, so he ended up showing the dance after the policeman had left. Hearing of this, the chief sent plainclothes officers to the theater to watch for the offensive scene, but the manager learned of their presence and "ordered the picture squelched." Once again the police departed, and once again "the Vampire danced as gleefully as before." In this case Everett and Jett decided not to bring formal charges against the manager, who defended his actions to the press, insisting, "The picture has been censored both by the local board of censorship and the national board. There is nothing harmful to it, or it would never have left New York. I was willing to act in accord with Mr. Everett, but I cannot jeopardize the popularity of my theater. When people began asking for their money to be refunded, I had to replace the dance in self-defense."[78]

This incident reveals the variety of entities whose voices might be heard on any question of censorship. Though the local censors and the theater managers were usually the most important parties in any dispute, everyone from movie patrons to the city police force to the national censorship board could be involved as well. Conflicts such as that over *The Vampire Dance*, however, were much more the exception than the rule, and the relationship between those who monitored the films and those who earned their livelihood from them was for the most part a relatively harmonious one, thus helping to earn Atlanta's reputation as a city with enlightened censorship procedures.

On the evening of December 6, 1915, patrons lining the sidewalk in front of the Atlanta Theater witnessed an unusual sight. A procession of men, draped in bedsheets, rode down Peachtree Street on horseback, firing rifle salutes into the air. They hoped to publicize their organization and recruit new members and evidently believed that the men waiting to enter the theater would be likely candidates, if not now, then when they emerged, overwhelmed, a few hours later. The association that the riders represented was the Ku Klux Klan, and the film that was causing such excitement was D. W. Griffith's masterpiece, *The Birth of a Nation*.[79]

If there was any single film that illustrated the broad popularity that movies had attained in Atlanta by the mid teens, that secured the respectable reputation of the medium in the Gate City, and that demonstrated the profound cultural power that motion pictures could exert, it was clearly *The Birth of a Nation*. Griffith's interpretation of the Civil War and Reconstruction, built as it was upon deep sympathy for the "southern" point of view and a profound belief in white supremacy, naturally appealed to the sensibilities of white Atlantans as a ratification of their "heritage" and as a justification of their racial prejudices.

Ironically, given the film's eventual success in Atlanta, a number of Atlantans were at first wary of allowing *The Birth of a Nation* to play in their hometown. In October 1915, Homer George of the Atlanta Theater asked Atlantans who had seen the picture during the long runs that it had already enjoyed in New York, Boston, and Chicago to "write us regarding the picture and its presentation here, and as to whether . . . any scenes should be eliminated." A few weeks later the *Constitution* reported that three local citizens had called on Mayor Woodward, urging him to ban the film because it might stir up "race prejudice."[80] Such concerns led black minister H. H. Proctor to appear before a sympathetic Evangelical Ministers' Association, urging its support in keeping the picture out of Atlanta.[81] After Woodward and the censorship board received additional protests, the city council passed a resolution asking the board to study *The Birth of a Nation* closely in advance of its scheduled Atlanta premier. Manager George and the censors subsequently traveled to Macon, where they attended a screening at the Grand Theater. Following the movie the Atlantans questioned audience members about their reactions to the production. Satisfied with what they had seen and heard, the men returned home convinced that Griffith's film could be safely shown in Atlanta.[82]

The Gate City's response to *The Birth of a Nation* was overwhelming. As the crowds who had thronged the theaters during the brief experiment with Sunday openings in 1913 had demonstrated, moving pictures were already an extremely popular form of amusement in Atlanta. Reporters who examined movie attendance in 1914 and 1915 concluded that from twenty-five thousand to thirty thousand Atlantans—or roughly one-quarter of the white population—visited the city's white theaters every day.[83] But *The Birth of a Nation* was strikingly successful even by these standards, in spite of ticket prices that ranged from fifty cents to two dollars for evening performances. This was a film self-consciously pitched to "respectable" middle-class audiences, the same people who paid similarly high ticket prices to attend legitimate stage productions, and in Atlanta such men and women turned out in force.[84] In actions unprecedented in the city's moving-picture history, the Atlanta Theater held the movie over for a second and then a third week. Newspaper reports claimed that more than nineteen thousand patrons saw the film during the first week—with as many as one thousand people being turned away from each matinee—and that thirty-five thousand had viewed it by the end of the second.[85]

Atlanta's film critics were ecstatic over the picture and passionately embraced its message. The *Georgian*'s Dudley Glass expressed puzzlement that anyone had worried about the film's reception below the Mason-Dixon line: "After seeing how strongly it defends the South I am only surprised that the North welcomed it so enthusiastically." As for his own reaction to the picture, Glass recalled, "I sat on the edge of my seat and hardly breathed. . . . I do not remember that I yelled, yet my throat was raw and my voice husky when the lights went on." Ned McIntosh of the *Constitution* began his review by affirming Griffith's newly won reputation as the American Homer, then went on to describe the emotions that the director's handi-work had evoked in him: "It makes you laugh and moves you to hot tears unashamed. It makes you love and hate. It makes you forget decorum and forces a cry into your throat. It thrills you with horror and moves you to marvel at vast spectacles. It makes you actually live through the greatest period of suffering and trial that this country has ever known." Above all it was Griffith's portrayal of Reconstruction—of a South "humiliated and crushed under a Black heel"—that had fired McIntosh's imagination and roused his anger. In the critic's words, "You live through a period of ruin and destruction in the country where you were born. . . . You sicken at the sight of an attempt to enforce marital racial equality. Again and again the unbearable hideousness of the days of reconstruction is borne in upon you. . . . You could shriek for a depiction of relief and—yes, retribution."

The *Journal*'s Ward Greene experienced similar feelings upon witnessing the picture's graphic depiction of the postwar years. "Loathing, disgust, hate, envelope you, hot blood cries for vengeance. Until out of the night blazes the fiery cross that once burned high above old Scotland's hills and the legions of the Invisible Empire roar down to the rescue, and that's when you are lifted by the hair and go crazy." Greene was not alone in his final assessment of *The Birth of a Nation:* "There has been nothing to equal it — nothing."

According to these reviewers, Atlanta audiences reacted to the film with a similar intensity. As Glass watched the movie, "the woman beside me was sobbing audibly, and the two men behind me were yelling like college boys at a football game." Of the response to the famous KKK rescue sequence that so moved Greene, McIntosh wrote, "The awful restraint of the audience is thrown to the winds. Many rise from their seats. With the roar of thunder a shout goes up. Freedom is here. Justice is at hand! Retribution has arrived!" Greene focused on the reactions of individuals: "A youth in the gallery leaped to his feet and yelled and yelled. A little boy down-stairs pounded the man's back in front of him and shrieked. The man did not know it. He was a middle-aged, hard lipped citizen; but his face twitched and his throat gulped up and down. Here a young girl kept dabbing and dabbing at her eyes and there an old lady just sat and let the tears stream down her face unchecked." [86]

Many of those who had lived through the travails recounted in the film emphatically expressed their approval of the picture and their pride in the manner in which it validated their experiences. The *Constitution* observed that at a showing of the film attended by more than a hundred Confederate veterans, "The realism of . . . the great moving picture . . . was enhanced almost to reality itself yesterday afternoon, when the 'rebel yell' rose above the music of the orchestra." Afterward some of the old soldiers assured a reporter that the movie was historically accurate and went on to recall events that the picture had brought vividly to mind. "I remember the day I went to the polls, and they wouldn't let me — me, a white man — vote," remembered one, still incredulous at the affront. [87]

Some Atlantans proudly claimed that they had once belonged to the Klan. A newspaper article told of a man, "about 60 years of age, well set up and genteel looking," who upon viewing the picture felt moved to relate his own youthful participation in the Ku Klux Klan. He explained that when, as a sixteen-year-old during "the worst of the reconstruction evils," he received word that his "band" was to go on its first night ride, he was so fearful that while en route to the gathering point he considered turning back. "But I didn't. . . . When a man has women folks to think of and the kind of hell we went through surrounding him it gives him a courage he doesn't get any other way." He was still apprehensive when he joined his comrades, but a brief speech by the Klan commander steeled his resolve. "Our captain said only a few words to us, but they galvanized us into a battery of determined men. I shed my youthfulness right there and I have never had that feeling since. It was a case of helpless woman and black brute, and 200 strong we rode to do our mission." [88]

Most white Atlantans already held strongly biased opinions regarding the Civil War and Reconstruction when *The Birth of a Nation* arrived in the city. But the film confirmed and elaborated these feelings in electrifying fashion. White Atlantans could now take even greater pride in the actions and principles of their forbears, as these ancestors were saluted in movie theaters all over the country. [89] Men who had belonged to the Ku Klux Klan or to similar terrorist organizations — or who now wished that they had — could publicly proclaim their old allegiances and expect to be admired as heroes. To the whites who packed the Atlanta Theater, *The Birth of a Nation* served as an inspiring confirmation of the superiority of white Americans over black and reinforced the deeply held conviction that only the diligence of white males prevented lustful black men from molesting white women. It is little wonder that a local insurance salesman and organizer of fraternal societies named William J. Simmons would seize upon the atmosphere created by the film to accomplish his dream of reviving the long-dormant Ku Klux Klan. And, given the Gate City's intense reaction to the film and its message, it is also no surprise that Atlanta remained central to the Klan's resurrection, serving as the "Imperial City" of the movement and home to Klan leaders. [90]

By the end of 1915, then, if not before, the movies had established themselves as the predominant form of commercial entertainment in Atlanta. As local theater executive Hugh Cardoza expressed it, the movies had "shot the stage — so far as legitimate productions are concerned — to literal pieces." [91] The motion picture appealed to men, women, and children of all social classes and had won an air of respectability that the stage had never managed to attain. There were still isolated voices speaking out against the medium — Methodist bishop Warren Candler carried on a rhetorical war against commercial amusements in general and movies in particular into the 1920s—but such criticism did not seem to hurt business.[92] Atlanta had become a big city with a burgeoning population that was increasingly inclined to accept commercial entertainment for the pleasure and excitement it offered rather than repudiate it for any threat it might have posed to traditional morality.

As Atlantans came more and more to take the movies for granted, and as the Gate City increasingly became an indistinguishable cog in a national motion picture industry, the movies become less revelatory of anything socially and culturally distinctive about the city.[93] Only rarely after Atlanta entered the nationally homogenized motion-picture-palace era of the 1920s did anything occur that appears idiosyncratically Atlantan.[94] Aside from the obsession with race that it shared with other southern cities, what is most distinctive about Atlanta in the 1920s, so far as motion pictures, vaudeville, and the theaters go, is how indistinct this "branch-office town" was, how interchangeable with cities of its size throughout the United States.[95] The unique and colorful city that Walter McElreath had loved in the late nineteenth century was no more.

The theater, vaudeville, the movies—all were designed to speak to the widest possible public. Their aim was profit, and however divided their audience might have been by race, gender, or class, the money each group brought to the box office was equal. Success was based on numbers, as in the crowds who lined up to witness *The Birth of a Nation* or packed the opera house to see Edwin Booth and Adelina Patti. For another type of entertainment prominent in the Gate City of this period, however, the criteria were different. While its promoters spoke of gaining a broad audience, its primary appeal lay in its reaching only the "gifted" few. Its backers claimed to reject sordid commercial calculation, but beneath the surface timeless questions of dollars and cents figured all the more mightily. In Atlanta's experience with classical music and opera, appearance always counted much more highly than did reality. It is to this rarefied world of "highbrow" music that we turn our attention next.

⤝ 4 ⤞

Music and the
White Atlanta Elite

T
he men who oversaw Atlanta's transformation from battle-scarred
village to southern metropolis were hard-nosed, aggressively ambitious members of a new generation that had seized control of
the region's fortunes in the decades following the Civil War. These merchants,
financiers, industrialists, and journalists linked their voices and destinies in
promoting the Gate City as the economic and political capital of the New
South. And as their campaign bore fruit, as Atlanta grew and thrived as a city,
these boosters prospered as individuals, gradually consolidating into an exclusive social class that enjoyed all of the perquisites attending wealth and
power: insular neighborhoods, ostentatious homes, lavish social clubs, and
imposing churches.[1] Arthur Inman, scion of one of the city's wealthiest families, later recalled the haughty cliquishness of this turn-of-the-century aristocracy: "Here was a fair-sized city not sixty-odd years away from its found-
ing date, and here was a portion of its population which somehow considered
itself socially superior banding together into the socially elite; and others were
persuaded to view them as living in a more desirable world. The conceit, the
vanity of the women who formed 'the upper set' was prodigious."[2]

Other cities had social elites and boosters, of course, but few possessed
leaders so obsessed with ceaseless self-promotion.[3] Driven by insecurities
deriving from Atlanta's upstart status and its location in an economically
backward region, the city's leaders extolled the Gate City with a zeal that
could reach ludicrous extremes.[4] In 1900 the *Charleston News and Courier*
satirized the excesses of the vaunted "Atlanta Spirit":

When expositions were about, it had an exposition or two. When big hotels were fashionable, it built the biggest one in the south. When sky-scraping buildings were in order, it put new stories on its offices and stores. When zoological gardens came in, it put an elephant and a camel, and a coon and some snakes into an enclosure and charged 25 cents to see them. Though it is 200 miles from the sea and about fifteen from the nearest river, it never rested till it got a custom house. It has the only Ponce de Leon spring on the continent, outside of Florida. When lynchings were going, it helped organize one at a nearby railroad station, and ran excursion trains for the accommodation of its sensation-loving citizens.[5]

In time, Atlanta's social elite came to embrace European high culture as part of its program of civic advancement. Wealthy Atlantans sought in part simply to emulate the business titans of the Northeast. But ambitious Atlantans also hoped to refute just the sort of irksome criticism leveled by the *News and Courier* and tradition-minded southerners, who regarded the Gate City as a bastion of superficial capitalists obsessed with appearances and the bottom line.

In their efforts to employ classical music as a means of social, cultural, and moral validation, Atlantans followed the examples of their counterparts elsewhere. By the end of the nineteenth century, "higher" forms of music were coming to be seen not simply as aesthetically superior to more mundane "popular" types, but as ethically superior as well. Advocates held classical music to be morally pure, even sacred, in its beauty and in its capacity to provide spiritual enlightenment. And if the music itself had sacred qualities, then the "better" people who genuinely understood and valued it were elevated as well, portrayed as a sanctified elect, free to worship at the altar of high culture while passing stern judgment upon the culturally unsaved.[6]

The "sacralizing" of music meant that the social elites of American cities—like European elites before them—could further distinguish and more effectively display themselves by liberally patronizing higher music. The most notable example of such support came in 1883 with the construction of the famed Metropolitan Opera House in New York City. Born of a rivalry between New York plutocrats that reached a crisis when the Academy of Music denied a box to Mrs. William Vanderbilt, the Metropolitan was in effect an ornate opera house constructed to showcase the occupants of a semicircle of thirty-five luxurious boxes. This "Diamond Horseshoe" regularly held some of the wealthiest and most powerful figures in America, who sat regally as the finest European talent that money could buy appeared on stage before them. The true performers were always the lords and ladies of the horseshoe, the real set their resplendent surroundings. "As compared with the opera house," a historian has dryly observed, "opera was a relatively minor matter."[7]

Atlanta, whatever the dreams of its leaders, was not New York City. The eminently practical, self-made men who made up the city's elite sprang for the most part from rural yeoman stock, and many of them initially balked at embracing the fine music that the Morgans and Vanderbilts patronized.[8] In fact, it was only when the New York Metropolitan Opera Company itself, the preeminent symbol of European taste and American opulence, agreed to visit the Gate City that a substantial number of Atlanta's leading residents began to realize the status and publicity—not to mention the financial rewards—that an assiduously promoted "appreciation" of high culture could bring to their class and to their city. Subsequently exalted by its local promoters as ethereally divorced from the worldly and mundane, high culture in Atlanta was in fact every bit as commercially oriented as movies, vaudeville, and the theater. Even economic considerations, however, were not enough to drive the great majority of Atlantans to a true acceptance—let alone an appreciation—of "high" culture. Ironically, as it turned out, this majority included many of the men and women who donned finery and filled the boxes for the Metropolitan Company's annual productions, along with those Atlantans who never dreamed of attending such fare.

From the beginning, a small group of musicians, music lovers, and businessmen worked to remake the bustling Gate City as an oasis of high culture. However grievous the boosters' setbacks, from the 1880s on Atlanta's critics and supportive newspaper editors proclaimed the city the "musical center of the south" and promised that her continuous cultural advances would soon make her the musical "peer of the northern cities." Melding love for music with civic boosterism, these supporters touted any supposed musical advance as a step along the path that would inevitably lead to cultural equality with New York City, Boston, and Chicago. Thus, the *Journal*'s appraisal of a concert by a newly organized (and characteristically short-lived) Atlanta Symphony Orchestra: "Atlanta, up-to-date in all things, is following in the footsteps of all the big cities. A first-class orchestra is one of the essential features of a great city, and this city can now boast of one of the finest organizations of this kind to be found anywhere." The quality of a community's musical life, the *Journal* claimed, provided an accurate gauge of the "intelligence, refinement, and progressiveness" of its citizens.[9]

Two events of the 1880s illustrate the aspirations that some Atlantans already held for their city, while at the same time revealing the long road that lay between the New South capital and its cultural salvation.[10] The Great Southern Musical Festival of 1883 was the first such enterprise in Atlanta's history. As would be the case with future festivals, local business-men and journalists—including in this instance such notables as Henry W. Grady, Evan Howell, Robert Maddox, and Samuel Richards—put up the guarantee money necessary to bring performers from the Northeast to At-lanta.[11] With this financial backing, local pianist Alfredo Barili and impre-sario August Doepp engaged Philadelphia conductor Carl Sentz and an or-chestra under his command; sopranos Letitia Fritch and Bessie Pierce; and, as the star of the festival, Jules Levy, the most renowned cornetist of the day. In addition, Barili and Doepp organized an amateur chorus made up of over two hundred voices drawn from all over Georgia. The directors scheduled these performers to appear in a three-day series of five concerts that were to present selections—many of them to be performed in Atlanta for the first time—by the world's most famous composers, including Mo-zart, Verdi, Schumann, Wagner, and Beethoven.[12] In another harbinger of the future, local newspapers, particularly the *Constitution,* heavily pro-moted the festival and in so doing pioneered the hyperbolic style that would characterize local coverage of major musical events for the next fifty years. Levy was the "greatest cornetist the world ever saw," the festival would be "beyond comparison the most important musical event ever re-corded in Georgia," and the audiences assembled for the concerts would be "the largest and most brilliant ever seen in Atlanta." The *Constitution* promised that the "jam" of people at each concert would "simply be im-mense" and implored its readers to purchase their tickets before it was too late.[13]

The festival did indeed draw crowds into DeGive's Opera House, but the audiences were not nearly so large as the promoters had hoped: financially, the enterprise failed to break even. This possibility had been a concern from the outset. After a month of lethargic advance ticket sales, the *Journal* had announced, "In response to a very general request, the manager [Doepp] has decided to reduce prices to the lowest possible figure, so that everybody can attend the Festival." Nevertheless, by the event's third day the *Constitution* was editorially reporting a "heavy loss for the management" and playing to its readers' sense of obligation: "Something is due to the gentlemen who stand behind the enterprise. Without the hope of profit they have put up their money."[14] But this appeal did not attract enough patrons to Saturday's final performance to pay off the festival's debts.[15]

Insufficient attendance was not the only thing that the event's promoters had to worry about; problems plagued the festival from the start. Jules Levy, for instance, arrived in town hounded by disclosures regarding his personal life that were sufficiently seamy to shock some female chorus members into announcing that they would not share a stage with him.[16] Railroad delays prevented the arrival of Sentz's orchestra until late on opening day, and when the tired musicians finally reached the Opera House, they found that DeGive could provide only a few music stands; most orchestra members had to attach their scores to the backs of the men seated in front of them.[17] In addition, the festival program mistakenly scheduled Pierce and Fritch to sing the same number, sparking an acrimonious dispute between the vocalists over who would actually perform the selection.[18]

Newspaper coverage of one backstage incident in particular reveals that despite its best efforts, the Gate City had not yet managed to cast off the unpolished provincialism of its youth. Reportedly, Levy "greatly admired" the singing of Letitia Fritch, and during Saturday night's concert the cornetist became irritated when a member of the Georgia amateur chorus enthusiastically cheered the performance of Bessie Pierce. According to witnesses, Levy "rudely accosted" the man, "abruptly" informing him that "he was making too much noise, and that if he wanted to applaud in that fashion he had better go out into the street." The rebuked chorus singer responded by seizing Levy, "with the evident intention of inflicting immediate punishment." Bystanders separated the two men, but moments later, Levy "again went up to the gentleman and said something in an undertone. Exactly what it was the bystanders failed to hear, but it was of such a nature to produce instant results. With the rapidity of lightning the Atlanta man's fist darted out on a straight line, plugging the great cornetist just over the eye, and knocking off his eye glasses." The *Journal,* which had already printed a mildly satirical review of the Friday night concert, poking fun at classical music and its followers, perceived a rough-and-ready moral to this incident. Choosing regional loyalty over refinement, the paper backed the Atlantan, advising Levy that he would "do well while traveling in this section to stick to his cornet, and not attempt to give our people lessons in etiquette." [19]

Whatever the festival's difficulties, the *Constitution* highlighted the positive, insisting that the enterprise was an artistic, if not a financial, success. Under the headline "The Feast of Melody," the newspaper maintained in a review of opening night that "no such music had been heard in the southern states as was given from the stage at DeGive's" the previous evening. Even the more skeptical *Journal* labeled the first day's concerts "The Grandest Artistic Triumphs Ever Seen In The South." [20]

The "triumph," however, was a mixed one on the purely musical front as well. Some critics expressed disappointment when the performers replaced scheduled selections by Beethoven and Mozart with lighter pieces. [21] The reaction of the concert audiences was more telling. It was not just that they could be as vocal in their approval at such concerts as they were at DeGive's regular stage presentations—the *Journal* complained that "the noisiest man" at the festival had been an elderly gentleman "who belabored the floor with a bludgeon, mean time whooping like a Comanche"—but that the audiences reserved their strongest reactions for the many popular airs mixed into the program. Reviewers remarked upon the "wildest of applause" that greeted such standards as "Yankee Doodle," "Coming through the Rye," "Home Sweet Home," "Nearer My God to Thee," and the inevitable "Dixie." [22] This reaction was not surprising given the lingering standards of the day. Whatever their feelings about classical music, most Americans still valued popular favorites as well, so even "refined" artists performed popular tunes, critics accepted them, and audiences responded to them with enthusiasm. But such attitudes increasingly seemed regressive to a growing number of musical partisans who drew sharp and impassable lines dividing "high" from "popular" culture. Atlanta, however, remained complacently oblivious to such trends. The city's concertgoers continued over the years to respond most fervently to programs that liberally mixed "middlebrow" with "highbrow" music rather than to the most purely refined music presented alone. In the future the Gate City's persistently democratic tastes would provoke the dismay of musically "discriminating" critics and performers alike.

Shifting critical standards and Atlanta's rising civic aspirations were apparent in the city's next musical extravaganza, the Wagner Festival of 1888. Constantin Sternberg, a pianist then residing in Atlanta, called in March of that year for a celebration of the composer's works, to be performed by local amateur and professional artists. In a letter to the *Constitution* announcing his idea, Sternberg explained, "thanks to the activity of our excellent local musicians . . . our musical life has reached such a state of advancement that we should no longer hesitate to form the acquaintance with the immortal works of Richard Wagner, and thus place us (musically) on a comparative level with the largest cities of the world." Sternberg thought himself uniquely suited to head such a project. As a newspaper noted, "Mr. Sternberg is a loving disciple of the great Wagner, and is familiar with every work he wrote. He has had the honor of Wagner's friendship. . . . He regards Wagner as the Shakspeare [*sic*] of music, and holds his name sacred." Armed with these qualifications and with a "disciple's" enthusiasm, Sternberg called for volunteers to help him take "this bold and important step in the musical history of Atlanta." [23] In addition to making history, the festival would have the added appeal of supporting charity: tickets would sell for seventy-five cents (or one dollar for reserved seats), and proceeds would go to the Women's Industrial Home. [24]

The *Constitution* eagerly embraced Sternberg's plan. "Wagner music is the most popular music of the day in cultured musical circles," the paper observed, and by paying tribute to the German master, "Atlanta will probably accomplish a musical feat that will—in significance—equal the Piedmont exposition [of 1881] and bring it to the front as a musical center at no distant day." Others were not so sure. The Gate City's perennially factionalized musical community offered Sternberg "little or no encouragement," and the "musical critics of New York" reportedly warned him against such a "foolish venture." A letter to the editor of the *Constitution,* signed "A Lover of Music," was particularly caustic. "The idea of giving a Wagnerian festival in Atlanta is absurdly impracticable and ridiculous," it began. Noting that previous American performances of Wagner had been confined to New York City and had employed imported German vocalists, the author insisted that to attempt to present Wagner's works in Atlanta using local talent would be the "height of folly": the writer asked, "Where has [Stern-berg] found the wonderful soloists that are willing to mutilate the great mas-ter's works?" The skeptic also recalled Atlanta's last major cultural enter-prise, the Great Southern Festival of 1883, reminding Sternberg that but for Levy's presence, "the festival would not have paid its advertising bills. Just think for one moment, from Levy to Wagner at one jump." The writer con-cluded by urging Sternberg to abandon his wild notion and stick to giving his less ambitious, free "drawingroom" concerts, if he was sincere in desir-ing to "elevate the musical taste in Atlanta." [25]

Despite such skepticism, Sternberg pressed ahead with his plans. He gathered as many volunteer vocalists as he could and commenced the diffi-cult chore of training his mostly inexperienced recruits.[26] While the singers labored at self-improvement, the *Constitution* worked to promote the festi-val. The newspaper described the usual "rush" to buy tickets, which "the literary and society people of the city" were supposedly purchasing in great numbers, and predicted a musical event of unsurpassed quality: "It is ex-pected that in many respects it will equal the great Wagner festival given in New York last year. One thing is certain—the singing will be the best ever heard in the south." [27]

The festival took place on two consecutive evenings in late May. On opening night, what the press described as a "large" audience "composed of the most cultivated people in Atlanta" assembled to hear choral selec-tions from Wagner's works accompanied by two pianos and an organ. The chorus appeared in tiers of seats on stage, the women seated in front in "brilliant and becoming toilettes," and the men ranged in the rear in "full evening dress." The *Constitution* politely reviewed the first night's perfor-mance but mildly suggested that the festival's patrons were not quite so cultivated after all, observing that Wagner's music "evoked much applause, which showed that it was keenly enjoyed if not thoroughly comprehended by the audience." Comprehending or not, the crowd displayed suitable rev-erence: "A large portrait of Wagner was suspended above the stage, and as the marvelous beauties of his works were unfolded the audience gazed in admiration at the picture." [28]

The *Constitution*'s appraisal of the following evening was again generally positive but revealed that in retrospect opening night may have left some-thing to be desired aesthetically, as the second evening's performance was deemed "a distinct improvement" over the first. The review also cast doubts over characterizations of the opening night's audience as a sizable one, since the second-night crowd was judged to be "about one-third" larger than its predecessor, although it still failed to fill the house. While the reviewer gamely concluded that the Wagner Festival was an "artistic triumph," the results at the box office were clearly more dubious.[29]

Some of the themes and elements present in these early festivals would disappear in time from Atlanta's musical culture. The tongue-in-cheek tone adopted by the *Journal* in its review of the 1883 festival, for example, in which the author derided the pretensions and jargon of classical music, would almost entirely vanish from newspaper coverage with the passing years.[30] Indeed, the critical detachment of Atlanta's newspaper coverage, such as it was, would precipitously decline in inverse proportion to the local elite's embrace of high culture. With the arrival of the Metropolitan Opera Company in the early twentieth century, the days of detailed critical reviews of any sort came to an end. Something more akin to unabashed gushing would rule the day.

But in many other ways, these early festivals prefigured the relationship that Atlanta maintained with classical music for at least the next half century. Take the problem of attendance. Just as they generally failed to patronize the more "elevated" dramas at the city's theaters, Atlantans did not typically support artistically "refined" music. There were exceptions: the performances of Walter Damrosch and his New York Symphony Orchestra attracted large audiences in 1893, and touring opera companies occasionally drew well also.[31] Far more typically, however, such performances played to small—sometimes dismally small—houses. Only 150 people turned up at the Grand Theater one night in 1902 to witness the work of the French Grand Opera Company of New Orleans, leading a despairing reviewer to conclude that "future efforts to bring grand opera to Atlanta must be seriously affected."[32] A similarly tiny audience that gathered a year later to hear Czech violinist Jaroslav Kocian also exasperated a local critic: "What an introduction to our 'Sunny South'—an uncomfortably cold opera house, a bleak and dreary stage and row after row of empty seats; this is what greeted Kocian, an artist for whom the musical world is going mad."[33] What a *Journal* columnist observed following a failed appearance by the Milan Italian Opera Company in 1885 remained true of the Gate City's response to all highbrow music: "Atlanta is not a city favorable to this class of entertainments. The number who have a taste for and appreciate this range of aesthetic and foreign music is too small to justify the production of grand opera and produce a paying audience."[34]

The complaints of Atlanta's musically informed frequently extended even to those who actually attended classical concerts. If these patrons seldom "whooped like Comanches," they nevertheless behaved in ways that deeply displeased music critics such as Louise Dooly of the *Constitution*. Atlanta audiences arrived late, left early, talked during overtures or even throughout entire programs, and worse. Dooly was at a loss, for instance, to explain how some of the Atlantans attending a production of Wagner's *Parsifal* "could find it in their hearts to regard the love feast as a feature of amusement." Equally troubling was the sheer boredom sometimes exhibited by Atlanta concertgoers, a case in point being the gentleman who, while seated near the stage at an opera, "read a newspaper wide before him . . . the actors having to send him a reproof through an usher." Such uninterested auditors could "benefit mankind in general and themselves and their neighbors in particular," Dooly acidly suggested, if they could at least spend the time they sacrificed at the concert "in the cultivation of their minds by studying the human nature around them, learning the ABC's backwards or devising some 'get-rich-quick' scheme. Their countenances would thereby lose the depressing and distressing expression of boredom that must influence their neighbors."[35]

Atlanta's theater- and concertgoing citizens did not dislike music. They simply did not respond in great numbers to the types of music that critics such as Dooly insisted that they *should* like. Rather, just as they had during the festival of 1883, Gate City concertgoers continued to react most enthusiastically to mixtures of highbrow and popular music. For example, while other opera troupes failed to attract audiences, Emma Abbott, the "populist prima donna," attracted droves of Atlantans because she was more than willing to insert popular favorites—such as "The Last Rose of Summer" or "Nearer My God to Thee"—into whatever opera she happened to be performing. In 1889 her company was the first to play the Gate City for an entire week, taking in some eight thousand dollars in the process.[36] Likewise Atlantans rousingly supported the music of John Philip Sousa for the better part of three decades. Sousa's band played classical and operatic selections—he offered a Wagnerian program in 1895—but he performed and fiercely defended popular music as well, sneering at those who disparaged it.

In a 1902 engagement at the Grand, Sousa presented a typically eclectic program, featuring numbers ranging from "A Roman Carnival" to "The Nigger in the Woodpile." Atlanta's audiences ardently approved. "Everything was encored," reported a reviewer. "Frequently the encores were encored."[37]

For a small but vocal group of critics and musicians in Atlanta, this sort of musical "appreciation" was not really appreciation at all. Like their counterparts elsewhere in the country, these authorities increasingly viewed classical music as a form of culture so elevated, so refined, so pure that only religious terms and imagery could adequately describe it. Thus, a music columnist warned in 1905 that the response of Atlanta audiences to coming appearances of the Henry Savage Opera Company would determine whether grand opera companies would continue to visit the city in the future: "It is for Atlanta, therefore, to work out her own salvation, and the general interest in the four operas that Savage will put on suggests that Atlanta will yet be saved!" When internationally acclaimed artists visited the Gate City later that year, a critic exulted that "the eve of the musical millennium of Georgia and the southeast is at hand." Other writers went even further, as when *Journal* correspondent Ann Stewart Etheridge wondered whether pianist Moriz Rosenthal was "man or god." All such critics shared a belief that classical music represented a revealed "truth" and beauty that could offer some benefit to the most humble, but that only the consecrated elect could fully comprehend. F. H. Richardson expressed this view in discussing the effects that a recent series of operas had had upon Atlanta audiences. "Not alone the aristocracy of culture in Atlanta . . . but also a host of people whom nature has not endowed with a deeper sense of the beauty and charm of music, who have never studied it and have little capacity for doing so successfully, feel today that they have been brightened and blessed by the revelations of these gifted children of song."[38]

These critics viewed the mingling of classical with mere popular music, the tainting of the sacred with the profane, as misguided at best and "sinful" at worst. As early as 1891, a *Constitution* writer reviewing an Opera House appearance by the Ovide Musin Concert Company charged, "Last night's programme contained several trashy pieces, and a number of others, if not trashy, rather light and flippant for such artists as compose the company." Eight years later, Joseph F. Burke—a former Confederate officer, no less—praised bandmaster Theodore Thomas for refusing to include popular songs such as "Dixie" in his southern concerts. Speaking for the "musicians of Atlanta," Burke observed that while "Some uncultured persons have thought there was music in 'Dixie,'" the "musicians of Atlanta have all along known better, and they wish to thank you for aiding them in enlightening the general public." Offering Thomas a ceremonial wreath, Burke asked the conductor to "Take this bit of laurel and wear it as a testimonial of your noble efforts to show the masses what true music is." Even performances consisting solely of classical music could be condemned if they were deemed insufficiently reverent. In reviewing an 1898 concert by the Boston Ideal Club, a local critic asserted that "to play the Intermezzo from 'Cavelleria Rusticana' on mandolins and guitars is artistic sacrilege. And to play Schumann's 'Traeumerei' . . . as a banjo solo, merits capital punishment, nothing less." [39]

More maddening to these critics than the taste of the masses for popular fare were the attitudes of Atlanta's leading businessmen, men who because of their wealth and opportunities for education and leisure clearly should have known better. The financial backing of such men was essential if expensive classical and operatic artists were to be brought to the Gate City, yet the apathy and even hostility of these capitalists was at times enough to drive local music lovers to distraction. Louise Dooly at one point complained bitterly that the "majority" of Atlanta's population—by which of course she meant the majority of that section of the population that counted in such matters—was composed of "shrewd, practical people who know what is for their own advancement in every line save that of refinement. They declare that they have continued so far in comparative enjoyment of life without partaking of its elegancies, and they are absolutely content to go on so to the end of their lives. They are utterly satisfied with themselves. They even boast of their own ignorance." Such philistines would be beneath consideration, Dooly continued, except that they "are often in such position that they have the privilege of expressing presumably the trend of public opinion and desire." Consequently, "the announcement is sent forth that the city cares only for such a class of music as can be hummed on the way home after hearing it, and the world outside believes therefore that the universal condition of the citizens is one of dense ignorance—the worst form of ignorance, which does not realize its own existence." [40]

Despite periods of deep frustration and near despondency, Atlanta's committed band of musical reformers did not lose heart. For as even poorly attended concerts and musical festivals had indicated, there had always been some people in the city who appreciated "artistic" music and some economic leaders willing to absorb financial deficits in support of it. So with the same faith in growth and progress exhibited by Atlanta's journalists and capitalists, the city's musical elite maintained hope that Atlanta's level of musical taste and refinement would increase just as did its economic standing.

In the end, it was a perceived link between economic and cultural progress that planted the desire for "refinement"—or at least the appearance of refinement—in the breasts of Atlanta's most influential citizens. The idea that high culture could enhance Atlanta's reputation regionally and nationally, that classical music could, as a *Journal* editorial put it, "advertise Atlanta far and near with her neighbors," eventually made classical music and opera much more attractive to the city's business elite.[41] Even the most tone-deaf merchant came to understand that high culture could attract paying visitors to the Gate City, while serving as well to refute once and for all that nagging criticism, bandied about by more tradition-minded southerners, that Atlanta was a crassly materialistic city, oblivious to the higher things and unnaturally modeled upon metropolises to the north.[42] Equally important, high culture, properly managed, could supply one more plank—along with their homes, churches, and social clubs—in the platform that set the newly risen Atlanta elite apart from its social inferiors and marked it as an aristocracy on a par with those who presided over the fortunes of the older, more established cities of the North and East.

Gradually, local financiers, industrialists, and merchants became more interested in the presentation of classical music as a promotional device. In fact, they came to believe that their resources and financial acumen entitled them to take charge of the local music scene, to displace the high-minded but fiscally inept Doepps, Sternbergs, and Barilis who had directed the city's cultural life in the past. In 1900 an officer of the Atlanta Concert Association, when questioned about the absence of musicians in the organization, told an interviewer that he recalled "no event conducted by musicians in this city in the last forty years which has not been disastrous financially. Our officers are cultivated gentlemen, fond of music, give a great deal of time and attention to the association, they are conservative business men, and have all made a success of their own affairs." Unlike their predecessors, these practical men realized that the true measure of musical achievement lay in ticket sales. "You may sometimes doubt your best friend," the officer explained, "but the statements of the box office are to be relied upon strictly." [43]

By the early years of the twentieth century, then, an alliance was building between a small band of musical enthusiasts and a larger group of businessmen, both intent upon making Atlanta a cultural center, albeit for different reasons. All that was needed now was a cultural entity that could cement and crown the budding union between the two groups, at once putting the Gate City on the national musical map and validating the cultural superiority of the local social elite. Enter the Metropolitan Opera Company of New York.

The Metropolitan Company appeared in Atlanta in 1901 and again in 1905, but in both instances the time was somehow not quite right. In fact, the Met's 1905 appearance in Wagner's *Parsifal* was later termed "disastrous." [44] Things had changed, however, by 1909. Just as Atlanta seems by this time to have crossed some invisible threshold into urbanity that allowed vaudeville finally to take root, the climate of the city seems to have changed musically as well. The partnership between music lovers and the business elite was strengthening, and the city was putting the finishing touches on a $250,000 auditorium-armory that civic leaders were eager to promote. Thus was born the idea of a "Great Southern Music Festival" that would bring to the Gate City the cream of the operatic world to mark the completion of the auditorium and to announce Atlanta's arrival as a world capital of culture and refinement. [45]

The *Atlanta Journal* was a driving force behind the enterprise. The newspaper claimed that "the idea of the festival was originally conceived in The Journal office," and its editors and writers spared no effort to ensure its success. [46] Indeed, *Journal* coverage of the festival offers a textbook example of civic boosterism in general and of the much-vaunted "Atlanta Spirit" in particular. It also shows the city's social, cultural, and economic leadership uniting in the use of high culture as a tool with which to enhance Atlanta's reputation, fill the coffers of its merchants, and consolidate the elite's own standing as a New South peerage.

Developers planned to secure the Dresden Philharmonic Orchestra and a number of leading operatic stars, including such Metropolitan luminaries as Enrico Caruso and Geraldine Farrar, for a series of five concerts to be held in early May. Any profit from the enterprise would go toward the purchase of a fifty-thousand-dollar concert organ to be placed in the auditorium. The campaign to bring off the Great Southern Music Festival was thus fought on two fronts. First, the artists had to be persuaded to come to Atlanta, and second, Atlanta had to be persuaded to pay the artists. Consequently, while a committee of leading Atlantans sought commitments from the opera stars, the *Journal* worked doggedly to attain the necessary financial guarantees from the city's wealthier citizens.[47]

Neither task was easy. Some of the stars had other commitments—Farrar was under contract to make recordings for the Victor Talking Machine Company on the dates set for the festival—and even when available, these artists did not perform cheaply. Farrar managed to obtain a release from her Victor contract but asked for twenty-five hundred dollars to appear in Atlanta. Yet Farrar was a bargain compared to Caruso, who demanded ten thousand dollars to perform in two concerts. Indeed, the total salary for all of the vocalists and the orchestra would come to about twenty thousand dollars, and this was the sum that had to be promised to guarantee the performers' contracts.[48]

This is where the *Journal* came in. The twenty-thousand-dollar guarantee fund would simply represent a backup source from which the performers could be paid should ticket sales fail to provide sufficient revenue. But many potential guarantors, cognizant perhaps of Atlanta's frequent failure to support highbrow music in the past, feared insufficient turnout. They were skeptical that Atlantans would attend the concerts in large enough numbers to make use of the guarantee fund unnecessary, and were therefore reluctant to pledge their own money. The *Journal* labored tirelessly to overcome this hesitancy. Beginning with the announcement of the proposed festival in February, the newspaper's editors and columnists spared no superlative in promoting the enterprise and the significance that it would hold for Atlanta's national reputation. The *Journal* promised the "greatest musical festival in American history, more brilliant than any the south ever dreamed of, more alluring in its variety than any the north or east ever dared undertake," featuring "the most brilliant array of great singers and performers ever dreamed of outside New York city or the largest music centers of Europe." In short, the festival would be "the richest feast of music which money can buy." Since it was therefore inconceivable that Atlantans would not swamp the box office, the *Journal* argued, there would be no need to touch the guarantee money. Indeed, given the large seating capacity of the new auditorium, "It is a simple calculation in arithmetic to show that there is not the slightest chance that any of the underwriters of this fund will ever be called upon to make up any deficit on account of the great music festival." [49]

The *Journal* avidly played up the cultural benefits that the proposed festival would bring. The event would be a boon in "stimulating the musical taste of the people," in making Atlanta the "musical center of the south," and in refuting the old charge that Atlanta was solely absorbed in crude mercenary pursuits. The city "famous for carrying out gigantic ventures in business and civic life" was now "pulling on her seven league boots and stretching her sinews to perform a marvel of art, a triumph higher than all her skyscrapers and as wonderful as all her growth." [50]

Despite this rhetorical emphasis on the festival's cultural value, issues of civic and individual self-interest were never far beneath the surface. The *Journal* heavily emphasized these themes to win the support of business-men who were not so interested in cultural refinement that they were willing to lose money in attaining it. The newspaper argued, "Thousands of music lovers will flock to Atlanta from all over the south, and from a financial point of view this feature alone will justify the entire outlay for the festival." At-lanta's reputation would be heightened immeasurably: "It is realized that a city which can successfully carry through an enterprise of this magnitude must be exhaustless in its resources and irrepressible in its determination. Thus the influence is spread abroad in other than musical channels." In addition, the opening of the Gate City's new auditorium—described with the usual modesty as "the greatest structure Atlanta or any other southern city ever bent her energies to build"—and the national publicity that the festival would provide for the building would help usher in "a new epoch in Atlanta's life. It will mean that she is to be not only the gateway of the south, but the resting place and Mecca of the whole section." [51] In more pedestrian terms, the city would instantly increase its appeal as a conven-tion center.

Such arguments eventually began to win over some Atlanta businessmen, who could be quite explicit in explaining their support. As Eretus Rivers, president of a realty company, put it, "Suppose we don't make a cent on the festival. As a property owner in this city I feel that the money I put into a subscription would be a splendid investment simply for the advertisement the festival would bring the city, and hence everything connected with the city." And so, even as the campaign to secure the fund dragged on without meeting its goal, the *Journal* continued to express confidence—or hope— that the "business men of the city, who are to profit in every particular from the festival and the crowds it will attract," would "rally" and subscribe the "entire amount" of the guarantee.[52]

This faith ultimately proved justified, as subscribers pledged sufficient funds to complete the guarantee fund in March.[53] The *Journal* could now turn to the task of convincing Atlantans to buy tickets—which they apparently did not do rapidly enough to satisfy the newspaper and nervous guarantors—and to the more enjoyable pastime of gloating over the Gate City's triumph in securing the festival.[54] "We have not been content to rise to the same height with other ambitious cities," the editor crowed, "but we have established a new precedent which will not be overshadowed for many years to come." In the future, "the very name of Atlanta will be to the world of music a veritable synonym of the highest artistic achievement." Atlanta's staging of the festival would mark "one of the most notable strides towards metropolitan eminence ever taken by this progressive city." Not content with repeated swipes at Chicago, which hosted a festival just in advance of Atlanta's, the *Journal* could not resist going further afield in its sallies, declaring cultural ascendancy—at least for the moment—over Paris itself. Asserting that the City of Lights had eagerly awaited Geraldine Farrar's return immediately following the end of her season in New York, the *Journal* reveled over Atlanta's coup, claiming that "a wave of disappointment" had swept over "the French metropolis now that it is known that the boulevardiere must wait, while Atlanta goes off with the prize." But the "gloom of the Opera Comique is the sunshine of the Atlanta auditorium, and what is too good for Paris is just about right for Atlanta."[55]

This jaunty tone continued in the coverage of the festival itself. Even Caruso's last-minute cancellation due to ill health did not dampen the ardor of the *Journal's* writers. They simply acclaimed the three lesser stars who agreed to replace him, going so far as to assert that the week of opera would be even greater without Caruso than it would have been with him.[56] Indeed, it is difficult to imagine how the Atlanta journalists who covered the festival could possibly have been more grandiloquent even had Caruso actually ap-

peared. In a front-page article describing opening night, a *Journal* writer
opined, "All that poets ever said or dreamed of music since Hellas' young
god strode singing through the dawn of the world came true again Tuesday
evening in the hearts of 8,000 southern people. . . . The vast auditorium,
crowned and girdled in color, shone with the light that gilds human faces
when the souls behind them wait upon the verge of a new, enchanted secret.
Even before the first half-spoken chord stole forth in the orchestra's overture, the whole expanse of listeners seemed to have been fused into some
new land, 'Where life no longer jolts or jars, but glides.'" Another article
further reflected the quasi-religious aspects of this first evening of grand
opera: "Never before in the history of Atlanta has such glorious tribute been
paid to any muse as that which Euterpe received Tuesday evening. . . . The
city and the assembled south bowed down and worshiped harmony. Magic
fingers touched the strings of a magic harp in the southland's soul, waked it
into being, and left it vibrant, living. It was an epoch in the city's history.
Hereafter through all time Atlanta will hold a place among the world's music
shrines." [57]

While the Gate City audience "bowed down and worshiped harmony"
(particularly, as it turned out, harmonies such as "Annie Laurie" and "Suwanee River," performed as encores), the *Journal* bowed down and worshiped the audience.[58] Although the performances themselves received far
more attention in 1909 than they would in subsequent years, it was already
clear that the real stars of the auditorium music festivals would be the men
and women in the boxes, particularly the women, whom the *Journal* un-
derstatedly described as "Beauteous southern womanhood swathed in glory
of raiment, gorgeously brilliant." From the earliest days of festival planning,
the newspaper had promised that the three-day gala would assume a paramount position in the world of society. "Hitherto the annual horse show
has been considered Atlanta's great society event," observed a columnist.
"But the horse show will not be comparable in this respect to the festival.
Belles from cities throughout the south will then be visiting here." Evoking
images of New York City's Diamond Horseshoe, the writer concluded that
the "auditorium is specially adapted through its long line of boxes and am-
pitheatre [*sic*] seats to give an effective mounting to the flash and sparkle of
fashion." [59]

The newspapers gave this "flash and sparkle" full play, providing copious details regarding who wore what and sat where at the concerts.[60] And as would be the case in future Opera Weeks, the papers also admiringly covered the myriad social events that took place outside the auditorium. On opening night of the 1909 festival, for instance, Atlanta's elite feted the opera stars and musicians at the Capital City Club, which sought to provide an atmosphere at once elevated and distinctively southern. As an orchestra played musical numbers that the program described, with an implied grin, as "a few classical selections"—including "In Dear Old Georgia," "My Old Kentucky Home," and, of course, "Dixie"—the guests sat down to dine before "attractively designed" place cards "depicting the familiar picka-ninny's face grinning from the heart of a watermelon."[61]

With the closing of the festival, attention turned gleefully toward tallying the receipts and to further vaunting the enterprise as "Atlanta's Most Brilliant Triumph." The *Journal* of May 7 proudly headlined, "Receipts of Music Festival, $31,500; Net Profit $11,500," figures that vindicated the underwriters and meant that a "substantial beginning" had been made toward purchase of the concert organ. This clear financial success and the opening of the auditorium meant "big things" for Atlanta. The papers promised that the festival would be permanent, becoming bigger and better with each passing year. These future festivals, along with other musical productions being planned for the new auditorium, would produce "a continuous and growing development of musical interest in the people of Atlanta." And for this inevitable improvement in public taste the city's elite could take full credit. As a correspondent from Macon noted in praising the Great Southern Festival, "The representative people of a state can do great things. They can make the best, the highest take the place of the low and evil, by giving their voice in its favor, making it fashionable to admire only the best. The masses follow their leaders, and are benefitted."[62]

It was reportedly at the suggestion of Geraldine Farrar that the Atlanta Music Festival Association, flushed with the triumph of 1909, resolved to invite the entire Metropolitan Opera Company to the Gate City for five performances in 1910.[63] The company's officers accepted the invitation—this time asking for a guarantee of fifty thousand dollars—and in the spring of 1910 made the first of a series of annual visits to Atlanta that would end only, temporarily, with the Great Depression.

But while the details would change with the passing years, the basic pat-

THE FIRST NOTES OF GRAND OPERA!

The *Journal* (March 31, 1910) playfully acknowledges that a night at the opera can be an expensive proposition. (Courtesy of UGA Photographic Services)

tern of newspaper coverage established in 1909 would remain the standard for treatment of the Metropolitan Company in Atlanta on through the 1920s. There were ever the same pleas to subscribe to the guarantee fund and, later, to buy tickets, pleas always couched in the same assurance that the guarantee would indeed be pledged and all tickets sold. There were the same unending boasts about Atlanta and its cultural parity with larger and older northern cities. There was the same extensive coverage of Atlanta "high society" and its functions, the same brief and unfailingly flattering reviews of the operas themselves, the same gloating over attendance fig-

ures, receipts, and Atlanta's rising reputation. The only consistent difference was that the newspapers portrayed each year of grand opera as being
unquestionably superior to that of the year before. The programs were always better, the audiences larger and more appreciative, the city more refined and culturally significant than had been the case a mere twelve months
earlier.[64]

This latter emphasis upon Atlanta's ever-heightening sophistication is
particularly striking. However much the newspapers promoted the enormous economic value that the Metropolitan Company's visits held in bringing prosperous visitors to the city and in advertising Atlanta nationwide,
and to whatever extent the papers exulted in the yearly exploits of the Gate
City's social elite, journalists always went out of their way to stress that more
important than all of this was the growing love for fine music that the Metropolitan's performers had inspired in Atlanta's citizens. As the *Constitution*
editorialized in 1916, "If Atlanta, in the beginning, accepted grand opera
from any 'child and new toy' motive, she has long since outgrown it; today
it is purely a question of the love of it, of genuine enjoyment of the music." This love was not solely the province of the city's wealthiest men and
women, as the same newspaper noted following a performance of *Aida* in
1919: "The fact that there were friends together one in decollette costume
and one in street attire but gave evidence to Atlanta's cosmopolitanism
which comes prominently to the fore on such occasions as Grand Opera
provides and entitles it to mention with the leading cities of the country." In
short, the Metropolitan Opera Company had ushered in a new "epoch"—as
the newspapers liked to say—in the cultural history of Atlanta. Gone for
good were the empty houses and the listless, unappreciative audiences that
had embarrassed local critics in the past. Atlantans of all walks of life luxu-
riated in a "spontaneous, deep-pulsing and now cultivated love of that art
which finds so marvelous a revelation in Metropolitan casts and productions."[65] Yet again, Atlanta had supposedly attained that quality so dreaded
by some and so craved by others, cosmopolitanism.

Actually, even a cursory examination of contemporary newspapers reveals that such statements greatly overstated the case. To begin with, despite
the renown of the Metropolitan artists and the "pulsing" love of the company's work by Atlanta audiences, the auditorium was rarely filled to capacity during Opera Week. When crowds did fill—or even almost fill—the

arena, they typically did so to see Enrico Caruso or Geraldine Farrar, great stars whose appeal far transcended the world of grand opera.[66] Factoring in the number of out-of-town visitors provides an even clearer measure of Atlanta's support for opera. In 1911, the *Constitution* claimed that twenty-five hundred men and women had come to the city to see the Metropolitan Company, and by 1916 local hotel men estimated that fifteen thousand people had visited Atlanta during Opera Week. That same year the manager of the auditorium calculated that visitors made up 50 to 60 percent of each night's attendance. And this at a time when Atlanta's opera-week audiences averaged just over five thousand persons a night.[67] Clearly, the love for grand opera was not as widespread in the Gate City as newspapers and civic leaders liked to suggest.

Even those Atlantans who did show up at the auditorium did not necessarily do so out of a consuming passion for music. Critics had long charged that operagoers were far more interested in being seen at than in seeing the performances. *Constitution* local-color columnist Bill Arp, who in 1895 attended a Wagnerian presentation by the Damrosch Opera Company, found himself unimpressed by either the singers or the audience. Arp recalled that the singing of Jenny Lind, whom he had seen as a young man, had "thrilled me and filled me with unutterable rapture and all I could do was to weep with emotion." This "German business," on the other hand, "tired me awfully and I slept right good at times." The language barrier was particularly irritating. "I wish they would sing in English," Arp grumbled. "I'll bet there were not ten in a hundred of that audience who understood a word that was sung. They go there because it is considered the thing to do. It is fashionable." Five years later, *The Concert Goer,* a national music magazine, surveyed Atlanta's musical scene and, like Arp, judged much of the city's concert attendance to be "fashionable": "The fact that a certain element is willing to pay extravagant prices . . . is not so much indicative of the genuine desire to hear the music as it is of the wish to be present and to be seen at a performance to which everybody goes." And Bishop Warren Candler, consistent in his condemnation of worldly amusements, agreed with such assessments. He defined grand opera as "a sort of fashionable diversion in which 'Macaroni' singers pour forth music to fashionably dressed men and women who do not understand what is sung."[68]

Such criticism did not end with the coming of the Metropolitan Company and the Gate City's supposed wholesale conversion to a love of the finer things. Negative appraisals sometimes even found their way into the normally boosterish newspapers. *Musical Courier* editor Leonard Liebling, for instance, argued in a 1916 letter to the *Constitution* that Atlanta's annual grand opera attendance figures interested him "only negatively," as they did "not represent the true barometer by which to gauge the degree of average musical culture in Atlanta." Rather, grand opera by its nature "has nothing of the essence of symphony, chamber music and choral performance, which are opposed to sensationalism and surface exploitation and necessarily appeal chiefly to those persons who love the work rather than the performers, and whose hero worship consists of reverence for the composers and not blind adoration of their headlined and Sunday-page featured interpreters." That same year, Mayor James G. Woodward, no friend to the respectable elite, offered a more pungent appraisal of the city's musical connoisseurs. Questioned by a local reporter after having attended three Metropolitan performances, the mayor opined that Atlantans "don't know B from bull's foot about grand opera, although they go and make a lot of fuss over it. . . . Further than that, I have nothing to say." [69]

Certainly Atlanta operagoers frequently behaved as though they were less than engrossed with the goings-on on stage. If they did not pitch coins and sausages as their less restrained brethren at the city's theaters sometimes did, Atlanta audiences continued to disrupt performances by arriving late and departing early, by engaging in loud conversations, and by cheerfully insisting upon applauding at inappropriate moments. Louise Dooly maintained her one-woman newspaper campaign against such conduct during the Met years, but with apparently limited success. Again and again Dooly found her evenings at the opera tainted by the distracting sounds of "low steady conversation . . . maintained almost throughout" the operas, broken now and again by loud comments, as when a young man asked his section of the auditorium, "Why don't they pick out good-looking women for those weepy parts?" Audience misconduct reached such levels during the 1912 Opera Week that a Music Festival Association official angrily complained to a reporter, "If opera-goers would keep their conversation bottled up until the opera is over or the curtain drops on the acts, they would add greatly to the pleasure of their neighbors who go to hear high-priced singers and not

Critics frequently castigated the behavior of Atlanta's operagoers. This cartoon appeared in the *Atlanta Constitution*, April 23, 1913. (Courtesy of UGA Photographic Services)

cheap conversation. I wish you'd put that in your paper where they can see it. It has been bad all the week, but at yesterday's matinee it was worse than ever."[70] Many Atlantans refused to allow the strains of European music to get in the way of a bit of socializing and, indeed, of some good-naturedly surreptitious drinking.[71]

A glance at Atlanta's cultural scene beyond the annual Opera Week confirms that no sudden love for "higher" music had swept the Gate City. To the contrary, as one unusually frank observer bluntly stated, "Atlanta has never been accused of an overtendency to the aesthetic." Metropolitan opera, even if only superficially supported in the city, was nonetheless, as Louise Dooly put it, "the only music Atlanta people go to hear." Just as in the decades prior to 1910, classical music continued to draw poorly in the city. The infrequent exceptions served only to highlight this fact. Dooly noted in 1914 that legendary prima donna Nellie Melba had "achieved last night the impossible in Atlanta; that is, the drawing of a concert audience." Two years later, another large turnout, this time for a Maud Powell violin performance, caused Dooly to wonder, "Why are Atlanta people not more frequent concert patrons? Why are high class concerts not more generally popular?"[72]

Even grand opera, now supposedly forever enshrined in the hearts of

Atlanta citizens, attracted negligible audiences when not performed by the prestigious Metropolitan Opera Company and its "high-priced" stars. In 1910, the very year that the Met ushered in Atlanta's musical millennium, the Bessie Abbott Grand Opera Company played to poor business in *Madame Butterfly* and *La Boheme.*[73] And when there was an exception to this pattern, there was generally a reason for it. In a 1913 review, Louise Dooly observed, "The beautiful opera which [Jules] Massenet founded on the Biblical story of 'Solome' [*sic*] was the attraction at the Atlanta [Theater] last night; or was the real attraction the well advertised fact that [Richard] Strauss's 'Salome' was suppressed several years ago in New York? The desire is not to be cynical, but certain it is that the production last night assembled a much larger audience than Atlanta ever sends to opera, except to the Metropolitan productions once a year."[74]

Local initiatives fared no better than did touring performers. In July of 1910 the Atlanta Musical Association inaugurated a series of concerts to be performed on the auditorium's newly purchased organ. There were to be thirty consecutive Thursday evening performances at which a small admission fee would be charged, and thirty free Sunday concerts aimed at providing music for poorer Atlantans and at instilling "taste . . . in those who have not had opportunity of becoming familiar with standard and most attractive music." The organist was J. Percy Starnes, whom Atlanta had characteristically acquired by offering him a thousand dollars more a year than he had been earning in New York City.[75] The program fell into trouble almost immediately; within a month of the first concert Dooly was already complaining that poor Thursday evening attendance would leave Atlanta "open to a natural question as to whether she does, indeed, possess any real musical interest."[76] The concert series staggered on for years, plagued by scanty support, noisy audiences, and recurring fiscal crises that perennially threatened cancellation of the project.[77]

Not surprisingly, given Atlanta's musical history, one of the most enthusiastically received Sunday organ concerts was made up entirely of the more respectable forms of popular music. "Say what you will," a reviewer observed, "the crowds like popular music. The organ recital of Sunday afternoon, composed for the most part of nationally known airs and national hymns, captured an audience in a measure seldom seen in the Auditorium since the first organ recitals were put on."[78] The broader Atlanta musical

public was not completely averse to or even always apathetic toward classical music; they simply preferred—just as they had in the late nineteenth
century—classical and popular musical forms blended together in a manner
seen less and less frequently as the years wore on. Thus, Irish tenor John
McCormack, who presented pieces ranging from Mozart to popular "heart
songs," consistently drew vast crowds to the auditorium at the same time
that more purely classical concerts failed.[79] John Philip Sousa continued to
play to throngs in Atlanta as well, his 1922 concert packing the auditorium
with an audience that included "people you would never see in a theater;
so many you never saw at Metropolitan opera."[80]

All of this is not to say that there were no men or women in the Gate
City during this period who sincerely loved and appreciated classical music
and grand opera; there were, of course. But as a long succession of poorly
attended concerts demonstrated, those Atlantans devoted exclusively to
classical music represented but a tiny minority in a rapidly growing city.
More than one observer noted as much. A press agent for a concert series
told the *Journal*'s Ward Greene in 1920—at a time when Atlanta's population had topped two hundred thousand—"This is a star-loving town, a
hero-worshipping town. There are two or three thousand people here who
actually like good music and who go to hear good music. But when the
auditorium is packed, the rest of the crowd is made up of star-gazers." A
writer who had visited Atlanta and other cities a few years earlier had come
to the same conclusion: "I am by no means sure that the regular spring visit
of the Metropolitan Grand Opera Company may be taken as a sign that
Atlanta is a peculiarly music-loving community. Indeed, I was told by one
Atlanta lady, herself a musician, that the city did not contain more than a
thousand persons of real musical appreciation, that a number of these could
not afford to attend the operatic performances, and that Opera Week was,
consequently, in reality more an occasion of great social festivity than of
devout homage to art." As the young woman explained, "Our opera week
bears the same relation to the life of Atlanta as Mardi Gras does to that of
New Orleans. It is an advertisement for the city, and an excuse for everyone
to have a good time."[81]

In large measure, however, such criticism was beside the point. For it
was primarily as an "advertisement for the city" that wealthy businessmen
sponsored the annual Opera Week in the first place. And they apparently

FLASHLIGHT PHOTOGRAPHS OF SOCIETY BEAUTIES

At left is Miss Constance Knowles and at the right Miss Helen Prior. These are | flashlight photographs made as the ladies were about to enter the Auditorium.

The *Georgian* (April 27, 1912) highlights two "society beauties" arriving at a 1912 opera performance. (Courtesy of UGA Photographic Services)

succeeded admirably in their efforts. As *Musical Courier* editor Leonard Liebling told the *Constitution* in 1916,

> the opera week is a commercial asset of phenomenal potency. I have just traveled through the entire southwest and south from Los Angeles and El Paso to Atlanta, and in all that territory I have not been in a city where I did not encounter constant mention of the opera week here. We heard persons making appointments to meet in Atlanta the end of April for the opera. . . . we saw signs in windows reading 'Gowns for the Atlanta Opera,' 'Gloves for the Atlanta Opera,' etc. . . . What the display of wealth

and fashion means to the business credit and standing of Atlanta, and what the expenditures for hotel outlay, entertaining and general purchasing accomplish financially here, I need not dwell upon, for those are elementary facts which must be clear even to those not accustomed to look for commercial returns in matters of music. [82]

Promoters of the yearly gala had hoped that the Met's appearances would help to soften Atlanta's reputation as a commercially keen yet culturally benighted city, but the idea of the festival would never have gotten off of the ground, much less survived, if the city's leaders had not calculated that there was a great deal of money to be made from it. There is a sense in which the city's leading citizens were never quite so materialistic as when trying to prove how much beyond materialism they were.[83]

But the men and women who occupied Atlanta's version of the Diamond Horseshoe did not confine their thoughts solely to questions of dollars and cents. They also dwelt on the image that they projected to their northern counterparts, to ordinary Atlantans closer to home, and to each other. The men who constructed the Capital City Club, the Druid Hills Golf Club, and the Piedmont Driving Club; who built and occupied the grand homes of Peachtree Street and Inman Park; who owned and read the *Journal* and *Constitution;* and who attended the Metropolitan's performances and entertained the company's stars were above all intent on casting themselves as a homegrown aristocracy, a social class justified in leading at home and in dealing as equals with the lords of other cities. So, in the end, for all the talk about stimulating the taste of a wider public and bringing a love of music to the masses, it was ultimately far more important that attendance at the Metropolitan's court be restricted to a fortunate few, a "representative" elect. Thus, however mundane and unaristocratic their origins, and however minimal their interest in the productions played out before them, if in the end they dressed like opera lovers and acted like opera lovers, they could claim to *be* opera lovers, with all the attendant glamour and social validation. For these men and women, high culture was a tool with which they worked to solidify their position as a culturally elevated, ultrarespectable ruling class. And when more run-of-the-mill Atlantans massed on the sidewalks opposite the auditorium to watch them alight from their cars and carriages on opening night—or rather to observe what one writer described as "royalty . . . the royalty which wealth and beauty gives and greater than all the royalty of heaven gifted in song and music"—Atlanta's leaders had at least partially succeeded in their purpose.[84]

Any hierarchy, of course, requires a bottom as well as a top. In the South, where class was always deeply intertwined with race, it stood to reason that African Americans would represent the lower end of the cultural pecking order, just as they formed the "bottom rail" economically and socially. If class is complicated by race, however, the reverse is also true. Atlanta's black community was anything but monolithic, and harbored deep class divisions of its own. Many elite blacks hoped to use culture as a means of sealing themselves off from those below while building bridges—founded upon mutual respect—with their white counterparts. But in the Deep South of the Jim Crow era, this would be a very difficult task indeed.

⇥ 5 ⇤

The Black Elite in a
Jim Crow City

While elite Atlantans looked to the New Yorkers who presided over the Metropolitan Opera House as exemplars of proper cultural ideals, they also required a negative standard by which to gauge and confirm their own status. Working-class whites came in for their share of cultural abuse and derision, but given the fiercely held racial ideology of the period, even the poorest among them were not entirely suited to this purpose. No matter how contemptuous elite whites might sometimes be toward their white "inferiors," this disdain was always mitigated by the realization that these unfortunates were, after all, white, and therefore possessed a cultural birthright that raised them—however slightly at times—above their black counterparts.

No, the negative cultural standard of the day was not to be borne by any white Georgian, no matter how lowly. In the South of the late nineteenth and early twentieth centuries, only one group could be safely, consistently, and thoroughly demeaned: African Americans. Disparagement of black culture brought whites together in an arrogant conviction of racial superiority.

Freedmen began pouring into Atlanta immediately following emancipation, and the river of black migrants continued to flow well into the twentieth century as farm families looked to the city as a refuge from deadening rural poverty.[1] The Gate City's black population rose from fewer than two thousand in 1860 to more than sixteen thousand in 1880, then to over forty thousand in 1900 and to just under sixty-three thousand by 1920. Eventually a number of educated and professional blacks settled around Atlanta's black institutions of higher learning, and middle-class blacks later established a business enclave along Auburn Avenue. These men and women, however, represented only a small percentage of the city's African American population. The vast majority of black Atlantans were semiskilled workers or common laborers, when they were able to find work at all. They typically lived in squalid slums such as Lightning and Beaver Slide, which were characterized by impassably muddy streets, proximity to reeking city refuse heaps, decrepit housing, outdoor toilets, and high crime rates. Always the last to receive city services such as water and sewage disposal, black Atlantans also faced woefully inadequate schools and hospital facilities.[2]

From an early date, racial proscriptions, zealously enforced by a callously brutal police force, served to exploit and humiliate black Atlantans while buttressing white supremacy. White Atlantans, for example, vigorously employed vagrancy laws to intimidate blacks into accepting low-wage employment.[3] But the white racial program extended well beyond economics. Custom, in league with a rigid system of Jim Crow laws developing during this period, dictated that blacks accept separate and usually vastly inferior facilities and services of all kinds. In the Gate City blacks were excluded from most hotels and from the public library. Bars, restaurants, and barbershops served one race or the other, never both. Blacks traveled in separate railroad cars and were not allowed to enter the train station by the front door en route to their separate waiting rooms. Black citizens used separate elevators, took a separate path through Grant Park Zoo, swore on separate Bibles in city courts, and, if arrested, rode in a separate vehicle to the stockade to be placed in segregated cells. This was all made worse by the insulting treatment that black Atlantans received from any white person with whom they had to deal, from sales clerks to city officials.[4]

The Atlanta Police Recorder's Court was ground zero for the enforcement of the city's racial laws and prerogatives. For many years Judge Nash R. Broyles ruled autocratically from the recorder's bench. According to the *Georgian,* a good recorder needed "Shrewd common sense . . . wide intelligence, undaunted courage and unswerving honesty."[5] The author might have added to this list of "absolute essentials" the quality of deeply held racial prejudice, which Broyles exhibited proudly and repeatedly. Praised liberally as a "Recorder with Backbone," Broyles made no secret as to his primary enemies in the continuing war against lawlessness. At a 1911 banquet in his honor, the judge grimly warned of the mayhem that might well afflict his countrymen during the dawning twentieth century: "Our children may live to see our citizens in terror, our country in flames! They may hear the victorious shouts of our American vandals as they ruthlessly trample upon the ruins of our civilization!" In explaining what his listeners might do to forestall such disaster, Broyles revealed the identity of these vandals: "First of all, we can set a good example to others by obeying the law ourselves. Just so long as the respectable citizen, silk-hatted and kid-gloved, slips his shining pearl-handled revolver into his hip pocket, just so long will the negro denizen of 'Hell's Halfacre' do the same thing. The negro is the most imitative race on the face of the earth, and he absorbs the white man's vices like a sponge does water."[6] Even when punishing erring whites, therefore, Broyles hoped to provide a stern lesson to "imitative" blacks who might otherwise "absorb" their sins.[7]

Broyles took his stand against civilization's decline from his bench at the recorder's court. Here black men and women of whatever station were ritually debased and mortified for the amusement of the judge, his underlings, and the courtroom audience. Broyles once boasted, "Sometimes we put on a bill here that would make a roaring hit on the regular vaudeville stage."[8] Benjamin Davis Jr., son of the editor of Atlanta's weekly black newspaper, provides in his memoirs a far less jovial recollection of the Progressive Era police court at work. On a visit home to Atlanta while a student at Amherst, Davis gave up his seat on a crowded trolley car to a pregnant black woman, then took a seat for himself in the white section of the car. For this offense police officers dragged him off of the conveyance and presented him with a summons to appear in the recorder's court the following day. At the appointed time Davis, accompanied by his well-known father, settled into the "Negro section" of the court and awaited his turn:

> What I heard during the long wait was enough to shock the most insensitive. The police court provided a form of entertainment, of sport, for the petty officials, at the expense of the hapless, humble Negro workers caught in the complicated toils of jim-crow laws. The vulgarity of the tin-horn magistrate was repellent, while the police and their hangers-on stood around making merry. One Negro woman was virtually stripped bare by the lewd language and gestures of the magistrate. The clerks and bailiffs fingered the woman's breasts as she stood there helplessly, her face bathed in tears of shame and agony.

When the Davises were called before the bench, the recorder listened to the policeman's account of the trolley incident, then heard what Davis's father had to say—the judge refused to allow the younger Davis to speak—before rendering his judgment: "Ben . . . you're starting your boy off on the wrong track. You sent him up no'th to school and he comes back thinking he's as good as a white man. You better get that stuff out of his head or we'll knock it out. You know the ropes here—this is a white man's country—no matter what it is up no'th. I'm gonna let him off this time, but I warn you we ain't gonna have no niggers down here sitting down with white people." When the judge imposed a ten-dollar fine, Davis's father "gulped audibly—swallowing his pride," and handed over the money. As he walked out of the courtroom the younger Davis was "furious," but "At the same time I felt ashamed and humiliated—not so much for myself as for my father and my people. If this could happen to me . . . what, indeed, would have been the fate of a Negro who had failed to get himself born into a 'well-to-do' family?" [9]

To spread these object lessons of black inferiority and white supremacy to a wider audience, reporters such as Gordon Noel Hurtel of the *Constitution* and Ward Greene of the *Journal* took the grim episodes enacted within the police court, sanitized and reworked them, then presented them to the newspapers' readers as "hilarious" anecdotes, rendering the court—as Broyles himself suggested—as a sort of real-life minstrel show. Regular columns such as Hurtel's "At the Police Matinee" and Greene's "Jedge Johnsing's Police Matinee" offered stories, accompanied by grotesque cartoons, of ignorant, childlike blacks who inevitably spoke in heavy dialect, receiving lessons in justice from an urbane and witty recorder. The authors particularly enjoyed satirizing black pretensions toward "respectability." Thus one matinee tale began, "There had been a dance down in Darktown in one of the most fashionable residences on Crooked Alley." In this case a black man attempted to distance himself from unsavory characters who had been present at the dance by insisting, "I is a quality nigger and doan soshurate wid dem." [10] Another favorite tactic was to have the learned recorder trip up or overawe defendants with legal terminology and literary allusions. In a typical instance, a "Darktown belle" was fined $1.75 for crossing beyond Decatur Street after dark, thus violating a racial boundary that the judge described to the uncomprehending woman as "our modern Rubicon." [11]

The attitudes epitomized in the recorder's court and broadcast through daily newspaper columns pervaded white Atlanta and were directed to one degree or another toward all of black Atlanta, law-abiding and law-breaking citizens alike. Thus the *Constitution* in 1910 called for a symposium of local white clergymen to deal with the pressing question, "What About The Half-Heathen?" The newspaper editorialized, "We have not sufficient confidence in the rudimentary intelligence of the average negro in America to let him govern himself, to let him operate the railroads he patronizes, to give him place or power in great concerns that supply commodities to the nation, to let him, unofficered by white men, fight under the American flag." Yet, incredibly, "In RELIGION and, largely, in EDUCATION, the keystone to all progress, the bulwarks of all civilization, the makers and preservers of races and of peoples, we virtually leave the negro to HIS OWN shifts!" [12]

Ultimately, such racism dreadfully cheapened the lives of all black citizens in the eyes of the city's whites. As late as 1928, a white store owner was not even taken into custody after murdering a black college student who refused to remove his hat in the man's presence.[13] And the wife of a *Journal* reporter, recalling her husband's earliest days working the police beat for the newspaper, told of the night he called the city desk to report three murders. The desk editor excitedly asked for the addresses of the victims, but upon hearing them inquired, "They all niggers?" The rookie answered that he did not know, but wondered if it really mattered; after all, they had been murdered just the same. "Look," replied the editor, "anytime there's this address or this section of town, just don't bother us. That's not news." [14]

Whites rationalized such views by placing the blame for the plight of the region's blacks on forces outside the South. African Americans were clearly an inferior race and were best understood by southern whites. Thus, the argument went that blacks had flourished under strict white control during the days of slavery, but the race had degenerated miserably since emancipation, or rather since black fortunes had been wrested by northerners from the patient and solicitous guidance of benevolent slave owners.[15] The inimitable Gordon Noel Hurtel nicely summed up this point of view in 1900 when he claimed, "Morality among negroes, as a class, is low, and . . . it is getting lower." Journalist Ray Stannard Baker encountered similar notions when he toured the South in the wake of the 1906 Atlanta race riot. "Many Southerners," he found, "look back wistfully to the faithful, simple, ignorant, obedient, cheerful, old plantation negro and deplore his disappearance. They want the New South, but the old Negro." As one fretful older Atlanta woman expressed it, "They don't sing as they used to. You should have seen the old darkeys of the plantation. Every year, it seems to me, they have been losing more and more of their care-free good humour. I sometimes feel that I don't know them any more. Since the riot they have grown so glum and serious that I'm free to say I'm scared of them!"[16]

To highlight this putative racial decline, the newspapers celebrated specimens of the "old-time negro" who had managed to survive in an urbanizing, industrializing world. In 1907 the *Georgian* somberly editorialized upon the death of Mary Webster, who for forty years had loyally served a white Atlanta family. Stressing the "mutual care and mutual consideration and . . . mutual affection" that had held servant and employer together, the author opined, "Northern people who were not raised in this environment can scarcely understand the tie that binds the old southerner to the old slave element of the race." A clear consciousness of place was fundamental to this warm relationship: "Never for an instant did this faithful woman overstep the boundary that marked the real division of equality between the races. And yet in that infinite tact of the old regime she lived on her side of this line as tranquilly, as happily and as heartily as the mistress of the household and her sons lived in mutual consideration and kindness upon theirs." Sadly, the editorial concluded, "One by one we are laying away these old and venerable links that bound the races to the only relation in which they were ever formed to live."[17]

By implication, of course, these worthy old darkies were giving way to younger generations of blacks who bore no affection for their superiors and who failed to recognize their rank in the racial order. As "Mammy" Georgia Bradwell, another old-fashioned servant, put it to an approving reporter, "Dese new-time niggers ain't no good for nusses. Dey don't keer about nuthin' but havin' a good time—dat's all. De chillun don't love 'em like dey do us old-timers."[18]

Paralleling these attitudes toward African Americans as a people were the opinions that white Atlantans held about black culture. Most whites believed that like the race itself, black culture had reached its apogee in the halcyon days of the Old South, when whites had guarded and nurtured their hapless charges. Thus, *Constitution* local color columnist Sarge Plunkett could argue that the singing abilities of slaves had been superior even to those of a white prima donna. At DeGive's Opera House in 1890, Plunkett's thoughts wandered back to olden times under the inspiration of Emma Abbott's rendition of "Old Folks at Home":

> It was sweet, mighty sweet, for er Yankee gal that never heard the old plantation niggers sing it; but when she opened on the chorus she touched it off with some of her opera 'trills' that spoilt it to my ear; but I liked the song anyhow, for it brought up memories of long ergo, and as she sang the next verse a tear stole into my eye, for it's these old songs the niggers used to sing at night as they came from the field on the other side of the river. . . . Them old plantation niggers could beat Emma's singing with all her art, and they were happier than she will ever be with all her wealth, but they are gone, never to be er gin.[19]

Plunkett's nostalgia represents a cultural version of the old versus new dichotomy that whites applied to black society and character in general. Likewise a puff for a 1910 appearance by "Polk Miller's Negroes" described the performers as "Four awkward, thick-skulled, heavy-handed negroes" who were "absolutely uncontaminated by education of any sort, musical or otherwise. . . . There is nothing of 'the new era' about them. They are of the genuine black corn field type, but they were born with music in their souls and they can sing." Unfortunately, a reviewer noted, this sort of music "is rapidly passing, going the way of the ante-bellum negro, its place being taken by ragtime and modern minstrel show stuff."[20]

The notion that blacks were "born with music in their souls" was a common one that survived the supposed degeneration of African Americans as a race. A white railroad man, contemplating a singing gang of black convicts excavating a building site, knowingly explained this characteristic to an attentive reporter. "Now, that sort of thing is born in a nigger. He does it naturally. I'll gamble some o' them convicts ain't been at that work two weeks, but they're on to the swing a'ready. It's just like this blamed dancin' of theirs; inside of every kinky skull somewhere is a bumpity, joggly pendulum that beats time. All kinds of time. Straight time sometimes, double-time by the yard, an' rag-time by the mile. An' any kind of work a nigger can do that has some kind of 'time' in it, he'll put it there. An' he'll do the work, too."[21]

Music in their souls, yes; native intelligence, no. To the contrary, whites refused to believe that blacks were or ever had been capable of any degree of independent creativity. In the 1890s, for example, the *Constitution* argued editorially and through an article by no less a supposed authority than Joel Chandler Harris that that quintessential African American musical instrument, the banjo, was not really a black invention at all. "The banjo as it is," an editor insisted, "is a white man's instrument; the banjo as it was belongs to the Arabians." [22] That the newspaper felt compelled to comment upon such an issue at all indicates how important whites felt it was to keep blacks culturally, as well as socially and politically, "in their place."

Along these same lines, while many whites were willing to concede that blacks were able performers of old spirituals and folk songs, few were equally prepared to allow that blacks might also have been capable of composing these songs. A *Journal* writer came close to giving blacks such songwriting credit but drew back at the last instant, asserting that after all, "No folksongs were ever deliberately created," and claiming instead that the old slave songs had somehow "burst" from "childish, imaginative hearts." [23] More typical were the comments of Virginian Polk Miller, who lectured on "The humor of the old southern darky" at the Opera House in 1894. Miller told his audience that although the "negro is fond of musical instruments and has a keen appreciation of musical sounds . . . Songs do not originate with the negroes . . . but are twisted from those they have heard." [24]

Others could be harsher in their assessments. A 1923 *Journal* editorial labeled as "tommy-rot" the claim of a *New York Times* correspondent that "Negro music represents the only native folk music of America." The *Journal* insisted, "The negro got his musical start from the white man, as he got everything else he had. . . . The negro having no ideals as a race gradually absorbed those of the whites." As for the spirituals that the *Times* singled out for special commendation, "The negro did not write or originate one of them," wrote the *Journal.* "Not one song of the ante-bellum south was written or composed by a negro." The editor refused even to credit African Americans with any provenance over jazz, a musical form consistently maligned by respectable southern whites as a corrupt product of degenerate postbellum black culture. In actuality, the editorial concluded, the true progenitors of jazz were the white country fiddlers who played "for the square dances of our fathers." [25]

Aside from black renditions of the old antebellum spirituals, whites responded favorably toward black culture only when it was belittled or satirized, as in the supposedly authentic "cakewalks" staged at the Grand, or in the minstrel shows that perennially drew swarms of white Atlantans to the city's theaters.[26] Beyond this, black performers could gain the praise—however patronizing—of Gate City whites only by performing highbrow European music, the same music rhetorically exalted by elite white Atlantans. But even here, as we shall see, white acceptance of black artistry was far from complete.

Atlanta's black citizens reacted in a variety of ways to these degrading attitudes. Particularly in the decades following the Civil War, as the postwar southern caste system took form, some local blacks openly opposed Jim Crow practices in the Gate City's theaters. Just after passage of the Civil Rights Bill of 1875, for instance, three black men sought to protest segregation in DeGive's Opera House by taking seats on the white side of the gallery. Hisses and catcalls issued from the white sections of the theater, the stage performance came to an immediate halt, and a group of white men roughly threw the interlopers down the gallery stairs. One of the aggrieved African Americans subsequently appealed to federal officials for help under the new law, but nothing came of his request. The *Constitution* concluded its account of the episode with a terse reference to the alleged black obsession with sexual "race mixing" that underlay much of the white drive for racial segregation, observing that it was "fortunate that none of the negroes tried to force their way among the ladies down stairs. Had they done so there, it would have been prevented." No doubt the newspaper was correct, for local whites seemed determined to preserve segregation—and thus their supposed racial "purity"—no matter what the U.S. government had to say; one Atlanta lawyer even carried a shotgun to the Opera House to forestall any misguided attempts at racial mingling.[27]

Six years later, in 1881, a near riot ensued when city police arrested John Burke, a "negro boy" from Griffin, Georgia, for attempting to enter "the part of the [Opera House] in which the ladies were." The initial *Constitution* report of the incident claimed that officers took Burke into custody after he knocked a white woman off the sidewalk while rushing into the theater, but a subsequent article allowed that Burke had first been ejected from the building after entering an area restricted to whites. In any case, Burke resisted arrest and was consequently clubbed with a police baton, leading an angry crowd of black Atlantans to threaten the policemen. Following a melee in which several other blacks were beaten, officers managed to get Burke to jail, but the protesters followed them there. A number of policemen then faced a fusillade of sticks and stones while forcing the mob to clear the street. Later in the day a U.S. soldier bayoneted a black man who had refused to move away from a stack of army weapons that happened to be near the Opera House, while another black Atlantan managed to elude police officers who attempted to arrest him after he delivered a fiery diatribe regarding police behavior toward African Americans. The *Constitution* regretted the lawless behavior of the city's blacks—especially on a day set aside for mourning the late President Garfield—and blamed the whole unfortunate row on "Burke's desire to aggravate the police by going where there was no other colored person."[28]

A more peaceable attempt to integrate the Opera House occurred less than two years later. On February 23, 1883, W. D. Moore, a black Republican and an employee of the Atlanta office of the Internal Revenue Department, entered the Opera House in the company of his wife and another woman, Hattie Epps. Moore and his companions took seats in the white section of the gallery, ostensibly to watch a performance of the Haverly Mastodon Minstrel Company. Whites in the area immediately protested, and DeGive asked a policeman to instruct Moore to move to the other side of the gallery. Moore, however, declined to go. The officer then called in a superior, who again informed Moore that he would have to leave the white section. Moore again quietly but firmly refused, noting that he was seated in the gallery and was therefore not "molesting or inconveniencing any white ladies." Although DeGive preferred that the police simply eject the trio from the building, Moore asserted that he would not leave unless he was arrested. In the end, the police obliged, detaining Moore and his companions for "disorderly conduct and refusing to comply with the rules of the opera house." Moore rebuffed DeGive's offer to refund his admission fee, promising that he would use the Civil Rights Act of 1875 to test the manager's right to segregate the theater.

Moore was immediately released on bond and ultimately turned the tables by having DeGive arrested for violating the federal law. But DeGive, who, like Moore, spent no time in jail, remained unswayed in his determination to maintain segregated seating in the Opera House. He argued, "If it is decided that the colored people can invade the white gallery there is nothing to keep them from occupying seats in the parquet or dress circle." And this would mean the ruin of the theater business, for white men would never bring "their wives and sisters" to a place where the women would "be seated for hours next to colored people of all grades, from the lowest even to the best of them." Rather, the "best" white people would stop coming to the theater, and "those white men who did go would go for the purpose of making it warm for the colored people."

Unfortunately for Moore, before DeGive could be brought to trial the U.S. Supreme Court invalidated the Civil Rights Act. News of the court's decision arrived in dramatic fashion at DeGive's Opera House, where, co-incidentally, Haverly's Mastodon Minstrel troupe was making its first appearance in Atlanta since the time of Moore's arrest. Word reached DeGive as he sat in his office counting the night's receipts. Someone then informed the Haverly company's manager, who stopped the evening's performance to announce to the "vast" audience that the Supreme Court had struck down the act, thereby ending the threat of integrated theaters, hotels, and restaurants. According to the *Constitution*'s account, the crowd "instantly grasped the full purport of the announcement and burst into such a thunder of applause as was never before heard within the walls of the operahouse [*sic*]. This was no sooner subsided than it was repeated and prolonged with even greater unction. The people smiled at each other with beaming faces and congratulations were exchanged all through the audience." This jubilation did not carry over into the "colored" section of the gallery, however, where the patrons "were silent and evidently smitten with dumbfounded consternation. Not a note of applause came from those solemn rows of benches, and their occupants evidently believed that the decision meant the total abrogation of the chief blessings that are involved in the facts of their emancipation and citizenship." As for DeGive, he expressed complete satisfaction with the ruling and hoped that black Atlantans would give up the struggle against segregated seating. Presaging the looming concept of "separate but equal," he told a reporter that "we have given them good places in the theater and protected them always in their rights in such places. They should be contented there, and now I believe they will be." [29]

However "contented" Gate City blacks may have been with these seating arrangements, the Moore incident marked the high point of attempts to integrate the Opera House. Indeed, when a group of black patrons complained to DeGive in 1885 about having to wade through a muddy alley to reach the theater entrance designated for their use, they carefully informed a *Journal* correspondent that they hoped their "white friends" would not "think this is a 'civil rights' kick, for it is not. We simply want a decent way of getting into the gallery, and do not desire in the least to go down among the white people." Far from it: "We are satisfied with the gallery." [30]

Atlanta's black citizens may have been forced to accept the fact that seating in the city's white theaters would continue to be segregated, but this did not mean that they could not protest the South's reigning racial ideology in other ways. Some black Atlantans, for instance, bitterly criticized the racism that imbued many local productions. The prime example of this came with the presentation of Thomas Dixon's *The Clansman* at the Grand in 1905. The Atlanta-based *Voice of the Negro,* a journal of African American news and affairs, castigated Dixon and his work for "stirring up race hatred," while praising white minister Len G. Broughton for similarly denouncing the play. The *Voice* later blamed the Atlanta presentation of *The Clansman* for helping to incite the savage 1906 race riot.[31] The *Independent,* Atlanta's black weekly, also vociferously attacked the play. City editor E. B. Barco asserted in the wake of the production's stay in Atlanta that the play and the racist attitudes it expressed had been so widely publicized that there had been "no excuse for any intelligent Negro" to attend the show.[32] A review by Professor James W. Woodlee, who did attend, further detailed Dixon's offenses against decency and good race relations. Woodlee charged that the very purpose of *The Clansman* was "to stir up the prejudice between the races and to arouse a deeper feeling of hate between them." He noted, "Everything to impress you with the inferiority of the Negro and to characterize him as a beast was prominently portrayed in every line. Everything that would show superiority of the white man spiritually, intellectually and morally was the climax of every act." Woodlee especially deplored the scene in which "a miserable black man was pictured sitting in a white man's parlor . . . dramatically exclaim[ing] that Negro rule means the extermination of the Aryan race and the perpetration of the nameless crime everywhere upon the wives and daughters of white men." This sort of demagoguery went beyond being unchristian and inhumane; it was dangerous. Woodlee recalled the "deep malice" that had settled over the audience at the Grand, the "scowles [*sic*] and frowns" that the whites in the gallery cast toward the blacks on the other side of the house, and the "look of contempt" returned by the black gallery patrons. He concluded that "had it not been for the presence of the officers of the law some would have given vent to their feelings, and an assault upon the colored people would have surely followed." Even leaving the issue of potential violence aside, *The Clansman* exerted a poisonous influence: "I dare say more white people left the Grand with a deeper feeling of hate for the Negro and more people of the Negro race left with a deeper distrust of the white man than the effect of all the political speeches since the Civil War has produced."[33]

As Woodlee's review suggests, black and white patrons took very different views of Dixon's work, giving rise to simmering animosities within the theater. In many cities across the South, local theater managers, hoping to avert violence, simply barred blacks from productions of *The Clansman.* Since DeGive did not take this step in Atlanta, blacks had the opportunity to take their seats in the Grand and to express their opinions. According to an account published in the *Independent,* these "Negro gallery gods" made their presence known through the "whoops and yells with which they greeted every appearance of a 'colored part' on the stage. These yells were derided by the other parts of the house by loud hisses." Worried police officers ordered that the house lights be kept on during the play and that the sale of soda water be discontinued, lest angry patrons hurl bottles at each other. During one especially dramatic moment in the production, someone on the black side of the gallery cheered loudly, bringing forth roars of disapproval from the white side: "There were cries of 'Put him out!' 'Shut him up!' 'Fix him!'" Later, during a scene in which a black character is tried before the Klan, whites in the gallery shouted "Lynch him!" This brought a cascade of hisses from the black side, and the police, deciding that they had seen enough, moved in. They arrested Frank Harper, a "Negro boy," on charges of disorderly conduct, but not without a fight that resulted in Harper being roughed up by the officers. The beating reportedly "had the desired effect, and greater quiet prevailed . . . after the ejection."[34]

By the early twentieth century, few Atlanta blacks overtly protested the regime of de jure segregation that had been rigidly fixed upon the South. Instead, in the coming decades the fight would be to obtain justice within the South's Jim Crow structure. By tending to their own segregated institutions and fortunes, the Gate City's black leaders hoped to create the possibility for dignified lives within a system geared by whites toward the diminishment of African Americans. There was always hope among many black leaders that an educated, cultured black middle class could be nurtured that would ultimately prove to the white elite that African Americans—or at least those who were "cultivated" and economically privileged—were worthy of respect and fair treatment. Given the acknowledgment and approval it deserved, this black bourgeoisie would then spearhead the "advancement" or "uplift" of the race as a whole. The infamous Atlanta riot of 1906, in which white mobs indiscriminately targeted blacks regardless of social class or cultural attainments, set back but did not destroy this dream that one day the "better" southern whites might in effect grant formal "recognition" to the more prosperous and refined of the city's African Americans, and that until that time elite blacks could carve out a satisfying existence for themselves in a "separate but equal" society.[35]

There were a number of uncertainties, inconsistencies, and contradictions involved in this program. How could the black elite "uplift" the lower classes while simultaneously maintaining its own prized exclusivity? Would it be possible to nourish an independent, self-sufficient African American society while eagerly aping white bourgeois values, implicit in which was a conviction of racial hierarchy?[36] Could the black leadership reach out for white acceptance without sundering its ties to and influence over the black working class? And finally—fundamentally—would whites ever deign to recognize a black social and cultural elite, no matter how diligently this elite followed the whites' lead?

Public entertainment frequently served as an arena in which such questions surfaced and played themselves out. Elite blacks, like their white counterparts, often used culture as a tool to enhance their status and to more clearly distinguish their behavior and values from those of the lower classes. Repeatedly, therefore, entertainment became a battleground in the struggle of the "better" class of blacks for social validation. Whether the issue at hand was seating arrangements, musical taste, or theater location, conflict over entertainment reveals the tensions and obstacles inherent in the attempt by Atlanta's fledgling black elite to subordinate race to class in the supercharged atmosphere of the New South.[37]

The twists and tortured ambiguities of this racial strategy are evident in the thought and activities of two of the Gate City's most important black leaders during the first third of the twentieth century: Benjamin Davis Sr. and Henry Hugh Proctor. The fiery, unpredictable, and controversial Davis edited Atlanta's black weekly, the *Independent,* which commenced publication in 1903. As a disciple of Booker T. Washington, Davis was not, at least into the 1920s, opposed to segregation itself. As he wrote in 1909, "To our mind the question of the social separation of the races is so sound, sane and godly, there is no question of its wisdom."[38] But at the same time, Davis believed that racial separation and black acceptance of Jim Crow indignities were two very different things. He bitterly criticized the willingness of many Atlanta blacks—especially those whom he disdained as a light-skinned local aristocracy—to partake of inferior Jim Crow accommodations within white institutions, as when black patrons were herded like cattle through filthy, saloon-lined alleyways to "colored" theater entrances.[39] And he railed against the rough treatment that blacks received from white ushers after clambering up to the gallery, or "buzzard's roost," as Davis liked to call it. Actually, Davis did not so much disparage these practices as he did black *acceptance* of these practices. In his mind, white men did not so much impose Jim Crow upon blacks as blacks willingly accepted Jim Crow. As Davis put it, "if there were no Jim Crow Negroes there would be no Jim Crow accommodations." Elsewhere he asserted, "We have no quarrel with the white man; he is going to provide Jim Crow places as long as Jim Crow Negroes patronize them." He even went so far at one point as to place the blame for white notions of black inferiority upon blacks themselves: "A self-respecting man admires a self-respecting people. The white man has not reached the conclusion that the Negro is a person of inferiority from any philosophical process of reasoning; but he has arrived at the conclusion because of the conduct of the Negro himself—and this conclusion has not been reached from a study of the common class of Negroes, but from the selected few—the talented ten, the educated and cultured class."[40]

As this passage indicates, Davis found the tolerance of Jim Crow practices by the South's black elite—the "talented tenth" promoted by Washington's nemesis W. E. B. Du Bois—to be particularly galling. Time and again he excoriated the black professionals, educators, and social leaders who accepted Jim Crow treatment for debasing themselves and their race and for setting a poor example for other blacks who looked to them for guidance. The *Independent* periodically threatened to publish the names of "respectable" black Atlantans seen crowding into alleys to attend the city's segregated theaters.[41] The paper also attempted to change the ways of black theatergoers by printing cartoons that held them up to ridicule. One, captioned "A Big Rush Among The Alley Bat Theatre Goers," showed a group of well-dressed black citizens variously labeled "Professionals," "Doctors," "School Teachers," and "College Students," all bunching up at the back entrance of a theater. As one policeman drags a black man out of the crowd, another officer, pistol in hand, shouts, "You niggers git in line or I'll bust your block—Shut up! Shut up!!"[42]

Davis hoped that the *Independent*'s editorials and cartoons would persuade his readers to abandon theaters and other white businesses that supported Jim Crow, and to give their patronage instead to black-run enterprises. To provide blacks with the opportunity to support their own, Davis played a major role in the creation of the Auburn Avenue black business district. He hoped to develop what he termed the "Auburn Avenue Negro," who would be "church-going, earnest, thoughtful, educated, industrious, and race-conscious" and who would help extinguish the stereotype of the degraded "Decatur Street Negro" that was harbored by many whites.[43] As part of this effort, Davis implemented the construction of the Odd Fellows Building, a three-hundred-thousand-dollar structure that took up an entire block of Auburn Avenue between Bell and Butler Streets. The building, which opened in 1914, was intended to be a black business center and headquarters for the Grand United Order of Odd Fellows, a black fraternal organization over whose Georgia branch Davis presided. The Odd Fellows Building also included an auditorium that could seat over thirteen hundred people and that would, Davis hoped, win over black patrons by providing them with the fair and courteous treatment they did not receive in Atlanta's white theaters.[44]

The Odd Fellows Auditorium, later known as the Paramount, was not the first Gate City theater that catered to blacks. From about the turn of the century, Bishop Henry McNeal Turner's Tabernacle had provided a stage for such famed artists as the Black Patti Troubadours, Billy Kersands and his Minstrels, the Whitman Sisters, and the Fisk Jubilee Singers.[45] Other traveling black troupes carried their "theaters" with them, performing under canvas on vacant lots, as did Pat Chappelle's A Rabbit's Foot Company in its 1905 appearance on the corner of Edgewood Avenue and Hilliard Street.[46]

During the early days of motion pictures in Atlanta, theaters that provided films and cheap vaudeville for black audiences had also sprung up—

and frequently, like their white counterparts, quickly disappeared. Clustered for the most part along Decatur Street, these movie houses were often, but not always, owned by whites.[47] Despite the fact that these theaters presented films to black audiences, the movies were typically the same as those shown in white theaters, with the same subject matter, the same white stars, and the same racist stereotypes.[48] When black theaters strayed from such "safe" material, they risked the wrath of white officials, as a couple of tiny articles buried in the back pages of the *Journal* indicate. In February of 1923, the Atlanta police received complaints that a movie entitled *The Gunsaulus Mystery* had shown at one black theater on Decatur Street and was about to appear in another, under the same management, on West Mitchell Street. The plot of the film, witnesses told police, closely paralleled Atlanta's infamous Leo Frank–Mary Phagan murder case of 1913, in which the Jewish Frank was lynched after being convicted in a farcical trial of having killed Phagan, a fourteen-year-old white girl who worked in his pencil factory. The main character in *The Gunsaulus Mystery* was said to be modeled after Jim Conley, the black man who had been the principal witness against Frank. The Frank case was still capable of igniting explosive sentiments in the 1920s, and in any case the Atlanta police force surely had no interest in revisiting the incompetent role it had played in the Frank fiasco.[49] So, police officers quickly converged upon the Mitchell Street movie house, tore down posters advertising the picture, and seized the film so that it could be screened for the city's censorship board. The censors subsequently decided that the movie was indeed based upon the Frank case, "with many identical details," and board chairman E. L. Harling ordered that exhibitors immediately ship the film out of Atlanta.[50]

Benjamin Davis would not have approved of *The Gunsaulus Mystery,* either, nor did he approve of the theaters in which such films were shown. Despite his regular skewering of the black "aristocracy," Davis was by no means a spokesman for the masses, nor did he reject the elitist values embraced by his enemies. His whole point in establishing and promoting the Odd Fellows Auditorium was to provide a theater where the "best" black people could witness the most refined white films while at the same time preserving their self-respect. But as it became depressingly apparent that the "better class" of black moviegoers would not flock to the new auditorium, that they would continue patronizing the galleries of the white theaters,

Davis became increasingly bitter and strident in his condemnation of such behavior. He provided a typical expression of his frustration in an editorial written nine years after the opening of the Odd Fellows Auditorium:

> Quite a half million dollars have been spent in Atlanta by Negro men to build up a first class picture house where our people can see something else on the screen besides wild west adventures, stage robberies, murders, and other tragedies of the under world. But so far, we have been unable to build up a constituency that would warrant further investment. Our best people would rather take their places in the peanut gallery and in the lofts among the rats in a white man's theater than to enter the front door of a black man's palace. . . . Any movie undertaking established for the best people of Atlanta among Negroes is doomed to failure. If you want to succeed in running a Negro picture house, you must establish your tent on Decatur or Peters Streets, or in some other segregated district and cater to those who form most largely the rabble of the race.

Sounding much like the white leaders who periodically bemoaned a lack of support for true art, Davis insisted that there were "enough good people in Atlanta to have at least one thousand theater goers every night," and he exhorted the "cultured, the educated, the refined to do as much for a house built for their entertainment, amusement, [and] education, as the people of the lower strata do for the houses on Peters and Decatur Streets."[51] But if Davis's continued editorial complaints are any indication, his plea brought little response. Many black Atlantans apparently remained willing to suffer the indignities of Jim Crow seating to see the brand-new films and live entertainment that white theaters were able to provide, while others were satisfied with the movies and cheap vaudeville featured in the unpretentious movie houses of Decatur Street.[52]

Like his bitter rival Benjamin Davis, Rev. H. H. Proctor of the First Congregational Church of Atlanta was vitally interested in grooming a new sort of Negro. But the two men differed dramatically in their emphasis and tone. Davis, the gadfly and firebrand, hoped to inspire the development of black men and women who were self-confidently proud of their race and who were independent of white leadership and control, even if they ultimately accepted middle-class white values. In other words, Davis believed that the races should be socially and culturally separate but equal. Proctor, more

representative of the self-consciously elite among black Atlantans, was intent on building interracial bridges. He explicitly urged his followers to
emulate the highest in white ideals as a means of earning white recognition and respect. Like Davis, however, Proctor hoped to enlist culture in
his cause.

The congregation of Proctor's church was made up of what Davis scorned
as the city's black aristocracy. As the *Constitution*—always far friendlier to
the agreeable Proctor than to the troublesome Davis—observed in 1910,
with equal measures of praise and condescension, "The membership of the
church includes some of the very best and most substantial colored people
of the city. They are known as a quiet, property-owning, home-loving
people. It is the rarest thing that an arrest is made of a member of the
Congregational Church. Their manner of worship is quiet and orderly. . . .
There is no excess of emotionalism. A high standard of living is insisted on.
A rigid form of discipline is exercised." Unabashedly class conscious, Proctor and his congregants sought to inculcate their own notions of propriety
and respectability in the black community at large. To this end, the Congregational Church—the first "institutional" church in Atlanta—offered a
wide variety of services to working-class blacks. The church provided a
library and reading room, a gymnasium, a "model" kitchen, a sewing department, a kindergarten, an employment bureau, a handiwork course for
the blind, a religious mission, a "ladies parlor," a "trouble department," and
"the only shower bath for colored people in the city, with one exception."
At the same time, Proctor was compelled to reassure his skittish parishion-
ers that "there is not the least danger in the plainest people mistaking our
kindly interest as an invitation to our private social functions."[53] As always,
socially and culturally, both among black and white elites, there was an
abiding tension between efforts to raise the lowly and a powerful desire to
remain clearly distinguished from them.

As part of his drive to "elevate" blacks and gain white approval, while at
the same time generating funds for the Congregational Church and its programs, Proctor and a committee of leading black Atlantans initiated in 1910
a series of annual "Colored Music Festivals."[54] Proctor considered music
to be "a great solvent of racial antipathies" and hoped that the festivals
would win white acceptance of the "better class" of black Atlantans while
simultaneously setting proper cultural standards to which blacks might aspire. As Proctor—sounding a bit like Judge Broyles—told a reporter, "The

always imitative negro too often attains notoriety by following whatever bad examples might be set for him. By organizing this music festival we wish to show that there is another class that is eager to follow the good and not bad in striving for the better things of life. We hope that this occasion will not only be of educational value, but will result in a great moral influence."[55]

Like the white Grand Opera Weeks, the Colored Music Festivals took place in the auditorium-armory. The programs blended European classical music performed by nationally renowned black artists, such as Harry T. Burleigh and Roland Hayes, with antebellum black spirituals and folk music, or rather with what was described as black folk music. In 1910 the Fisk Jubilee Singers offered a selection of "Negro melodies" that included such white-penned numbers as "My Old Kentucky Home," "Suwanee River," "Old Black Joe," and "Massa's in de Cold, Cold Ground."[56] The elite blacks who organized the festival largely accepted prevailing white cultural notions: European music provided the true standard of beauty and excellence, and black Americans had made their only real cultural contributions before the Civil War, as slaves.

However, Proctor and his peers did not buy into white attitudes completely. Although granting that black culture had crested during the antebellum period, Proctor was less willing to concede that blacks had degenerated as a race since the war. The drama *Up to Freedom,* which Proctor wrote and then staged at the 1912 and 1913 festivals, illustrates his ambivalent view of his people. Described as a "passion play of the negro race," *Up to Freedom* contained three acts, entitled "Paganism," "Slavery," and "Freedom," and was constructed around the theme of black racial progress, from the jungles of Africa through enslavement and emancipation to "education." While the black race's greatest gains, in Proctor's view, came as a result of white tutelage and support, strides had nevertheless been made and continued to be made in the present day.[57]

Promoters of the Colored Music Festivals modeled their advertising on that used by Atlanta whites for their own Opera Weeks. One blurb for the 1910 festival promised that it would represent the "greatest musical entertainment in the history of the South," and a newspaper ad claimed that Atlanta was "ablaze" over the approaching festival, that people were coming "from all over Georgia" to see it, and that the "culture, beauty and refinement of the race" would fill the auditorium for the concerts. Tickets were also said to be "selling rapidly," and it looked "as if every reserved seat" would be sold before opening night. Festival directors hoped that some of these seats would be filled by whites, who, of course, would not be expected to mingle with even the "culture, beauty and refinement" of black Atlanta. The *Constitution* noted before the 1910 festival that "1000 special reserved seats have been set apart for white patronage," carefully emphasizing that these seats were completely "separate from the others and in no way in contact with the main body of the Auditorium."[58]

Atlanta's white newspapers responded favorably, if patronizingly—and likely, from the minister's perspective, disappointingly—to Proctor's efforts, praising the concerts less as a flowering of middle-class black culture than as a wholesome influence upon a race in dire need of wholesome influences. The city's dailies worked to build white interest in the festivals by pointing out what they deemed to be the true value of the concerts. The *Constitution,* for instance, predicted that the 1911 festival would "have a morally uplifting effect upon the colored race as a whole. It should prove an antidote to the wave of crime that has been sweeping over the colored people in this city. To turn their minds away from that which is low to that which is high will be for the benefit of the entire city." In 1913 the same newspaper followed the request of the Colored Music Festival Association in urging its readers to allow their black domestics to attend that year's performances. "In some cases," the *Constitution* observed, "employers have purchased tickets and given them to their employees. There are so many places in this city that tend to drag down the colored servant that any occasion of this type that is elevating in its nature proves of benefit to the whole city life, which is so much affected by the character of its servants."[59]

White reviews of the concerts similarly combined approval, condescension, and a distressing reluctance to endorse Proctor's clear-cut distinctions between elite and common black citizens. The *Journal* reported in 1910 that the festival "was a real pleasure to all the white people who were present, and it was an encouragement to what is best and soundest in the colored people." The festival was particularly praiseworthy in that proceeds would go to Proctor's Congregational Church and would "thus be instrumental in fostering thrift, love of law and greater efficiency among the Negroes of this community."[60] The article did not refer to the "poor" or "uneducated" African Americans of the community, but to blacks in general.

The Colored Music Festivals represented but one example of an attempt by respectable black Atlantans to strike some sort of balance between white and black cultural standards, between racial deference and racial pride. In 1911 the Colored Music Festival Association brought to Atlanta the Tuskegee Band, Orchestra, and Glee Club, which performed a mixture of classical music, "Plantation melodies," and patriotic airs such as "The Star Spangled Banner" and, oddly enough, "Dixie." A preview of the concert in the *Independent* noted that bandleader Captain N. Clark Smith "is almost a pure-blooded man of his race" and promised that "there will not be a Negro in the house that night who will not be prouder of the fact that he is a Negro after he sees the work of the Captain than he was when he went into the great audience." In December of 1917, black schoolteachers and students, perhaps inspired by Proctor's *Up to Freedom*, took to the auditorium stage to present a historic "pageant" entitled *Choosing the Better Part*. Written and directed by Burnell T. Harvey Jr., the play, as described by the *Constitution*, illustrated "various stages in the development of the negro . . . until the present time." The days of the Old South and the Civil War received special attention: "The loyalty of the negroes, especially in the civil war period, when the slaves remained at home and guarded the wives and the children of their masters, who were away at the front in battle, was particularly stressed." And the white reviewer felt that "One of the best features was a plantation scene which was presented in a very realistic style, the dancing, especially of the buck and wing variety, being especially good." Another black auditorium production took place in 1918, when the Georgia Music Festival Association, successor to Proctor's earlier musical organization, presented a concert featuring "Negro folk songs." The program included genuine black folk music, as well as the usual white-authored tunes such as "Suwanee River," referred to by the *Constitution* as "the negro's anthem." [61]

Both the historical pageant and the folk concert appeared before audiences composed predominantly of black men and women, and both were held to raise money for the support of black soldiers stationed at Camp Gordon, near Atlanta. Clearly, a substantial number of black Atlantans, among them Proctor, his friends, and their followers, more or less accepted the portrayal of black culture found in these productions. They believed that, in addition to creating profoundly moving spirituals, the slaves of the

Old South had happily danced the buck and wing and had diligently protected their masters during wartime. Other blacks doubtless rejected such notions entirely, while still others may have dismissed the ideal of the happy slave while realizing nonetheless the power that such an image might have over potential white patrons and philanthropists. In his memoirs, Benjamin Davis Jr. recalls the resentment that he had felt as a young Morehouse student over repeatedly being compelled to perform black spirituals for white visitors: "If religion is designed to deaden the militant dissatisfaction of the masses, it also becomes a potent weapon in wangling donations from white philanthropists who are titillated at the sight of a 'healthy corps of religious, spiritual-singing Negroes.' Negro college presidents became past masters in the use of this weapon." To Davis, "This singing of spirituals for money was . . . undignified, subservient and a perversion of indigenous Negro folk music." He went on, "I wondered why these philanthropists were not equally eager to find students who were brilliant mathematicians and to offer them jobs as actuarial assistants in, say, the Metropolitan Life Insurance Company. Didn't these fellows count unless they could sing 'Swing Low, Sweet Chariot'? It was a subtle way of telling the young Negro that no matter what he learned and how well he learned it, he was still a singer of religious spirituals at the bidding of the master." [62]

It was perhaps inevitable that in their vulnerable social and economic position within the southern caste system, middle-class blacks would find it difficult to escape entirely the "bidding," the allure, the judgments of white culture. Blacks such as H. H. Proctor and his followers believed that respectable white culture contained much of value and hoped that by embracing it they could gain a measure of acceptance from their white counterparts, that they could thereby confirm their position as an elite within black society. In many respects, however, their pursuit of white validation proved a vain one. Certainly Proctor won some white patronage and support for his efforts, although this was largely because elite white Atlantans saw the reverend's work as supporting their own interests. But whites would only go so far, even in support of the "best" black citizens, as the rigidly segregated seating at the auditorium attested. Indeed, as editor Ben Davis realized, simply by accepting this seating the black elite unwittingly helped to reinforce white notions of black inferiority. Despite the dreams of men such as Rev. Proctor, the best that the "better" blacks could ever hope to attain from even the most well-disposed whites would be a distant, quali-fied, and deeply condescending nod of approval.

While white and black elites jostled for recognition and social supremacy, working-class blacks and whites went about the business of living their lives. The Louise Doolys and H. H. Proctors of the world might don their "love" for "refined" music like an expensive suit of clothes, but the cultural garb of less elevated Atlantans tended to have a more comfortable, lived-in look. For them, culture was less a purchased symbol of self-conscious superiority than a vital means of daily sustenance and self-expression. Scorned or ig-nored by their "betters," these men and women never saw themselves as harbingers of any musical millennium. Nevertheless, in their unassuming way, they helped to forge a musical revolution far more substantive and long lasting than anything generated by the local cultural "elect."

᙭ 6 ᙮

Atlanta as a Regional
Music Center

I n 1986 the MacMillan Press of London published the four-volume *New
Grove Dictionary of American Music.* Volume 1 includes a thousand-
word essay by contributor John Schneider on the history of music in
the Gate City. Although the project as a whole treats popular as well as
classical music (the entry for Atlanta follows that for country music guitar-
ist/producer Chet Atkins), Schneider does not cast his own net so widely.
He touches upon various milestones in Atlanta's experience with classical
music and opera, he mentions local organizations dedicated to the promo-
tion or performance of highbrow music, and he notes the different music
training programs offered by the city's colleges and universities. The essay's
final paragraph is but one sentence long: "By the early 1980s, a number of
recording companies specializing in popular music had been established in
Atlanta."[1]

Schneider's brief history brings up to date attitudes held by Atlanta's
social elite during the late nineteenth and early twentieth centuries. In this
view the Gate City is now, as it was then, a beacon of taste and refinement,
its leaders struggling to bring the blessings of European high culture to their
city, state, and region. Popular culture, on the other hand, barely merits
mention and, if Schneider is to be believed, played no significant role in the
city's cultural life prior to 1980.

This accounting of Atlanta's musical history may not be particularly surprising, given Schneider's biases, but it is also embarrassingly incomplete.
For by the 1920s Atlanta was one of the most important cultural centers in

the United States. This significance was not due, however, to the tireless efforts of the ladies in the music club or to appearances by the Metropolitan Opera Company. Rather, Atlanta owed its newfound place in the sun to advances in technology, to the acumen of New York businessmen, and to a ragged but talented group of men, black and white, who brought their guitars and fiddles to town seeking a livelihood.

Atlanta's laboring classes, of course, had always been around. For the most part, however, the vibrant black and white working-class cultures of the early twentieth century have come down to us obscured and distorted by the biases of middle-class newspaper editors and reporters. Rarely—very rarely—members of the laboring classes were able to speak publicly for themselves, as when a man signing himself "Mechanic" wrote the *Journal* to complain about Laurent DeGive's pricing policies and the morally unsavory atmosphere that reigned in the gallery of DeGive's Opera House, where the presence of "females of bad reputation" meant that no one would sit there "with his wife or with any respectable female friend." [2]

But much more commonly, to the extent that working men and women received attention from the daily newspapers, the middle class spoke for these people, asserting elite authority to guide its "inferiors" culturally, socially, and politically. Take the case, for example, of the residents of the North Georgia mountains, in many respects the white Georgians most disdained by respectable upper-middle-class Atlantans. Female reformers in particular found themselves at once drawn to and repelled by the "plight" of the hill folk. [3] In 1919 the *Constitution*'s Isma Dooly discussed "The Problem of the Mountain People" in her weekly column "Current Events from a Woman's Point of View." After cautioning that "To make sweeping statements about the illiteracy, lack of morality, or general lawlessness of the mountain people would be unjust," Dooly made a series of unjustly sweeping statements. She indicted the North Georgians for their "lawlessness of spirit," supposedly bred by geographical isolation, which manifested itself in moonshining and other unsavory behaviors, proving that the standards of civilization had been "entirely forgotten" by mountain men and women alike. She implored her readers to combat this "menace" by supporting "extension work through churches, schools and the agencies for public health and sanitation" that might "reach these people," or rather reach those adults not "past redemption." Mrs. S. B. C. Morgan had urged a similar approach eight years earlier when she told the Georgia Federation of Women's Clubs that although the Georgia mountaineer was as a rule "Proud, suspicious," and gripped by "an almost irritating spirit of independence," he nonetheless possessed a "brain quick to utilize every chance for betterment . . . if only a guiding hand is held out to point the way." For those mountain folk who migrated to Atlanta in search of economic opportunity, that "guiding hand" took the form of mill-district settlement houses, such as the one near the Fulton Bag and Cotton Mill, which worked diligently "to build up character and create ambition" among those who have "little or no advantages, having come from remote places in the country or the mountains, and [who] are ignorant, uncultured and extravagant." [4]

Whether discussing Enrico Caruso or North Georgia subsistence farmers, for privileged whites such as Isma and Louise Dooly the vocabulary and the goals were the same. At issue was not mere poverty or economic distinction, but "morality," "culture," "character," "civilization," and the possibility of "redemption." Atlantans such as the Doolys were ever willing to assist those who needed "guidance," to promote civilized behavior among those unacquainted with it. Whether this guidance took place through an opera performance, at a settlement house, or at a free Sunday afternoon concert, the motive was always to impose the elite's standards upon all of the white South, to persuade the "unsaved" to defer to the elect. [5]

In the case of the North Georgians, this task would be made easier because of the mountaineers' positive attributes. For all their alleged flaws, these proud folk were still heirs of the pioneers who had courageously opened up the South for white settlement and fought the Revolution to free the country from British tyranny. [6] Thus, every negative stereotype disgustedly applied to the North Georgians was matched by a more positive generalization. According to a 1927 *Journal Sunday Magazine* piece, the same people portrayed by Dooly a few years earlier as depraved illiterates were in fact noble guardians of "the vital elements of national greatness," namely "strictest honesty, love of freedom, protection of women and children, love of home, ability to wrest from the soil the necessities of life, loyalty and helpfulness to neighbors, [and an] interdependence upon one another that was characteristic of early American life." [7]

This ambivalence about the people of North Georgia extended to their culture, such as the music performed in the annual "old-time fiddling conventions" that took place, beginning in 1913, in Atlanta's auditorium-armory (the very same auditorium-armory, by the way, that hosted the Metropolitan Opera Company).[8] Most of the performers who competed for prizes at these concerts hailed from northern Georgia, either directly or by way of the mill villages of Atlanta, and a large portion of their audiences had similarly rural origins. The music that the fiddlers played consisted of traditional folk tunes; written music and more modern genres were banned.[9] Of course, such fare was beneath the consideration of columnists such as Louise Dooly. The reporters who did cover the conventions treated the fiddlers with a mixture of good-natured condescension and genuine respect. On the one hand, these writers employed some of the same stereotypes as did those who criticized mountain culture: they exaggerated the remoteness of the fiddlers' rural homes, they played up the mountaineers' colorful behavior and predilection for flasks of "peculiar white liquid which bore no evidence of acquaintance with a revenue stamp," and they harped upon the "wild," uninhibited behavior of the musicians and their audiences.[10]

On the other hand, accounts of the conventions emphasized as well the heartfelt sincerity of the performances, the mesmerizing effect that the fiddlers could have upon listeners, and the widespread appeal of the music. Time and again reporters commented on—and doubtless overstated—the extent to which Atlantans from all walks of life eagerly looked forward to and attended the contests. A correspondent for the *Constitution* claimed that the convention audiences were "the most democratic known in any Georgia affair" in that they were composed of "every type": "The devotees of grand opera, the lovers of jazz and ragtime, the city folks who were reared in the country and remember the merry dances of their youth; the men and women from the mill districts, old folks who haven't ventured away from home for a year—all go to at least one session of the fiddlers' convention."[11]

The key to such success, observers agreed, was the manner in which the conventions recollected an ostensibly virtuous and uncomplicated past that the big-city dwellers of Atlanta had left behind. Indeed, the fiddlers appealed quite consciously to the memories and sentiments of the "rural refugees" who made up the great majority of the Gate City's population and who often found that life in Atlanta was not what they had hoped it would be.[12] On one occasion the rustic musicians decorated the auditorium stage with "an old-time log cabin, a picket fence and . . . live chickens which roosted high and refused to be awakened even when several of the fiddlers broke into an impromptu clog dance." [13]

Much of the writing about the conventions had a lighthearted tone, as when a *Constitution* reporter joked insightfully about the relationship between musical preference and social class. He observed that fiddlers in the upcoming convention would play "old favorites" such as " 'Soldiers' Joy,' 'Billy in the Low Grounds,' 'Chickens Before Day,' 'Bacon and Collards,' and a score of others your granddaddies used to dance to in the country cabins before they moved to Atlanta and got rich in real estate and turned into grand opera lovers." [14] A similarly humorous example of such cultural divergence occurred in an account of a musical clash between "fiddlers" and "violinists." Four fiddlers in town for the yearly convention visited the Kimball House Hotel in their spare time to hear the house musicians. "For a time they listened in bored tolerance to the 'Melody in F,' 'The Barcarolle' and other classics rendered by the Kimball orchestra, until finally Shorty Harper could stand it no longer, and the regular orchestra was startled to hear the strains of 'Billy in the Lowground,' with the accompaniment of patting feet. 'The Barcarolle' began to wane, until finally it died altogether, and left the fiddlers in triumphant possession of the audience." [15]

But alongside such humor ran a strong strain of sentimentality. For Ralph Jones of the *Journal,* the antique tunes brought to mind "the feel of the old red hills of Georgia and the little old cabin with the golden corn swaying in the wind across the patch and the sour mash still bubbling out its distilled sunshine just over the brow of the hill, where the revenoors haven't looked yet. Shut your eyes and you forget you are in Atlanta's big Auditorium. You can see the rafters of the old barn and smell the hay up in the mow and 'most hear the lowing of the cattle and the rustle of the hen who complains about her disturbed nest." [16]

The music sawed out by the fiddlers invoked images of an agrarian past held in common by many Atlantans, and probably by most of those who attended the conventions. But these audiences shared more than their rural heritage: they were powerfully bound together by race as well. The traditional songs, the memories that they conjured, and the sentimental portrayals of the fiddlers and their music in the newspapers provided a source of cohesion and pride for a white population that was increasingly divided socially, economically, and culturally. From this perspective it is telling that a *Journal Sunday Magazine* piece on the fiddling conventions began by quoting two lines from the old standard "Run, Nigger, Run":

> Run, nigger, run, de patter-roller comin'
> Run, nigger, run, it's almost day.

The article explained, "The old tune harks back to the plantation days, when the darkies who strayed away from the quarters after nightfall needed to keep a pair of sharp eyes open for the 'patrol.'" [17] The old-time fiddling conventions received the attention they did because they allowed white Atlantans to look back fondly to the years before the Civil War, to a glorious era—as it was distorted and romanticized in the civil religion of the New South—in which whites lived in harmony and racial hierarchy held fast. [18] As we have seen, elite Atlantans bent their energies toward creating an ostentatious cultural exclusivity. Given all that conspired to pull the classes apart, an occasional celebration of white unity served important political and psychological functions. At the yearly conventions the lowliest mill worker and the most exalted financier could come together—however briefly and superficially—in recognition of their shared rural heritage and racial birthright.

Like their white counterparts, working-class African Americans in Atlanta enjoyed a rich cultural life, although readers of white—and even black—newspapers might never have known that this was the case. While middle-class black leaders assiduously sought white recognition of their cultural and social accomplishments, for the great mass of the Gate City's black population—poor, uneducated, and "unrefined"—the possibility of white acceptance simply did not exist. To whites of all classes, these men and women represented the nadir of southern culture and served as the targets of the most vicious stereotypes and dehumanizing caricatures. Fortunately, these Atlantans did not see themselves through white eyes, so they went about living their lives as best they could under a grim array of restraints. And, like other segments of the city's population, they sought out entertainment to lighten their burdens and brighten their nights and days.

Even the poorest blacks found access to some form of amusement, such as the music that pervaded African American culture. Street musicians, for example, both black and white, were a common sight in Atlanta. As early as

1879 a correspondent for *Harper's New Monthly Magazine* managed during a brief evening's stroll to run across two black string bands playing on street corners to crowds of "happy darkies," and he saw other blacks performing in a patent medicine show. Some fifteen years later, the *Constitution* discussed the spread of singing "beggars" throughout the city, complaining that "there is scarcely any relief from their pitiful tales, pinched faces and harsh music." The article described in particular a Decatur Street accordionist, "small of stature but loud of voice," who was "strictly modern and thoroughly familiar with the latest airs. His favorite piece, 'I've been hoo-dooed by a big black coon,' is a theme suitable to the locality in which he moves, and the darkies gather around him in droves."[19]

Other Atlanta blacks hosted "rent parties" in which they cleared one room of a house to make space for dancing to the music of a piano or guitar. Admission was low—fifteen cents at most—and the host provided food. The availability of bootleg liquor also served as a drawing card at some of these functions. In addition to much-needed recreation, these parties accorded opportunities for up-and-coming young musicians, such as future blues and gospel great Thomas Dorsey, to earn a living and develop their styles. Hosts, musicians, and revelers alike, however, had to keep a wary eye out for the police, who frequently raided such get-togethers.[20]

The Gate City's raucous black dance halls aroused even greater hostility and scrutiny on the part of local officials. The gambling, alcohol, and un-inhibited sexuality characteristic of these halls brought strident criticism from whites and middle-class blacks alike. Nevertheless, these venues—at least during years in which they were not banned by city law—were a popular and important outlet for working-class African Americans, who welcomed the release that came from socializing and dancing together to the strains of a band or a ragtime piano.[21]

The center of black working-class culture in the city was Decatur Street, Atlanta's "Bowery," with its restaurants, dance halls, theaters, clubs, gambling houses, pawnshops, cheap hotels, and brothels. The *Journal* referred to Decatur Street as "the melting pot of Dixie": "Here bearded mountaineers from Rabun County brush shoulders with laborers fresh from the Old Country. Jewish shopkeepers pass the time o' day with the clerk of the Greek ice cream parlor next door. The Yankee spieler cries his wares and the Confederate veteran buys 'em, and through it all negroes, yellow, black and brown, thread their laughing shiftless way, types of the south which could be seen in no other city in the land in all their native picturesqueness."[22] Famed—and reviled—for its nightlife, Decatur Street served as the Gate City's version of Beale Street in Memphis. As the lyrics to "Atlanta Blues" put it:

> They got plenty good liquor,
> And everything for sale,
> If you get in trouble,
> You won't have to go to jail.
>
> Step out in Atlanta,
> Any time of night,
> You'll get your lovin' on Decatur Street,
> In Atlanta, down on Decatur Street.[23]

By the 1910s, the center of Decatur Street, so far as live entertainment went, was the 81 Theater. Owned by Charles P. Bailey, a white man, the 81 belonged to the Theater Owner's Booking Association, a major black vaudeville circuit, so the theater showcased some of the best in black popular music, including performers such as Ma Rainey, Ethel Waters, and, above all, Bessie Smith.[24]

Later known as the "Empress of the Blues," Smith came to Atlanta in 1913 and worked to establish herself at the 81, which she later used as a home base as she toured in vaudeville. She was enormously popular in Atlanta. One observer who saw her perform at the 81 Theater at the beginning of her career recalled, "She was just a teenager, and she obviously didn't know she was the artist she was. She didn't know how to dress—she just sang in her street clothes—but she could wreck anybody's show. She only made ten dollars a week, but people would throw money on the stage, and the stage hands would pick up about three or four dollars after every performance."[25]

This awkward teenager who practiced in the theater's backyard quickly won over black audiences throughout the South. She began her recording career in 1923 after moving to Philadelphia, which, like other northern cities, had a black population of potential record buyers swollen by the Great Migration. A temperamental rebel, Smith sang songs of social protest and frank sexuality, expressing the concerns and emotions of her listeners and in the process becoming a symbol of black racial and cultural pride. Widely regarded then and now as the greatest female blues singer, she sold six to ten million records and did more than anyone else to bring blues into the mainstream of popular music.[26]

The exuberant reception accorded Smith was but an exaggerated example of the rambunctious behavior that characterized the 81's patrons, providing exceptions to arguments holding that audiences nationwide were politely subdued by this time. One Atlantan remembered a typical night at the theater as "rather a loud-talking, foot-stomping, booming affair. People did pretty much as they pleased until it got so bad they had to acquire some policemen to keep order."[27] The crowds at the 81 were not exclusively working class, nor were they even exclusively black. Clearly, however, the 81 was no place for the refined and respectable.[28]

"Respectability" was not the province of the middle class alone. Decatur Street and its attractions were considered to be well beyond the pale not only by most better-off blacks, but by many working-class citizens as well. Domestic worker Alice Adams recalled, "It was just a rough place, and we just didn't hang out over there. Because my peoples told me when I came to Atlanta, 'Stay off Decatur Street.' And I did just that. It wasn't no place for me. I stayed on the safe side." In words that would have pleased Ben Davis, Adams explained, "I would go to Sweet Auburn Avenue. That was my street, Sweet Auburn Avenue."[29]

For an untold number of working-class Atlantans, black and white, the notion of leisure itself, especially in its commercialized forms, was suspect. Fiddlers, banjoists, blues singers—all could seem tools of the devil to strictly religious men and women. Willie Rakestraw, wife of a steelworker, remembered, "We didn't do nothing. I've been a Christian all my life and I never wanted to go to dances or things like that. I just stayed at home with my children."[30] These people did not write newspaper columns detailing their beliefs, so their voices have been almost entirely lost, but the evidence that remains serves as a cautionary reminder that it would be simplistic to portray working-class citizens of either race as thinking, feeling, or behaving uniformly.

As indicated by the efforts of Ben Davis and H. H. Proctor to promote the "best" black citizens of Atlanta, sharp class divisions ran through the city's black community. Like Atlanta's leading whites, who used high culture to distance themselves from more ordinary citizens, respectable black citizens frequently sought to solidify their tenuous social position by denouncing the cultural degeneracy of the "rabble" beneath them. Indeed, middle-class blacks could equal southern whites in their contempt for lower-class African Americans. Rev. Proctor, for example, bowed to no one, white or black, in his verbal assaults upon black dance halls, going so far in 1915 as to blame them for the 1906 riot and to argue that the city council's decision to close the halls in the wake of the bloodbath had facilitated "peace between the races for nine years." To reopen the halls, Proctor argued, would be to risk once again inspiring black men to rape white women, thereby making another horrendous riot extremely likely.[31] Thus the highly proper Proctor acceded to one of the central and most poisonous myths of white society, that of the black man obsessively lusting over white women.

Other black Atlantans took aim at black music. Most African American critics expressed appreciation of and fondness for the old slave spirituals, but like white critics, they decried the manner in which black culture had decayed since emancipation. Thomas Jefferson Flanagan declaimed in the *Independent* against "Jazz stuff, the Blues, and all such rot" while lamenting that female singers with real musical talent had "given themselves over to the fad of singing this trashy stuff for a few dollars and cents." *Independent* music critic Frederic Hall was even harsher, insisting, "There is no factor today that is more detrimental to the cultural development of the American youth than this jazz." Echoing white criticism of the genre, he claimed, "In the dens, the dives, the cabarets and the underworlds of the country, we find jazz a hand-in-hand companion of the other evils and vices." He went on in the vein of Judge Broyles and Rev. Proctor to complain, "Too often members of the Negro race imitate the weak, foolish things carried on by the whites while some of their traits that they should emulate are allowed to pass by unnoticed. The symphony orchestra could afford to lose Paul Whiteman; there were hundreds to take his place. We as a race cannot afford to lose one genius of ours to jazz. We have not one to spare."[32]

White Atlantans, of course, had long made an art form of savaging working-class black culture. Like Proctor, they particularly loathed the cheap dance halls. In 1881 a *Constitution* correspondent visited a black beer and billiard parlor in the slum known as Beaver Slide. In the rear of the building he found a large room where, "by the light of a few smoky oil lamps, and to the soul-harrowing music of a string band, the colored beaux and dusky damsels, who rarely speak to a white person, trip the light fantastic toe, not forgetting to refresh themselves at the saloon counter when each dance is ended." After exploring similar black haunts elsewhere in the area, the reporter concluded that these "dens" formed the "nests where the worst forms of crime are born and bred, and every true Atlantan must long for the good time coming when they will be choked out of existence by the demand for Atlanta space which will come from a better and more respectable class of people."[33] A later and more lighthearted—if equally racist—look at Decatur Street dance halls by the *Journal* furthered the association between these establishments and crime. Reporter Milt Saul stated that the owner of one particular hall was of great assistance to the Gate City's police force, as "scores of dusky criminals have been caught in the place." He elaborated, "When the police get after a 'dusky,' they notify the proprietor . . . and in nearly half the instances the bird walks in to indulge in his favorite pastime only to be transferred to his natural pastime of pecking rocks."[34]

For all of the contempt that white Atlantans heaped upon African American culture, some among them nevertheless found black entertainment to be irresistibly alluring. A few of the more daring whites even ventured onto Decatur Street itself in search of the emotional power and uninhibited sensuality that characterized the black entertainers of the day. In particular they came to the 81 Theater, which by the 1920s sought out their patronage by offering whites-only "Midnight Frolics" on Friday evenings, featuring leading black artists like Bessie Smith.[35]

But whites attended the 81 on other nights as well. In 1916, *Constitution* columnist Britt Craig, whose journalistic persona was that of the worldly man-about-town, decided to expose Leo Ornstein, a visiting concert pianist and composer, to Craig's favorite brand of entertainment. After picking up Ornstein at his room in the Piedmont Hotel, Craig began the evening by taking the pianist to the city jail, where with pocket change the reporter persuaded some black inmates to give an impromptu blues performance. As Craig smugly described it, the prisoners "sang like they were singing for liquor they knew they weren't going to get." Ornstein was entranced. "To think," the composer exclaimed, "that such as this existed and I never heard it until now." After visiting the black women's ward of the jail, the two men headed off to the 81 Theater to see a vaudeville show. According to Craig, Ornstein practically came unraveled here. The combination of a "buck and wing dancer" and a ragtime piano player filled the composer with uncontrollable ecstasy: "Before I knew it, Mr. Ornstein was swaying his shoulders and rolling his eyes toward the ceiling," Craig wrote. When a "big, fat high-yellow" subsequently came on stage and belted out a blues song, "Mr. Ornstein shouted with glee. He was like a boy seeing his first circus. Pretty soon he got to be as big a show to the negroes as they were to him. But he didn't care. He was having the time of his life." Following the show, Craig returned the dazed and enraptured composer to his hotel room. As the columnist walked down the hallway toward the elevator, he heard Ornstein's piano wildly pounding out the song that the singer had ripped through at the 81. Craig coyly concluded his story with an implied wink at the reader: "I hope I didn't do anything wrong carrying him down along Decatur street. Reckon I did?"[36]

Craig, the cocksure, streetwise reporter, fills his article with the reigning stereotypes of the day. The classical pianist is overly intellectual and somewhat effeminate, the blacks that the two men encounter are invariably capable of rendering soulful songs in exchange for a coin or two. Craig takes a patronizingly proprietary delight in confronting the effete composer with the earthy energy of Atlanta's black underclass. But however clouded with distortions and laced with condescension, Craig's account suggests the vitality that the best of the black singers and musicians of the day possessed. In whatever manner whites—and blacks, for that matter—sought to ostracize Decatur Street and all it represented, by condemning it, ignoring it, or condescending to it, the force and the beauty were there. And if the arbiters of good taste in Atlanta were utterly incapable of recognizing this, there were others—many others, as it turned out—who could.

As their treatment of the fiddling conventions showed, elite whites took it upon themselves to explain and evaluate white working-class culture and to use it as they saw fit. Middle-class newspapermen sought to define the goals and desires of the fiddlers, to characterize them as amiable hayseeds loyally bound to their social and economic superiors through mutual whiteness, wistful for an Edenic rural past but happy about their opportunities in the capital of the New South. Likewise white Atlanta adopted a similar—if much harsher—interpretive privilege with regard to working-class black culture, authoritatively assessing its origins and moral worth. Separated socially, working-class whites and blacks were equal in their inability to speak publicly for themselves.

In the 1920s, however, Atlanta's working-class citizens, black and white, gained an unprecedented opportunity to bring their own voices—or at least the voices of the most musically talented among them—before the wider public. On March 15, 1922, WSB radio took to the air for the first time. A creation of the *Atlanta Journal*, WSB was the first radio station in the South and had a tremendous range. As early as 1923, the station's estimated nightly audience already exceeded two million, and WSB's advance programs were being mailed to newspapers in more than thirty states. "The Voice of the South" reached even farther at times, with Nevada being the forty-eighth and final state to notify the *Journal* that WSB's signal had been picked up there.[37] WSB claimed that its "Transcontinental" program, broadcast at 10:45 in the evenings, reached listeners "from sea to sea."[38]

The young station required a never-ending flow of entertainers to fill its airtime, and a strikingly varied group of men and women answered the call. In fact, early radio re-created something of the atmosphere that had once marked the American theater, in the days when entertainers of all stripes appeared on the same stages before socially diverse audiences. Once again, as in the youthful years of the theater, one medium sought to please a broad population. It was not at all unusual on WSB for a "hillbilly" string band to go on the air sandwiched between a classical pianist and a jazz saxophonist.[39] And, crucially, WSB extended its welcome across the color line, giving local black musicians undreamed-of access to a nationwide audience. The 1920s saw an amazing array of black artists appear on WSB, from famous singers such as Bessie Smith to more obscure groups such as the Cornfield Chorus, singers of "oldtime" melodies. Even the Jolly Four, black inmates at the Atlanta Federal Penitentiary, sang on WSB. Remarkably, black convicts—in white southerners' eyes the lowest of the low, the most despicable of the despised—had the opportunity to sing across airwaves that reached much of the country.[40] WSB played a critical role in giving a national voice to men and women who had previously gone largely unheard.

At the same time that WSB established itself as the South's leading radio station, and in large measure because of WSB's presence, Atlanta became the leading hillbilly and blues recording center of the 1920s. By this decade, northeastern record companies, reeling from the commercial assault launched by radio, were seeking out new audiences and new performers who could reach them. Some in the business sensed that black Americans and southern whites represented two potentially lucrative markets, and so engineers set out, portable recorders in hand, to test the waters. A major beneficiary of the exodus of black and white farm folk away from the countryside, Atlanta had long harbored a wealth of musical talent, as the fiddling conventions had demonstrated, and the presence of WSB drew many other musicians to the area. The Gate City thus inadvertently served as something of a musical hothouse where various rural musical styles met, cross-fertilized, and flourished.[41] At the same time, Atlanta appealed to record-industry men because as a rail center it was easily accessible and offered a "big-city" atmosphere to recording technicians and talent scouts accustomed to the amenities of New York. And Atlanta's success built upon itself; as artists sang on WSB and made records here, other musicians got word and set out for the Gate City to seek their fortunes.[42]

On June 19, 1923, the commercial history of country music began as Fiddlin' John Carson, hero of many a local fiddlers' convention, entered a vacant building on Atlanta's Nassau Street to record "Little Old Log Cabin in the Lane," an old song lamenting the passing of rural life, for the New York–based Okeh Record Company. Okeh Records executive Ralph Peer, who was present at the session, berated Carson's performance as "pluperfect awful," but the original five hundred copies sold out quickly in Atlanta (with the help of an Elks convention that heard Carson perform), forcing Peer to reconsider his hasty evaluation and order a repressing. Carson was not the first artist to record country music—Texan Eck Robertson and Virginian Henry Whitter had narrowly preceded him—but Fiddlin' John somehow caught on where they had not, and an industry rose in his wake.[43]

Carson was a pivotal figure in the cultural history of Atlanta and the nation not only because of what he did, but because of the past and the traditions he represented. Born just after the Civil War in North Georgia's mountainous Fannin County, Carson labored variously as a farmer, railroad hand, jockey, moonshiner, mill worker, and house painter. He brought his family to the Atlanta area in 1900 to work in the Exposition Cotton Mill, and in 1911 the family moved into a four-room company house in Cabbagetown, a community adjoining the Fulton Bag and Cotton Mill with which John and other family members signed on to toil twelve hours a day. During a 1913 mill strike, Fiddlin' John earned change as a street musician, "busking" for coins on Decatur Street and in other likely locations. Indeed, 1913 was a banner year for Carson not only because of the strike, but because the first of the fiddling conventions that would win local fame for him took place then, and because 1913 was the year of the notorious murder of Mary

Phagan. Carson's ballad "Little Mary Phagan" caught fire at the time, especially among mill workers infuriated by the murder and outraged by what they perceived as Leo Frank's attempt to buy his way out of responsibility for it. On the day of Frank's lynching, Carson sang the song for a crowd gathered at the Marietta courthouse—Phagan had lived and was buried in Marietta and Frank was murdered there—until he was hoarse. The ability that Carson showed here to encapsulate and express the feelings of displaced farmers made him a valuable tool for rurally oriented politicians such as Tom Watson and Eugene Talmadge. Performing at their rallies, Carson, much of whose repertoire and performing style was rooted in the nineteenth century of his youth, served as a symbol of the lost virtues of an agrarian past.[44]

Fiddlin' John's local renown made him a valuable commodity for newly established WSB. Three months after the station's birth, in September of 1922, Carson became the first country fiddler to appear on radio. Thereafter he was a frequent guest, and WSB began a long-running tradition of holding a special program each year on Carson's birthday. For his part, Fiddlin' John acknowledged the power of the new medium, explaining, "Radio made me. Until I began to play over WSB . . . just a few people in and around Atlanta knew me, but now my wife thinks she's a widow most of the time because I stay away from home so much playing around over this part of the country."[45]

The idea of recording Carson, less than a year after his first radio appearance, originated with Polk Brockman, an Atlantan who ran the section of his grandfather's furniture store that sold phonographs and records. By 1921 the store—James K. Polk, Inc.—was the South's largest outlet for the Okeh Record Company, doing particularly well in the sales of "race" (African American) records. But within a couple of years, under the onslaught of radio and more general economic problems, record sales lagged. In June of 1923, while sitting in the Palace Theater in New York, Brockman was inspired by a newsreel of a fiddlers' contest in Virginia. In a memo pad he jotted down "Fiddlin' John Carson—local talent—let's record." Peer approved the idea of a recording session in Atlanta, and Brockman rented space on Nassau Street and invited a variety of acts—including Carson—to participate. No one present in the studio that day could have anticipated the cultural phenomenon they were launching.[46]

In the months and years following Carson's initial success, other local notables such as Riley Puckett and Gid Tanner made recordings in Atlanta, as did famed out-of-towners such as Jimmie Rodgers—the "Father of Country Music," who recorded in Atlanta with a local band—the Carter Family, and bluegrass music founder Bill Monroe. Country music recording sessions occurred in other locales during the 1920s, from New York City to Bristol, Tennessee. But Atlanta, with its powerful radio station and rich vein of talent, was foremost. As one music historian observes, "Most of the genuine country music recorded in the 1920s came from Atlanta. It was the Nashville of its day, and all the major record companies had studios there."[47]

The Gate City was equally important to blues recording. Growing out of the grim struggles of African Americans at the turn of the century, the blues offered meaning, direction, and a sense of communal support to individuals blasted by segregation, poverty, and the transition from country to city. Blues singers served as secular "preachers," and rent parties as the secular equivalents of churches, helping alienated and disoriented rural migrants adjust to and survive their often harsh lives in the unforgiving city. At the same time, the blues allowed black artists to affirm their individuality—their very humanity—in a society that was in too many ways dehumanizing. Through music, one of the few areas of their lives in which they exercised control, blues singers could simultaneously express themselves and reach out to others. Running the full range of human emotions, from exuberance to bitter despair, the blues charted the unfamiliar experiences in unfamiliar territory that characterized the lives not of just African Americans, but of all men and women in the troubling and disconcerting world of the twentieth century.[48]

Atlanta served as a blues "melting pot" and as the South's foremost blues recording center of the 1920s.[49] Few of the artists who put Atlanta on the map were actually born in the Gate City, but like innumerable other black and white migrants of the day they came to Atlanta to find work or to ply their trade as musicians. Just as the major record labels set up shop in Atlanta to tap the city's supply of hillbilly musicians, the labels used Atlanta as a base for recording the region's abundance of blues singers. The city consequently provided recording opportunities for a host of early blues artists, including such luminaries as Peg Leg Howell, Barbecue Bob Hicks, Curley Weaver, Buddy Moss, and, greatest of them all, Blind Willie McTell.[50]

The advent of blues recording was not, however, an unalloyed triumph for black musicians. White businessmen garnered most of the profits, and their commercial demands worked at times to stifle individuality in the name of "respectability" and the replication of proven successes. Still, commercial recordings brought undeniable benefits. Records preserved traditions, allowed for the interchange of styles, and provided millions of listeners, black and white, with access to music and performers they might otherwise never have heard. And for all of the influence that white executives and recording engineers might ultimately have exerted on black performers, as often as not in the early days of the 1920s—the period that represents Atlanta's heyday as a recording center—the performers themselves remained sufficiently able to impose their tastes and values on their employers. The demand for artists at this time made it easy for performers to get auditions, and the whites who ran the sessions, largely ignorant of the music they were recording, usually allowed the singers to go their own way. So even while the phenomenon of recording worked to fix and standardize certain black styles and forms, a wealth of African American sensibility and experience found permanent home on record.[51]

Blind Willie McTell exemplified many of the trends in Atlanta's black musical life. Born in 1898 in rural McDuffie County, McTell attended schools for the blind in Georgia, Michigan, and New York City before settling in Atlanta. Never one to give in to his disability, McTell could confidently negotiate the streets of the busiest city; a cousin described him as "ear-sighted." His economic options severely restricted as a blind black man, he earned his living as a street singer and by performing for traveling tent shows, carnivals, and medicine shows. A master of the twelve-string guitar, McTell performed a wide variety of music to appeal to different audiences, including the whites for whom he often played. It was as a bluesman, however, that he earned his lasting reputation. He created and recorded such classics as "Statesboro Blues," "Broke Down Engine Blues," and "Mama, 'Tain't Long 'fo' Day." McTell was a heroic figure to his fellow musicians. As one blues chronicler put it, "People not given to speaking in awe of anyone at all spoke of McTell in hushed tones." Despite his immense talent, like many other early blues singers he saw little in the way of wealth during his career and fell upon hard times in his later years. Viewed in his old age as an anachronism by a younger generation of blacks, McTell spent the 1950s drinking, playing for whites in the parking lots of restaurants such as Ponce de Leon's Pig 'n' Whistle, and delving more deeply into religious music. He died in 1959, a ward of Atlanta's charitable Lighthouse for the Blind.[52]

In his move from the country to the city, in his hardscrabble life, in his opportunity to record, and in his obscure death, Blind Willie McTell typified the experiences of countless other blues singers of the day. Significantly, his career also indicates the manner in which recordings provided a stage for the expression of opinions, insights, and grievances born of his experiences as a black man in 1920s and 1930s Atlanta. In "Death Cell Blues," McTell laments the lack of justice in the segregated South:

> They got me killed for murder, and I haven't even harmed a man. . . .
> They have me charged for burglarin', I haven't even raised my hand. . . .
> They got me 'cused for forging, and I can't even write my name.[53]

Other blues singers echoed these sentiments. In the mid 1930s, song collector Lawrence Gellert recorded black singers complaining that

> Niggers ain't got no justice in Atlanta,
> Down in Georgia where you better live right . . .
> Lord you better not gamble and you better not fight.
> Niggers ain't got no justice in Atlanta. . . .
> Well, he lockin' up the niggers, let the white folks go.
> Niggers ain't got no justice in Atlanta.

Another singer resolved,

> I'm gonna leave Atlanta;
> I don't want to see this white man's town no more,
> Cause hard time got here and prosperity is slow.[54]

Obviously, such sentiments would never have seen newsprint in the *Constitution*, the *Journal*, or the *Georgian*, nor would the feelings of blues singers have been of any interest to Ben Davis of the *Independent*. If not for sessions in contrived studios presided over by white technicians and collectors, songs like these would not have received wide circulation, and much of the "oral literature" of ordinary black men and women would be lost to us.[55] Ironically, in pursuit of profit, white record companies provided a national platform for the sometimes subversive messages of men and women at the bottom of the social hierarchy.

African Americans were not the only artists to use their music to question, criticize, or ridicule reigning social, political, and economic ortho-doxies. The hillbilly performers of the day were quite capable of this as well. Consider the case of the Skillet Lickers, Atlanta's most famous hillbilly band. Three Georgians made up the group's core: fiddlers Gid Tanner and Clayton McMichen and blind guitarist Riley Puckett. The Skillet Lickers cut their first records in March of 1924, less than a year after Fiddlin' John Carson had paved the way. Most of the forty-four records (eighty-eight "sides") that the group made for Columbia Records between 1926 and 1931 consisted of traditional string band fare, but the Skillet Lickers' most popu-lar material turned out to be a series of recordings that Columbia billed as "Entertaining Novelty Records." Structurally rooted in the minstrel show, these skits alternated humorous dialogue with short bursts of music drawn from the group's other recordings. Here, in these Prohibition-era "rural dramas," the musicians joyfully tweak the noses of the respectable and flaunt middle-class conventions.[56] "A Corn Licker Still in Georgia" runs fourteen sides and features moonshining, liquor running into Atlanta, an agreeably bribable police officer, a brief stay in jail by the protagonists, a "revenuer" fleeing for his life, an attempt by the group to establish a restau-rant/speakeasy, and plenty of unrepentant drinking and slurred speech. Likewise, "A Night in a Blind Tiger" follows a post–fiddlers' convention foray into a presumably fictional Atlanta dive—Gasoline Alley Pete's Place—where our heroes take "snorts," argue about who should truly have won first place at the convention, and hold an extemporaneous rematch with a good-natured policeman as judge.

Much more typically, of course, blues and hillbilly music alike dealt—often with a hard edge and realism missing in mainstream American popular culture—with the day-to-day joys and heartbreak of ordinary lives.[57] The similar themes in black and white music, and the similar rural-to-city back-grounds and recording strategies of the artists, testify to the close kinship of the black and white vernacular music of the period. Theaters, schools, and hospitals may have been strictly segregated, but working-class culture was not, in Atlanta or elsewhere in the South. Hank Williams of Alabama and Kentucky's Bill Monroe, the paramount figures in the history of coun-try and bluegrass music, respectively, each readily acknowledged the deep and abiding influence that black musicians had on their own musical devel-opment. And the influence did not run in one direction. The Country Mu-sic Foundation recently released a three-compact-disc compilation entitled

From Where I Stand: The Black Experience in Country Music, which documents some seventy years of African American involvement in country music, from the hillbilly string band era to the polished Nashville output of today. Included in the liner notes are quotes from black country performers about their youthful musical experiences in the rural South. Oklahoman Stoney Edwards recalls his family using his father's truck battery to power a radio, but only in short increments and for important broadcasts. "I'll just tell you the truth," Edwards related in an interview, "the battery was only took out of the truck for Bob Wills, Grand Ole Opry, and when Joe Louis fought. That was it." Cleve Francis of Louisiana remembered that he was "introduced to Hank Williams by my father. I mean, Hank was his favorite singer. . . . My father was a big Hank Williams fan."[58] In fundamental ways that the heavy hand of Jim Crow could not prevent, white music touched black rural life just as black music affected white experience.

In retrospect, it should not be surprising that poor whites and poor blacks, rurally rooted groups in such geographic and cultural proximity, groups both economically disadvantaged and existing on the fringes of "respectable" society, should have shared to a large degree each other's musical sensibilities and overall worldview. An instructive account by music historian Charles Wolfe of a 1927 Atlanta recording session and its results shows how confusingly intertwined black and white culture could be.

In November of that year, Frank Walker led a field unit that was busily recording black artists for Columbia's 14000 series of race records and white singers for its 15000 hillbilly series. On record, as in society, the races were segregated, but Walker recalled that the cultural boundaries between the races were much more porous: "If you were recording in Texas, well, you might have a week in which you recorded your country music. . . . And the next week might be devoted to so-called 'race music,' because they both came from the same area, and with the same general ideas." On this early November day in the Gate City the roster of scheduled artists was typically diverse, including hillbillies such as Clayton McMichen and Riley Puckett; local bluesman Charlie Lincoln; and two artists, the Allen Brothers, who were more difficult to categorize. White musicians from near Chattanooga, the Allen Brothers had deeply immersed themselves in blues—three of the songs they recorded that day were "Chattanooga Blues," "Coal Mine Blues," and "Laughin' and Cryin' Blues."

Their work in the makeshift studio completed after a couple of hours, the Allens left Atlanta to return to their workaday lives as touring musicians, and Walker shipped the wax masters they had cut to New York for pressing. Thus far the process had gone as normal, but things went awry when the northerners back in Columbia's New York office decided after listening to the recordings that the Allens were black. The duo's next issue was subsequently released in December on the 14000 series, and the brothers' jubilation over getting their new record out so quickly faded when they learned that it was being sold as a race record. The result of all of this was a $250,000 lawsuit filed by the Allens against Columbia for "damaging their reputations." Wolfe notes that the circumstances that produced this episode were not so unusual at the time, given the cultural dynamics of the South and of the recording industry. At field recording sessions, "Black songsters sat waiting next to white gospel quartets; black blues singers took their turns with white fiddle bands. The give and take between white and black music 'in the field' was always greater than the segregated race series implied; what had upset the Allen Brothers . . . was not so much that their music had been mistaken for the work of African-Americans, but that they themselves had been mistaken for blacks." [59]

Bewildering as such cultural interaction might have been to northern technicians, it was precisely this blending of two rich yet nominally separate traditions that gave southern popular music its fire and power and that, for a time, made Atlanta center stage in a budding musical revolution.

Not, of course, that Atlanta's status-hungry elite noticed. The Gate City's social and civic leaders had long sought to make Atlanta a hub of southern cultural activity, but their notions of what constituted "culture" were far too restricted to allow for the efforts of a Gid Tanner or a Fiddlin' John Carson, much less those of a Blind Willie McTell. For their part, the newspapers portrayed the hillbillies, when they considered them at all, as they had pictured participants in the fiddling conventions—as quaint and colorful relics of a simpler past, rather than as creative figures in their own right or as harbingers of new forms of cultural expression. African Americans remained, as always, caricatures and cultural ciphers from the newspapers' point of view.

However oblivious or condescending the city's respectable citizens may have been, men like Carson and McTell effected a major shift in Atlanta's cultural role. Prior to the 1920s, Atlanta had always been something of a funnel into the South for culture produced elsewhere, whether in the Northeast, Europe, or Hollywood. But in 1922 the situation began to reverse. Through the broadcasting power of WSB and the portable recording machines of northeastern engineers, Atlanta began to attract indigenous southern folk culture and to funnel it to the rest of the country, where its lasting significance was much greater than anything the city had previously produced along cultural lines. The irony is that when Atlanta finally became the influential cultural center that its advocates had long promised it would be, there were no boosters about to trumpet the fact, or to profit from it, or in fact to feel anything other than embarrassment about their city's new claim to fame.

This pronounced disdain on the part of local men and women with money and influence helps to explain why Atlanta ultimately lost its cultural centrality, as do more national trends such as the centralizing of the radio industry. Just as the scattering of locally based theatrical troupes of the early nineteenth century gave way to a consolidated system of traveling combination companies based in New York, so radio stations that began as local, autonomous, wildly eclectic entities quickly evolved into satellites of the major national networks. In January 1927, WSB officially affiliated with NBC. Henceforth network programming would leave less time for shows featuring local talent, and a new sense of cosmopolitan sophistication may have changed the attitudes of WSB officials toward the station's more rustic offerings.[60] In any event, as a chronicler of country music in Atlanta has noted, "The era in which a fiddler or banjo picker could drop by the station and go on the air on short notice had now ended."[61]

What apathy and respectability did not finish off, desperate economic times did. The Great Depression laid waste to the recording industry, with sales dropping more than 80 percent between 1927 and 1933. Labels discontinued field recordings in the South, and some, like Paramount and Okeh, went out of business altogether. Blues recordings were particularly hard hit. The average race record, which had sold around ten thousand copies in the mid 1920s, sold only four hundred in 1932.[62]

By the time the record business rebounded, Atlanta's day in the sun had largely passed. But the blues and country music industries that Atlanta had helped launch went on to firmly establish themselves and to profoundly influence other American musical forms, thereby playing an essential role in creating the American popular culture that swept the globe in the twentieth century.[63] Atlanta's contribution to this phenomenon was admittedly limited, but it was also crucial and worthy of acknowledgment, especially from a city forever starved for cultural importance and legitimacy.

⇥ Conclusion ⇤

Atlanta's history between 1880 and 1930 can be broken into three phases that mark its development from small southern town to big U.S. city. The years 1880 to 1895 show an aspiring but still idiosyncratic city striving for a national reputation while laboring to shed—or to preserve, depending on who was doing the talking—a strong measure of provincialism. The Cotton States and International Exposition of 1895 signaled the beginning of a new phase of startling growth in which Atlanta grappled with big-city ills and debated its future. By 1915, when *The Birth of a Nation* symbolically "reunited" the country, the Gate City's course was more or less set: it bounded toward metropolitan status and cultural homogenization, though not without catching a glimpse of a road not taken. These dividing points are of course arbitrary to a degree, and there is a great deal of overlap between the periods, but by focusing on the salient trends and events in each, we can provide answers to those questions posed in the introduction: What does Atlanta's experience reveal about the history of American entertainment? And what does the history of American entertainment reveal about Atlanta?

The first period, 1880 to 1895, saw Atlanta emerging from the traumas of the Civil War and Reconstruction to assume leadership of the New South Movement. Here we see concrete indications that the South has its own unique tale to tell. The region's social, economic, political, and cultural history differs in important ways from that of the Northeast and Midwest— Henry Grady's New South crusade was itself an acknowledgment that the South was fundamentally different, in many respects disadvantageously so—

and consequently the context in which commercial entertainment evolved in this part of the country is different as well. Atlanta therefore provides a generally overlooked perspective, a Deep South perspective, on the growth of commercial culture in the United States. This is not to claim that the entirety of Atlanta's experience was distinctive—it was not—nor to assert that in every respect the city's divergence from the northern experience is attributable to Atlanta's "southernness." But the regional context of Atlanta's story is crucial, helping both to flesh out the larger national story and to modify a number of assumptions rooted in the tendency of historians to focus their attention on the big cities of the North.

The South of the late nineteenth century presented distinctive challenges to those who wished to profit from leisure below the Mason-Dixon line. Much less populous than the North, and with far fewer sizable cities, the South offered a markedly smaller pool of potential patrons for commercial amusements. The region's widespread poverty and recurrent economic misery shrank the pool still further, while long railroad jumps and discriminatory rates increased ticket prices for a population already less able than its northern counterparts to pay for entertainment. As a result, theaters, which depended for their survival on traveling performers, struggled to schedule high-quality productions on a regular basis—many companies simply decided that expensive tours of the South were too risky, especially given the scarcity of potential patrons. The often-inferior troupes that braved the odds and came south anyway alienated local audiences and critics, making the financial prospects for future tours even dimmer.

There were other obstacles, less tangible than ticket costs and railroad schedules, but formidable all the same. The region pulsed with the values of evangelical Christianity, which was generally hostile toward commercial amusements, in particular those presented on stage. This animosity deepened in the waning years of the century due to an increasingly desperate sense among many evangelicals that their standards were under assault and that the South represented a last lone bastion against a corrosive broader culture awash in soulless materialism. These men and women saw Atlanta as a southern "city on a hill" that required vigilant protection against all who would sully and debase her.

Again and again, commercial entertainment provided a target for ministers and others angry about what they perceived to be a collapse of morality. The theater seemed intent on undermining what many evangelicals saw as key pillars of civilization. In its exploitation of sexuality, for example, and its subversion of traditional notions regarding women's roles, the stage seemed especially reprehensible to many clergymen and their followers, especially since the theater aroused people's passions and misdirected their energies for no better reason, ultimately, than to fill some businessman's pockets. It was in opposition to such an encroaching amoral, free-market ethos that Atlanta ministers would later rally to prevent Sunday motion pictures.

Looming over all thought and activity in the South, of course, was the specter of race. The North would later experience explosive racial conflict as well, but during the period under study—the period when the mass entertainment industry was establishing itself in the United States—the African American population was overwhelmingly concentrated in the South, and it was here that racism assumed its most intense, pervasive, and codified form. Race affected every aspect of the entertainment business in the South, just as it molded southern culture, politics, and economics. Audiences were strictly segregated, black performers were expected to remain firmly within "their place," and any production that deviated from white southern racial norms was deemed antagonistic to civilization itself. This was particularly true of obvious "enemies," such as *Uncle Tom's Cabin,* but even works that heartily endorsed the "southern way of life," such as *The Clansman* and *The Birth of a Nation,* could arouse anxieties if they threatened to upset the delicate balance of regional race relations.

All of these factors—race, religion, gender, geography, demography— interacted in such complicated ways that the "highbrow/lowbrow" dichotomy applied recently by historians to the United States does not fit comfortably in the South of this era. There are of course parallels between the South and the rest of the country. In Atlanta just as in New York City, for instance, we see the white elite employing highbrow music to define and elevate itself, to clearly distance itself from cultural "inferiors," to redefine the city in its own image, and to link itself with its peers across the nation. But for all the similarities, even here distinctions need to be made. The quest by the Gate City's nouveaux riches for cultural ascendancy occurred in a particular context of regional insecurities and crass commercial considerations that set these men and women apart from the Vanderbilts and

Morgans of the North. In addition, unlike the northern elites studied by Lawrence Levine, the Atlanta upper crust was at best only sporadically "highbrow"—generally only during Opera Week—and even a pretended "refinement" was beyond the capacities of most, as the much-lamented behavior in the Municipal Auditorium too frequently indicated. By the same token, Atlanta's less "elevated" patrons did not precisely fit the highbrow/ lowbrow pattern either. Frequently their tastes and behavior did not differ in any fundamental way from those of their "betters," and they were never segregated into "lower-class" theaters to sit quietly in meek acceptance of what was offered them on stage. Atlanta simply saw no sharp, impermeable division between high and low during the five decades under study, despite the grimly determined efforts of some of its "better" citizens.

Moreover, the wild card of race deeply complicates the picture in the South as it did not in the Northeast. More than one social and cultural hierarchy existed in Atlanta. The pecking order might vary according to context, but virtually all whites, of whatever social class, viewed themselves as superior to all African Americans. It was never necessary for a white Atlantan—whether a financier or a day laborer—to spend an evening at the opera to demonstrate this basic fact of life. Among white southerners, in other words, when push came to shove, race trumped class. Even the most socially pretentious whites conceded—and at times even celebrated—some sort of bond, however tenuous, with lower-class whites; white supremacy depended upon at least a semblance of racial unity. There was always a tension, therefore, between the white elite's desire to distance itself from its white "inferiors" and its need to remain allied with them. Within the black community, likewise, the aspiring social elite found itself torn between a longing to "uplift the race" and a powerful yearning to be accepted by upper-crust whites as a cultured, refined class of ladies and gentlemen sharply distinguishable from working-class blacks.

In short, while Atlanta did witness a great deal of social climbing marked by the ostentatious wielding of "high" culture, most citizens—even the well-to-do—were too contentedly "middlebrow" to replicate New York's Golden Horseshoe in anything more than short, frenetic bursts. Furthermore, in the distinctively biracial South, the white elite's struggle for cultural supremacy was at once eased by a bedrock assumption of black inferiority and weakened by the pressing political and psychological requirement that a link be maintained with the white working class. The game in the South was similar to that played elsewhere, but the teams and the rules were very different.

The Cotton States and International Exposition of 1895 ushered in a new age for the Gate City, in both economic and cultural terms. As a later generation of Atlantans liked to say about the 1996 Olympics, the exposition "brought the world to Atlanta"—in what turned out to be both welcome and less welcome manifestations—and symbolized Atlanta's increasingly rapid shift from nineteenth-century town to twentieth-century city. Over the following decades Atlanta's rate of population growth skyrocketed and its economy expanded in ways that provided eager entrepreneurs with both a more welcoming environment and a larger pool of entertainment-hungry patrons. This period observed the rise of an array of cheaper amusements—vaudeville, burlesque, and, above all, movies—that captured a broader audience than the theater had ever been able to claim.

Dramatic change, however, only intensified social conflict, symbolized by the 1906 race riot and the Leo Frank lynching of 1915. Atlanta seemed to have arrived at a crossroads, and its citizens disagreed over which path it should take. Down one road, oriented geographically toward the Northeast and temporally toward the future, seemed to lay the Emerald City of "cosmopolitanism," alluring to some, repugnant to others. More conservative southerners pointed toward a southerly route favoring the past and called for a sort of cultural retrenchment, a rejection of the deceptive baubles of northeastern commercialism. Entertainment frequently occupied center stage in these battles. Indeed, perhaps no other lens is as helpful in bringing into focus the social, cultural, and ideological conflicts of this era as is that provided by commercial amusements. To many, burlesque, Sunday movies, and cheap vaudeville gave body to more abstract concerns about Atlanta's future and the transformations it would entail. As a result, repeated clashes over amusements vividly illustrated the divisions and anxieties that animated this period.

But amidst the strife, Atlanta by the early twentieth century was also experiencing an increasingly widespread acceptance of commercialized leisure—or at least of leisure conducted within "proper" bounds. The movies provide a telling example. The ministers who were outraged in 1913 by Sunday movie screenings conceded that they had no quarrel with the presentation for profit of decent motion pictures, so long as this business, like others, rested on the Sabbath. Over time, broadsides against movies or the theater as institutions dwindled in number, ferocity, and influence. Rather, morality-minded Atlantans narrowed their focus to individual productions, evaluating these movies and plays in terms of the allegiance that they paid to the core values of the white South. And in the all-important case of the movies, such judging would no longer be done by fiery late-nineteenth-century ministers but by businessmen and lawyers imbued with a Progressive Era worldview. In these men's eyes, if a film explicitly or implicitly upheld white supremacy, evangelical propriety, and traditional notions of patriarchy, it could be, as Judge Broyles had approvingly described some plays, "as good as a sermon." But if a given work was seen as challenging— or even questioning—this holy trinity, then the city's censors sprang to action, whether this meant banning a film, excising unacceptable scenes, or, as in at least one case, ripping down posters and ordering a film out of town.

Ultimately there was no stopping the cultural and economic force represented by inexpensive mass entertainment. The revolutionary consumer culture then taking firm root all over the nation represented too mighty a force to bend for very long to the will or the traditions of any single city or region. Indeed, once Atlanta accepted and became accustomed to institutionalized commercial amusement, the battle for the city's future was in a very real sense over. "Cosmopolitanism" had come to stay, in one form or another, and movies, vaudeville, and later radio and television helped tremendously to ensure its triumph.

With cosmopolitanism would come the tradeoffs that defined the twentieth century from a cultural standpoint, as local distinctiveness more and more gave way to nationally standardized amusements. As we have seen, there was definite good in this process for all Atlantans: they gained access to what at its best was high-quality entertainment. No single city was likely to produce performers equal in talent to the Charlie Chaplins and Buster Keatons who now regularly tripped across the Gate City's screens. On the other hand, much of an essentially human character—something beyond the fact that local audiences would no longer be able to hurl sausages at feckless actors—was lost as well. The transition from a local, face-to-face popular culture—personified variously by Scott Thornton, Yellowstone Kit, and an assortment of fly-by-night dime museums—to a nationalized, impersonal mass culture—symbolized by proliferating cineplexes and flickering television screens—has embodied a multitude of societal profits and losses that have yet to be tallied.

The years 1915 to 1930 highlighted, on the one hand, the Gate City's participation in the national trend toward cultural homogenization. Atlanta became a "metropolis," but also just another "big city," resulting in less and less in the way of culture that was distinctively its own. The annual opera visits were secure, the motion picture palaces rose apace, and civic leaders beamed with pride, but all the while Atlanta came more to resemble a "mass-produced" city not very different in most ways from cities "coming off the assembly line" in every section of the country.

On the other hand, a tantalizing but ultimately unfulfilled alternative to this drive toward national "sameness" appeared with the emergence of Atlanta as a regional musical center in the 1910s and 1920s. For the first time, Atlanta was offering a cultural product to the rest of the country rather than importing it from the outside, and thus the Gate City served as a harbinger of the limitless influence that southern culture would have upon American culture as a whole during the twentieth century. True, the product—working-class music—that Atlanta helped to introduce to the nation's consciousness would eventually face the same commodifying and standardizing pressures that afflicted all such cultural eruptions, but for a time, unbeknownst to its "leaders," Atlanta achieved a measure of the cultural singularity and importance it had always sought for itself. The moment was, however, all too brief—it was terminated in the end by a combination of local apathy and the Great Depression. Although it had lasting significance, Atlanta's role in the evolution of American popular music has been largely forgotten, certainly by the city's cultural elite. For all too many Atlantans, southern culture has always been something to run from in headlong pursuit of praise elsewhere, rather than something to nourish and display with pride. The result has been yet another painful tradeoff, noted by anyone who has ever wished that the city had preserved more than a handful of its historic buildings. In its prolonged and frenzied scramble to become a modern, respected, "international city," Atlanta has sacrificed the better part of its soul.

Atlanta's history between Reconstruction and the Great Depression embodies a complex tangle of social trends and contradictions. But it is possible—

especially using the spotlight of public entertainment—to lift and examine individual strands, intricately intertwined though they are, within this web. Atlanta was at once a southern city lurching toward the national mainstream, a provincial city shedding its distinctiveness, a religious city embattled with secularism, a deeply racist city at war with equality. From yet another perspective the entire period from 1880 to 1930 can be seen as a series of conflicts, not always overt—indeed, not even always conscious—between an ostentatiously respectable elite strenuously (and usually ineffectually) attempting to foster cultural "appreciation" in Atlanta, and ordinary folk unpretentiously going about the business of living their lives and expressing themselves. To say this is not to flip the traditional highbrow-versus-lowbrow hierarchy, putting the bottom rail on top, or to make meaningless comparisons between Enrico Caruso and Fiddlin' John Carson. It is simply to point out that culture is not restricted to any one group's terms or definitions. Beauty can arise just as easily from a mill-town shack as from a concert stage, from a bluesman's guitar as from a gleaming grand piano. This was always clear to the men and women who took culture and sincere self-expression for granted. But it was never evident to the people who dominated Atlanta's officially sanctioned cultural life. And it is not entirely clear to Atlanta's social elite many decades later. There is a sense in which Atlanta's cultural spokespersons remain north of the South today.

⋙ NOTES ⋘

ABBREVIATIONS

AC   *Atlanta Constitution*
AG   *Atlanta Georgian*
AI   *Atlanta Independent*
AJ   *Atlanta Journal*
NYDM   *New York Dramatic Mirror*

INTRODUCTION

1. W. E. B. Du Bois, *The Souls of Black Folk,* in *W. E. B. Du Bois: Writings,* The Library of America (New York: Literary Classics of the United States, 1986), 415.

2. *AC* 2 September 1915, p. 11 of magazine section.

3. For another discussion of Atlanta as a "city of contrasts," see Blaine A. Brownell, *The Urban Ethos in the South, 1920–1930* (Baton Rouge: Louisiana State University Press, 1975), especially 13–14. Elsewhere Brownell and David R. Goldfield have observed, "Southern cities served as repositories of regional culture—including, many would argue, the primitive values and instincts of rural society—and as links between the traditional South and the contrary influences of northern capitalism and the American 'mainstream.'" Brownell and Goldfield, "Southern Urban History," 8.

4. Rabinowitz, "Continuity and Change," 97.

5. Rydell, *All the World's a Fair,* chap. 3; Mary Roberts Davis, "Atlanta Industrial Expositions"; Martin, "Biggest Event," 91–94.

6. For Atlanta's early-twentieth-century "economic awakening," see Preston, *Automobile Age Atlanta,* 17–19, 44. For the sharp increase in population growth, see Brownell, *Urban Ethos in the South,* 12–13, 16.

7. For descriptions and analysis of the Atlanta riot, see Dittmer, *Black Georgia,* 123–31; Godshalk, "In the Wake of Riot"; and Mixon, "Atlanta Riot of 1906." For a chilling first-person account of the riot, see White, *Man Called White,* chap. 1.

8. For more on the Frank episode as a product of local tensions, see Dinnerstein, *Leo Frank Case;* MacLean, "Leo Frank Case Reconsidered," 917–45. For the Ku Klux Klan and Atlanta's role as "Imperial City," see Jackson, *Ku Klux Klan,* especially chaps. 1–3.

9. Brownell employs the concept of a "commercial-civic elite" in *Urban Ethos in the South.* For the beginnings of Atlanta's gargantuan traffic problems see Preston, *Automobile Age Atlanta.* Preston notes the granting of metropolitan status on page 150.

10. Levine, *Highbrow/Lowbrow;* Kasson, *Rudeness and Civility,* 216–51.

11. For discussions of Atlanta's dance halls and amusement parks, see Hunter, *To 'Joy My Freedom,* chap. 8; Hickey, "Visibility, Politics, and Urban Development," 269–77.

12. See, for example, Gorn and Goldstein, *Brief History of American Sports;* Riess, *Sport in Industrial America.* See also the discussion of baseball in Nasaw, *Going Out,* chap. 8. For an Atlanta example of the close relationship between sports and broader community life, see the description of the Gate City's reaction to the famous 1910 Jack Johnson–Jim Jeffries heavyweight championship fight in Dittmer, *Black Georgia,* 69–71.

13. Fort, "History of the Atlanta Journal"; Golson, "Accuracy of Atlanta Newspapers," 47–67. By the end of the 1880s, the weekly edition of the *Constitution* had a nationwide circulation of close to two hundred thousand, making it "perhaps the largest weekly in the nation." Harold E. Davis, *Henry Grady's New South,* 52. For more on the widespread influence of Atlanta's newspapers, see Ayers, *Promise of the New South,* 87; *AJ* 14 July 1909.

14. For an analysis of the perspectives the three dailies took on the Leo Frank affair, see Dinnerstein, *Leo Frank Case,* 29–31.

1. THE THEATER IN ATLANTA

1. *AC* 27 October 1894; *AJ* 25 October 1894 and 26 October 1894; and *NYDM* 10 November 1894.

2. *AC* 30 October 1894; *AJ* 29 October 1894, 30 October 1894, and 31 October 1894.

3. *AC* 5 November 1894; *AJ* 3 November 1894 and 5 November 1894.

4. *AJ* 5 November 1894.

5. Ibid.

6. *AC* 9 November 1894.

7. This account of the trial is drawn from *AC* 9 November 1894; *AJ* 7 November 1894, 8 November 1894, and 9 November 1894. On the calling of newspapermen

as experts, see *AC* 6 November 1894, 8 November 1894; *AJ* 6 November 1894, and 7 November 1894.

8. *AC* 10 November 1894.

9. *AG* 17 March 1910.

10. This account of DeGive's life and the opening of his theater are drawn from Garrett, *Atlanta and Its Environs*, 3:30–31; Gough, "Entertainment in Atlanta," 63–64; and *AC* 17 March 1910. On Davis Hall, a large but "primitive" facility, see Gough, 40–44, 49.

11. For Atlanta's theatrical history before DeGive, see especially Gough, "Entertainment in Atlanta"; Garrett, *Atlanta and Its Environs*, vols. 1 and 2; Taylor, "From the Ashes"; Orr, *Alfredo Barili*, 53–55; *AC* 5 November 1882; and *AJ* 18 June 1883.

12. *AC* 22 January 1870; Gough, "Entertainment in Atlanta," 64–66; *AJ* 9 September 1884; and *AC* 22 January 1870. For Opera House renovations and expansions, see *AC* 15 January 1888.

13. *Atlanta Daily Intelligencer* 14 June 1870, cited in Taylor, "From the Ashes," 406.

14. *AC* 8 April 1888; *AG* 10 March 1910.

15. One southern theater owner presented the problem to an Atlanta newspaperman in defending the admission prices that DeGive charged. He first described a typical week's tour of the East, which would involve fifty miles of travel. The tour would go from "Boston to Lynn, Lynn to Haverhill, and thence to Lawrence, Salem, Loring—railroad fare $1.50 per head." On the other hand, a week's tour of the South would involve traveling from "New York to Lynchburg, thence to Charlotte, thence to Atlanta, thence to Montgomery, thence to Mobile or New Orleans. Now count up the fare and distance," the manager concluded, "and is it not real good management on Mr. DeGive's part to give Atlanta seats at the same rate as Boston?" *AJ* 2 May 1883.

16. *AC* 2 December 1881. For more on railroad rates and their effects on theatrical touring, see *AJ* 7 July 1907, 5 February 1908, 6 February 1908, 7 February 1908, 11 February 1908, and 26 February 1908.

17. See DeGive's letter to the editor in *AC* 3 March 1889. For more criticism of his ticket prices, see the reply in *AC* 6 March 1889.

18. Theater admission prices appeared frequently in newspaper advertisements. The prices cited are from *AC* 4 January 1880; *AJ* 4 November 1886, 10 November 1903, and 3 January 1904.

19. *NYDM* 23 January 1892.

20. *AJ* 23 October 1896. See also *AJ* 15 August 1896, 28 November 1896, and 6 August 1898. As if such economic problems were not enough, the theatrical

business in the South occasionally fell victim to even more arbitrary disasters, such as outbreaks of yellow fever in 1888, 1897, and 1905, which caused skittish companies to cancel tours. See *NYDM*, quoted in *AJ* 6 November 1897, and *AJ* 16 September 1906.

21. *AJ* 28 October 1884. During the 1898 season the *Journal* noted that "More than one company has gone to pieces in the south, and many more have barely managed to pay railroad fares and board, salaries often being an unknown quantity to the player folk." *AJ* 26 March 1898. For an account of a small company's foundering, see *AG* 7 September 1906.

22. *NYDM* 1 January 1881. For similar occurrences, see *AJ* 6 December 1884, 8 December 1884, and 16 March 1885. Even when companies managed to show up, DeGive sometimes had to take legal action to obtain his rent. See *Atlanta Herald* 27 November 1874, cited in Taylor, "From the Ashes," 279.

23. Bernheim, *Business of the Theatre*, 79–80.

24. *AC* 1 March 1885; *AC* 8 November 1885.

25. Cited in Taylor, "From the Ashes," 279. See also *AJ* 30 January 1895; *AC* 23 November 1915. Some companies attempted to counter cynicism about traveling companies through advertising. One production promised "Every Inch of Scenery—Every Comedian—Every Soubrette—Every Chorus Girl—Everybody and Everything identically as produced at the New York Theater." *AG* 12 February 1910.

26. *AC* 14 May 1890, p. 3; *AJ* 30 October 1894. See also *AG* 12 September 1911; *AC* 1 April 1912.

27. *NYDM* 3 January 1891.

28. Bernheim, *Business of the Theatre*, 80.

29. McArthur, *Actors and American Culture*, 130. Atlanta's Rev. C. D. Holderby viewed a 1912 recommendation by Methodist bishops that the bans on theatergoing, dancing, and card playing be lifted as "a clear compromise with the devil." *AG* 13 May 1912. For examples of condemnation of the theater by denominational organizations in Georgia and Atlanta, see *AC* 11 December 1887; *AJ* 18 February 1907.

30. DeGive had faced clerical attacks from his earliest days as manager of the Opera House. See Taylor, "From the Ashes," 202. In fact, Atlantans had argued over the morality of the theater before DeGive arrived on the local scene. See Gough, "Entertainment in Atlanta," 4, 28–30, 106, 188.

31. Rev. J. B. Hawthorne, quoted in *AC* 12 September 1892.

32. Newman, "Vision of Order," 2. See also p. 128.

33. This is the primary theme of Newman's "Vision of Order." See especially pages vii, 29–30, 146, 155. By the second decade of the twentieth century, Atlanta's churches were no longer able to keep pace with the city's surging population. Newman, 153.

34. Minnix, "Atlanta Revivals of Sam Jones," 5–34; Bauman, *Warren Akin Candler*, 131, 205; and Godshalk, "In the Wake of Riot," 193–94, 250–51.

35. Quoted in Newman, "Vision of Order," 126–27.

36. *AG* 22 February 1909; Bauman, *Warren Akin Candler*, 51–53, 171; Rev. J. B. Hawthorne, quoted in *AJ* 5 November 1894.

37. *AJ* 21 March 1896 and 27 March 1896.

38. *AJ* 1 June 1901.

39. See Minnix, *Laughter in the Amen Corner*, 74–80, for a discussion of Jones's style and his use of "religious theater."

40. *AJ* 25 February 1899.

41. *AJ* 29 November 1886; *AC* 29 October 1894.

42. *AG* 6 December 1912. See also *AG* 22 February 1909, 19 February 1909, 20 February 1909, and 24 January 1910.

43. *AJ* 2 November 1905. See also *AJ* 4 February 1905 and 6 November 1905.

44. *AJ* 10 February 1907 and 5 February 1907. "There was a time when I was narrow about the theater just like Dr. Broughton," Nation explained. "But that was because I was ignorant. I've learned since then that not all plays are bad and that there are as good people on the stage as elsewhere." *AG* 4 February 1907. Besides, Nation responded to those who questioned her activities in the theater, "I am fishing and I go where the fish are." *AG* 2 February 1907. See also *AG* 26 January 1907, 5 February 1907, 6 February 1907, 7 February 1907; *AJ* 4 February 1907, and 22 February 1909.

45. *AJ* 7 March 1898. See also chapter 3 of this book.

46. *AJ* 8 December 1900, 22 December 1900; and *NYDM* 22 December 1900. See also *AJ* 22 September 1900 and 8 March 1898.

47. This account is drawn from *AJ* 21 February 1899, 22 February 1899, and 24 February 1899.

48. *AJ* 5 November 1906. On at least one occasion the EMA expanded the scope of its offensive against all things theatrical by attempting to suppress a book upon which a scandalous play was based. See *AJ* 14 March 1900, 15 March 1900, and 2 April 1900.

49. The Sam T. Jack Company had rushed back to the Gate City to take advantage of the poster flap, realizing that, as the *Journal* put it, "they have been far better advertised by this general discussion than they could have been by their own most strenuous efforts." *AJ* 5 November 1894. On *Ben-Hur*, see *AJ* 4 March 1903 and 8 March 1903. *Ben-Hur* continued to draw enormous audiences during its subsequent visits to the Gate City. See *AC* 7 December 1913.

50. *AG* 25 February 1909.

51. *AG* 26 February 1909.

52. *AJ* 3 March 1909, p. 4. See also *AG* 8 December 1909. The EMA was not the only evangelical organization to oppose the theater. In 1900 members of the Salvation Army drew a warning from Atlanta police for haranguing men and women entering the Columbia Theater with taunts of "Paying 50 cents to go to hell." *AC* 1 March 1900, cited in Deaton, "Atlanta during the Progressive Era," 63. For debate over whether ministers themselves should attend "good" plays, see *AG* 31 January 1907, 4 February 1907, and 5 February 1907.

53. According to an 1888 newspaper interview with Jake Tannenbaum of Mobile, southern managers calculated that only 7 percent of a given city's population attended the theater over the course of a season. *AC* 8 April 1888.

54. Levine, *Highbrow/Lowbrow;* Kasson, *Rudeness and Civility,* 216–51.

55. *AG* 3 November 1909; see, for example, *AC* 28 February 1889, 12 March 1889, and 18 September 1911; *AC* 4 December 1892.

56. *AC* 23 September 1894.

57. *AJ* 11 February 1893.

58. *AC* 29 October 1894. For examples of melodrama performed at the Grand, see *AJ* 22 March 1893 and 29 January 1895. For an example of the presentation of a prize fight film, see *AC* 14 January 1900.

59. For a critical assessment of the American theater in the late nineteenth century, see Reardon, "American Drama and Theatre in the Nineteenth Century," 170–86. See also Nasaw, *Going Out,* 41–43.

60. Toll, *On With the Show,* chap. 6; Nasaw, *Going Out,* 41.

61. *NYDM* 11 November 1905 and 2 December 1905.

62. *NYDM* 9 March 1889.

63. *AJ* 4 March 1898. A leading actor of the day claimed that the entire South was at fault, lamenting to a *Constitution* reporter, "I am pretty well discouraged. Here in the South the problem is narrowed down to about this: Shall I continue to try to educate the people up to these plays, or shall I give them the stuff they want?" *AC* 23 February 1900. See also Sidney Ormond's discussion of the "pitifully small" audiences that attended the Shakespearean productions of the Stratford-Upon-Avon Players in 1914, despite laudatory reviews in all three daily newspapers. Ormond agreed with a theater policeman who observed, "I notice that more people in Atlanta like minstrel shows than Shakespeare." *AC* 22 February 1914.

64. According to a reporter, DeGive was "not a believer in the old remedies." *AC* 10 November 1895. See also *AJ* 14 October 1905.

65. For a discussion of the rise of the "star system" and of the increased emphasis on stage realism in the American theater, see Bruce A. McConachie, "Pacifying American Theatrical Audiences, 1820–1900," in *For Fun and Profit: The Transformation of Leisure into Consumption,* ed. Richard Butsch (Philadelphia: Temple University Press, 1990), 47–70.

66. *AJ* 16 March 1895.

67. *AG* 29 January 1907.

68. After the noted actress Hortense Rhea and her famed counterpart Adelaide Ristori attracted the largest audiences of the season during one week in 1885, the *Mirror* held this up as proof that even at advanced prices, "good attractions will draw in spite of short crops and the stringency in money matters." *NYDM* 14 February 1885.

69. *NYDM* 18 February 1882; *AC* 18 January 1888 and 22 January 1888. See also *AC* 17 January 1888. For a reference to an earlier visit by Booth and the excitement it generated, see *AC* 5 November 1882.

70. *NYDM* 12 February 1887.

71. *NYDM* 27 January 1894. See also *AC* 11 January 1894.

72. *AC* 5 December 1880; *NYDM* 1 January 1881.

73. *AC* 4 February 1881 and 5 February 1881; *NYDM* 19 February 1881.

74. *AC* 16 February 1881.

75. *AC* 17 February 1881; *NYDM* 26 February 1881; *AC* 8 June 1881. Bernhardt played to a packed house again in 1906, this time at the Peachtree Auditorium. See *AJ* 28 February 1906; *NYDM* 31 March 1906. See also accounts of Atlanta's frustrated attempt to turn another star's planned visit to account. *AC* 18 January 1882 and 24 January 1882.

76. Atlanta's population may simply not have been large enough to provide an adequate audience for a theater catering solely to "higher" aesthetic standards. This seems to have been the case earlier in the century in the Upper South cities examined by Patricia C. Click in her book, *The Spirit of the Times*.

77. McConachie, "Pacifying American Theatrical Audiences"; Levine, *Highbrow/Lowbrow*, especially chap. 1; Kasson, *Rudeness and Civility*, chap. 7; and Allen, *Horrible Prettiness*, 70, 72–73.

78. *AC* 18 September 1911.

79. *AJ* 25 October 1883; Gough, "Entertainment in Atlanta," 28–29; cited in Gough, "Entertainment." See also *Atlanta New Era* 23 January 1869 and 26 November 1869, cited in Taylor, "From the Ashes," 273. A *Constitution* reporter writing of Atlanta in the immediate postwar years recalled that "About this time Atlanta had much the style of a western border town of the present day." *AC* 5 November 1882. See also Orr, *Alfredo Barili*, 52–53.

80. Lucien York remembered as much when recalling for the *Journal* his early days working for DeGive at the old opera house. He started out in 1884 as a program boy, but "The next season there was a vacancy on the balcony and gallery door and I asked Mr. DeGive for the place. He hesitated at first, saying he did not think I was old enough to handle the rough crowds which sometimes surged up to the gallery." *AJ* 18 March 1910. A frequenter of the gallery fondly recalled the

"rushes we used to make" up the stairs of the Grand in a letter quoted in *AG* 11 November 1915. The presence of prostitutes in the gallery—and elsewhere—was also an occasional source of complaint. See *Atlanta Daily New Era,* 30 March 1870, quoted in Gough, "Entertainment in Atlanta," 66; letter to the editor in *AJ* 18 November 1886.

81. For examples of newspaper comment on crowd behavior and police presence in the theaters, see *AJ* 27 March 1883, 23 January 1884, 27 March 1885, 11 May 1886, 24 March 1896, 15 December 1896; *AC* 9 November 1889; *AG* 3 September 1907, 12 November 1907, 12 May 1908, 1 October 1908, and 7 April 1910. Evidently some theaters were cracking down by 1913, when a college student was brought to police court for whistling a tune in the gallery. Recorder Broyles dismissed the case. *AG* 30 January 1913.

82. *AJ* 8 April 1895.

83. *AC* 14 December 1890.

84. For coverage of Thornton's travels through Georgia, see *AC* 2 May 1891, 8 May 1891; and *AJ* 4 July 1896. The *Albany Herald* is cited regarding Thornton in *AC* 2 October 1893. For Thornton's belief in his talents, see his obituaries in *AJ* 24 November 1897; *AC* 25 November 1897, and 26 November 1897. Walter McElreath recalled Thornton as "perhaps, the best example of the near genius which Atlanta ever produced. He was a Shakespearean scholar of no mean ability and just missed being a great tragedian. With the delusions of grandeur characteristic of his temperament he was utterly oblivious of the interest which a cruel public took in his histrionic talents." McElreath, "When Atlanta Was Just a Big Town," 85–86.

85. *AC* 31 March 1896.

86. *AJ* 11 May 1895.

87. On the degeneration of southern race relations during this period, see Ayers, *Promise of the New South,* chap. 6.

88. Dinnerstein, *Leo Frank Case,* 148.

89. For examples of the "Police Matinee" column, see *AC* 18 February 1900, 1 April 1900, 1 July 1900, and 28 March 1915.

90. Baker, *Following the Color Line,* 9–10, 18.

91. For references to segregation in theaters in the United States, see Sampson, *Ghost Walks,* 47, 57–58, 140–42, 195, 233, 287–88, 292, 321, 426, 440–41, 443–44, 462, 531. On the banning of blacks from southern theaters, see ibid., 140–41, 543.

92. *AJ* 24 February 1897.

93. Ibid. See also *AJ* 6 April 1895.

94. *AJ* 23 March 1896.

95. Sampson, *Ghost Walks,* 88–89.

96. *AJ* 23 January 1895 and 24 January 1895; *AJ* 25 January 1895.

97. *AG* 17 March 1910; *AJ* 6 January 1893; *AJ* 7 December 1898.

98. Toll, *On with the Show*, 153–55; Gossett, *Uncle Tom's Cabin*, 370–71. According to Gossett, "In 1879, the *New York Dramatic Mirror* listed the routes of forty-nine of what had already begun to be called 'Tommer shows.' . . . By the 1890s, there were, according to one estimate, approximately five hundred companies producing Tommer shows." Estimates of the number of productions that had been given in the United States ranged from 250,000 or more by 1912 to up to one million by 1952. Ibid., 371–72. On the muting of the play's message, see ibid., 372–73, 387.

99. *AC* 12 January 1881.

100. The advertisement is in *AC* 3 April 1881.

101. *NYDM* 23 April 1881 and 30 April 1881. Basing his claim on an earlier erroneous source, Gossett in *Uncle Tom's Cabin* mistakenly states that it was in Atlanta that the audience consisted of two boys. See 373–74.

102. *AC* 9 April 1881; *NYDM* 23 April 1881.

103. *AC* 18 February 1915, 19 February 1915. According to a puff for *Old Plantation Days* in the *Constitution*, "The biggest features of the production will be a regular old-time negro jubilee of singing and dancing by any number of local Georgia dancers and singers, with plantation scenes of before the war." Duly noted was the fact that "Mr. Baldwin has given his assurances that there will be nothing about the performance to which anyone could take the slightest objection." *AC* 21 February 1915. In fact, Baldwin's forced expurgation of the play was so successful that the production, far from provoking anger, in fact aroused among white Atlantans a sentimental interest in the Old South and its plantations. *AC* 21 March 1915, magazine section. For similar protests against *Uncle Tom* in Kentucky, see Gossett, *Uncle Tom's Cabin*, 375–76

104. *AJ* 17 February 1903, p. 8. The reviewer was Grantland Rice, later a famed sportswriter.

105. *AJ* 22 October 1905.

106. *AJ* 6 November 1905; *AJ* 8 November 1905.

107. Baker, *Following the Color Line*, 4.

108. *AG* 19 January 1907 and 27 January 1907.

109. *AJ* 9 October 1909; For more on matinees, see, for example, *AJ* 7 November 1901 and 21 January 1910.

110. *AC* 10 December 1891. For other examples, see *NYDM* 10 December 1887; *AC* 10 November 1891; *AC* 14 December 1890.

111. *AC* 16 April 1905. For the application of similar standards to women in literature, see *AC* 13 July 1890; *AC* 14 September 1890.

112. *AC* 8 January 1905; *AJ* 1 January 1903. For another example of this sort of review, see *AG* 5 January 1907.

113. For a discussion of the role assigned women in upholding Victorian culture, see Budke, "Assessing the 'Offense of Public Decency,'" chap. 2.

114. *AJ* 29 January 1895. For later apprehension over the same issue, see *AG* 23 November 1911; *AG* 14 March 1907.

115. *AJ* 14 December 1909.

116. *AJ* 25 December 1899, 27 December 1899, and 30 December 1899. See also *AJ* 29 December 1899, 8 February 1900; and the editorial in *AG* 14 March 1907.

117. *AC* 24 November 1895.

118. *AJ* 29 October 1895.

119. *AJ* 1 April 1896 and 28 December 1895. In the early days of the exposition, the *Journal* had gone so far as to compare Atlanta with Paris. See *AJ* 19 September 1895.

120. See *AC* 2 October 1894, 7 October 1894; and Bernheim, *Business of the Theatre,* 43–44. For background information see Bernheim, 40–52. The firm Klaw and Erlanger was formally known at this time as Jefferson, Klaw and Erlanger.

121. *AC* 7 October 1894; *AJ* 8 April 1895. For the date of the contract, see *AJ* 10 May 1910.

122. In addition, the New Lyceum was significantly smaller than the Grand, it was less conveniently located, and Greenwall had difficulty supplying it with quality attractions. On the Edgewood Avenue Theater, see *AC* 23 April 1891 and 1 October 1891. For the DeGives' description of its problems, see *AJ* 8 April 1895. On the New Lyceum, see *AC* 6 October 1894, 30 April 1895; and *AJ* 27 April 1895. For examples indicating its decline, see *AJ* 1 November 1899 and 14 December 1900. For its destruction, see *AJ* 7 November 1901.

123. Bernheim, *Business of the Theatre,* 46, 52.

124. Ibid., 52.

125. Ibid., 59.

126. See, for example, *AJ* 29 January 1898.

127. *AC* 12 December 1897. This review was cited in a survey of anti-Syndicate editorials in *NYDM* 1 January 1898. See also Jacques Futrelle's sharp criticism of the Syndicate in *AJ* 12 January 1901, magazine section.

128. For background on the theatrical war and for its outbreak, see Bernheim, *Business of the Theatre,* 46–70; *AJ* 9 April 1909, 13 July 1909, 14 July 1909, 15 August 1909, 10 May 1910, 11 May 1910, 12 May 1910, 13 May 1910, 15 May 1910; *AC* 15 May 1910, 22 May 1910, 12 June 1910; and *New York Times,* 13 May 1910.

129. *AJ* 17 March 1910.

130. This letter is reprinted in *AJ* 10 May 1910.

131. *AC* 10 April 1910.

132. See *AJ* 2 September 1910 and 10 October 1910.

133. *AC* 16 September 1912.

134. Bernheim, *Business of the Theatre,* 75, 79–81. For references to the blows delivered to the "legitimate" theater by popular-priced theater and vaudeville, see *AG* 9 April 1910 and 12 November 1909.

2. CHEAPER AMUSEMENTS

1. McElreath, "When Atlanta Was Just a Big Town," 82–88.

2. Quoted in Rabinowitz, "Continuity and Change," 104.

3. *AJ* 3 July 1886.

4. *AJ* 6 July 1886. Leon was the second tightrope-walking "professor" to entertain Atlantans. Professor Bond gave a series of impromptu performances between 1868 and 1870. Gough, "Entertainment in Atlanta," 149.

5. *AJ* 26 July 1886.

6. *AJ* 7 August 1886 and 14 August 1886.

7. *AJ* 28 August 1886; *AC* 28 August 1886. A dime museum also touted an endorsement from Leon. *AJ* 31 August 1886.

8. Cited in Moore, "Negro and Prohibition," 52–53.

9. *AC* 9 November 1887.

10. *AC* 11 November 1887, 24 November 1887, 25 November 1887, 26 November 1887; and Moore, "Negro and Prohibition," 52–53.

11. *New York Times* 25 November 1887.

12. *AC* 25 November 1887, 26 November 1887; and Moore, "Negro and Prohibition," 53.

13. *New York Times* 27 November 1887; and Moore, "Negro and Prohibition," 52–53. The *Times* refers to a "stampede" of blacks to the wet side, but Kit's role in this—to the extent that it actually occurred—was probably exaggerated. Black Atlantans had other reasons for opposing the prohibitionists. See Moore, 51, 53, 56–57; Dorsey, "'To Build Our Lives Together,'" 197–200. On the overall divisiveness of the campaign, see Harold E. Davis, *Henry Grady's New South,* 45–48.

14. A couple of months after Kit left Atlanta, word came back of a black Montgomery editor being driven from town because of criticism of Kit, who had been appearing there for several weeks. And a few years later rumors reportedly spread in Atlanta's black community that Kit would soon return to the Gate City. See *AC* 10 February 1888 and 22 September 1891.

15. McNamara, "'Congress of Wonders,'" 216–17, 222. See also Dennett, *Weird and Wonderful.*

16. Gough, "Entertainment in Atlanta," 151–53.

17. *AJ* 12 December 1884, 30 April 1886; *AC* 31 December 1892; Gough, "Entertainment in Atlanta," 149–53. For other examples, see *AC* 4 December 1881, 30 March 1882, and 2 April 1882. McNamara notes that "the freak show was the chief attraction at most dime museums." "Congress of Wonders," 223.

18. *AJ* 3 February 1885; *AC* 5 October 1887.

19. This paragraph is drawn from *AC* 24 November 1892, 17 December 1892, 30 December 1892, 31 December 1892; and *AJ* 3 January 1893.

20. See *AJ* 17 January 1885, 4 May 1886, and 31 August 1886.

21. McNamara, "Congress of Wonders," 222; Dennett, *Weird and Wonderful*, 45, 61–65.

22. *AJ* 24 January 1909; *AG* 23 January 1909. For a similar Atlanta museum, see *AJ* 10 April 1883 and 11 April 1883. Dennett notes that through their presentations of criminals, "dime museum waxworks served the same function as today's television docudramas; they immortalized the latest crime stories." *Weird and Wonderful*, 114.

23. *AJ* 3 February 1885.

24. This paragraph is drawn from Snyder, *Voice of the City*, 3–37. The quote is from pp. 12–13.

25. *AG* 30 January 1909. For a review of an evening's bill at another local vaudeville house, see *AG* 14 December 1915.

26. Gough, "Entertainment in Atlanta," 100–110. The newspaper quote, from the *Daily New Era* of 3 February 1870, appears on p. 106.

27. For the City Trocadero, see *AJ* 17 September 1895. For the Casino, see *AJ* 16 November 1895. And for the Imperial, see *AJ* 6 April 1895 and 11 December 1895. Frank is described in *AC* 21 April 1895.

28. For ticket prices, see *AJ* 24 September 1895, 16 November 1895, and 1 January 1896. For the supposed quality of the shows, see *AJ* 28 September 1895, 29 September 1895; and *AC* 15 December 1895.

29. *AC* 29 September 1895; *AJ* 28 September 1895. See also *AJ* 11 December 1895; *AC* 15 December 1895.

30. *AJ* 4 January 1896.

31. *AJ* 7 January 1896 and 7 February 1896.

32. On the nature of vaudeville performances, see Toll, *On With the Show*, chap. 10; McLean, *American Vaudeville as Ritual*, 14–15. For information on the considerable physical and economic distance that still lay between Atlanta and the larger northern cities it hoped to emulate, see Preston, *Automobile Age Atlanta*, chap. 1.

33. At this time vaudeville was still a novelty in the South. Even as late as 1911, according to impresario Jake Wells, only Atlanta, New Orleans, and Memphis

among southern cities could begin to support "first-class vaudeville." This meant that there was even a greater problem with long railroad "jumps" than existed in the legitimate theater business, and the problem was made worse by the fact that vaudeville performers, unlike actors in legitimate drama, had to pay their own railroad fares. See *AC* 16 October 1911; DiMeglio, *Vaudeville, U.S.A.,* 87. See also note 36 below.

34. On Wells's holdings and plans, see *AC* 23 December 1900; *AJ* 14 January 1901.

35. *AJ* 6 February 1899; *AJ* 5 January 1901.

36. *AJ* 15 January 1901. The audience included a wide array of Atlantans, including the usual contingent of African Americans in the gallery.

37. *AJ* 19 January 1901. For ticket prices, see *AJ* 15 June 1901. The *NYDM* also reported "packed houses" for the New Lyceum. See 2 March 1901. See also *AJ* 20 April 1901.

38. *AJ* 31 October 1901 and 7 November 1901.

39. *AJ* 23 January 1902. For a review of opening night at the Bijou, see *AJ* 16 September 1902. For ticket prices, see the same issue. On the Bijou's reopening as a ten-cent house, see *AJ* 15 March 1909.

40. *AJ* 15 January 1901. For the dearth of vaudeville theaters in the South, see the vaudeville house listings in *NYDM* 26 March 1904, 2 December 1905, and 26 September 1906. For the difficulties in luring vaudeville performers to the South, see *AC* 16 October 1911.

41. For the history of the Orpheum, see *AJ* 8 September 1907, 13 September 1907, 17 September 1907, 8 March 1909; and *AC* 10 April 1910. For ticket prices, see the advertisement in *AJ* 6 October 1907.

42. Inman, *Inman Diary,* 1:33.

43. The information in this paragraph is drawn from Doyle, *New Men, New Cities, New South,* 39–46; Preston, *Automobile Age Atlanta,* especially 17–19, 44, 91; Brownell, *Urban Ethos in the South,* 12–13, 16; and Brownell, "Urban South," 128. The phrase "economic awakening" is Preston's. See pp. 19 and 44.

44. Bolden, "Political Structure," 75–76, 177. On the smoke problem, see *AG* 13 January 1912, 15 February 1912, 30 November 1912, 2 December 1912, and the cartoon in 15 December 1915. See also Preston, *Automobile Age Atlanta,* 188–20.

45. On the importance of the burgeoning numbers of white-collar workers to the amusement industry, see Nasaw, *Going Out,* 4–5, 40. In his autobiography, Walter McElreath recalls that the "clerks, installment furniture collectors, and money sharks" that he roomed with in 1894 spent most of their evenings hanging around the boarding house, "except on the nights when they indulged themselves in gallery seats at the Grand." Saye, ed., *Walter McElreath,* 123. Such men would

very likely have eagerly patronized the new, inexpensive amusements that cropped up after the turn of the century.

46. Quoted in May, *Screening Out the Past,* 51. Of course, the South remained a poor region, its per capita income far below the national average. So while Atlanta was growing bigger and more prosperous, there were certainly thousands of Atlantans who could not have afforded even a cheap vaudeville show. On per capita income, see Preston, *Automobile Age Atlanta,* 20.

47. *AG* 13 February 1909. The Atlanta city government also helped the cause of commercial amusements at this time by lighting streets and sidewalks in the Peachtree Street and Five Points areas in an effort to create a "Great White Way" that would attract consumers to downtown stores and theaters after dark. See Hickey, "Visibility, Politics, and Urban Development," 247–49. See also Hickey's article "'Meet Me at the Arcade,'" 5–15.

48. *AJ* 17 September 1907; *AJ* 6 June 1909.

49. For the growth of vaudeville in the South, see *AJ* 13 November 1908, 17 February 1909; and *AC* 21 January 1912.

50. See DiMeglio, *Vaudeville, U.S.A.,* 21.

51. *AG* 3 February 1910. For an example of local censorship, see *AJ* 10 March 1903. See also *AC* 9 October 1911.

52. *AG* 8 September 1908.

53. For the Forsyth Theater, see *AC* 10 April 1910; and *AJ* 12 April 1910. For an example of its popularity, see *AC* 1 January 1912. For the Lyric, which opened in 1908 as a popular-price playhouse, see *AJ* 18 September 1908. On its role as a larger house in which Keith vaudeville could be played, see *AC* 18 September 1917. On the opening of Keith's Georgia, see *AJ* 15 November 1926 and 16 November 1926. Marcus Loew's rival brand of cheaper vaudeville took up residence at the Grand Theater in 1916. See *AC* 15 October 1916 and 31 October 1916. In 1926, Loew's, Inc. leased the Grand theater block from the DeGives for sixty years for an aggregate rental of six million dollars. See *AJ* 20 December 1926. On the relationship between Keith-Albee vaudeville and that of Loew, see DiMeglio, *Vaudeville, U.S.A.,* 20.

54. As early as 1911, Atlanta's theatrical critics were reduced to expressions of relief over the unusual fact that, for the time being, the local managers of the city's three principal theaters were southerners, though none was a native Atlantan. *AC* 4 September 1911 and 9 October 1911.

55. *AJ* 5 October 1898.

56. According to one historian, "Vaudeville and burlesque were negative reflections of each other. Each defined itself in terms of what the other was not." Allen, *Horrible Prettiness,* 179. The coochee-coochee dance, or "hootchy-cootchy" dance, was premiered by the performer Little Egypt at the Chicago World's Fair of 1893 and ultimately helped to "establish the burlesque show as a separate form of

American show business." Toll, *On With the Show,* 225. The dance appeared in Georgia by 1894; a state legislator was outraged to find it being performed at the state fair in Macon. See *AJ* 12 November 1894. For local reaction to the coochee-coochee dance, see *AJ* 25 October 1895, which notes the vote of the state house of representatives to ban such "obscene" dances. Also see *AJ* 8 October 1895 for criticism of a song about the dance. For more on the Cotton States Exposition's midway, known as "Midway Heights," see Rydell, *All the World's a Fair,* 87–88, 94–97; and Martin, "Biggest Event," 91.

57. Allen discusses Thompson at length in *Horrible Prettiness.* For the establishment of American troupes, see Toll, *On With the Show,* 221.

58. Apparently the dancers drew a large male crowd. DeGive responded to the criticism by explaining that "As I have a very limited knowledge of the theatrical world . . . I can be easily imposed upon." Taylor, "From the Ashes," 279–80.

59. *AC* 18 February 1881, 20 February 1881; and *NYDM* 5 March 1881.

60. *AC* 3 November 1881. The troupe members who were arrested were male. For an advertisement and puff preceding the company's appearance, see *AC* 1 November 1881.

61. See the review in *AJ* 22 October 1896, which relates that a man stepped out before the curtain prior to the previous evening's show to tell the audience that "smoking would be permitted and that everyone could do just as he pleased—there were no ladies present—so long as he behaved himself 'to a certain extent.' The talk closed with an injunction to those in the audience to 'be men, not geese.'" There is unfortunately little evidence with which to determine precisely who made up Atlanta's burlesque audiences. In his history of the genre, Robert C. Allen claims that burlesque succeeded by appealing to the audience that the theater and vaudeville had "excorporated," namely "white working- and lower-middle-class males who continued to seek commercial entertainment apart from women and their families. This core audience was augmented by more miscellaneous single and family men on a night out with 'the boys,' farmers taking in the sights of the big city, and even a few intellectuals. . . . Burlesque offered them an aesthetic form and a place of their own." *Horrible Prettiness,* 192. A rare mention of the occupation of Atlanta's burlesque patrons occurred when the *Georgian* ran the story of two young "railroad men" arrested after they brawled with the ushers who had kicked them out of the Star Theater. *AG* 8 September 1906. A 1908 article claimed that the Star drew its audiences from Decatur Street "and its environs," suggesting a clientele of young, single men attracted to the area's rowdy nightlife. *AG* 28 September 1908.

62. *AJ* 29 December 1896, 2 February 1897, 15 November 1898, 12 December 1899; *AC* 7 January 1900.

63. *AJ* 21 February 1898 and 31 October 1898.

64. *AJ* 5 October 1898.

65. *AJ* 11 October 1898.

66. *AJ* 2 February 1897. For a similarly critical review in the *Constitution,* see 2 February 1897.

67. *AC* 31 December 1896; *AJ* 5 January 1897, 10 March 1897, and 29 March 1898.

68. This account of the trial is drawn from *AC* 18 January 1900; *AJ* 18 January 1900. For years Truehart remained the only person ever arrested and convicted for violating Atlanta's obscene dancing ordinance. *AG* 12 January 1912.

69. The Imperial was renamed the New Star in 1901. After the New Star burned, it was succeeded by the Star, which became the Lyceum in 1908. The Lyceum in turn burned in 1909. See *AJ* 4 May 1901, 4 September 1901, 29 December 1902, 28 September 1908, and 30 January 1909. For changes in ownership and management, see *AJ* 16 December 1897, 3 September 1898, 8 February 1899, 4 May 1901, 25 November 1901, 29 December 1902; *NYDM* 15 January 1900, 22 September 1900, 22 December 1900, 1 March 1902; *AG* 8 April 1908, 5 September 1908, 28 September 1908, and 2 October 1908. For references to the fortunes of the theater, see *AJ* 17 November 1900; *NYDM* 2 March 1901, 14 September 1901, 15 March 1902; and *AG* 30 January 1909.

70. *AJ* 26 October 1906 and 28 October 1906.

71. *AG* 8 October 1907; *AJ* 19 November 1907.

72. *AJ* 30 November 1908.

73. *AC* 21 September 1913. Also see the advertisement in *AC* 14 September 1913, giving ticket prices of fifteen, twenty-five, and fifty cents; stating that the Columbia was for "whites only"; and featuring a drawing of a scantily clad dancer. For a racier ad, see *AC* 26 October 1913.

74. *AC* 23 November 1913. See also *AC* 24 November 1913 and 12 December 1914.

75. *AC* 19 April 1914.

76. *AC* 13 February 1916; *AJ* 13 February 1916.

77. *AC* 2 December 1917 and 4 December 1917.

78. *AJ* 21 February 1909, 16 March 1909; and *AC* 25 September 1911. See also *AC* 13 February 1911. The Bijou later tried burlesque again, resulting at least once in police intervention and a court appearance for the manager. See *AC* 30 March 1916; *AJ* 30 March 1916, 3 April 1916, and 4 April 1916.

79. *AC* 1 September 1914 and 4 October 1914.

80. This phenomenon, which forced burlesque itself to present ever-more-daring material, is treated in Toll, *On With the Show,* 208, 225–26, 237–38; Allen, *Horrible Prettiness,* 244–46.

81. *AJ* 24 February 1920.

82. *AJ* 21 September 1920. The shimmy was a "black torso-shaking dance" that aroused controversy in New York City as well at this time when it was taken up by white dancers. See Erenberg, *Steppin' Out*, 249–50.

83. *AJ* 24 February 1909. See also *AC* 25 September 1911.

84. *AC* 29 September 1914. For a review that similarly stresses the looks of a lightly clad actress, see *AG* 12 April 1910. For a brief history of the chorus girl, see Erenberg, *Steppin' Out*, 218–21.

85. Erenberg makes a similar point in *Steppin' Out*, 85–86.

3. ATLANTA AND THE MOVIES

1. This account is drawn from Kelkres, "Forgotten First," 45–58; Musser, *Emergence of Cinema*, 103–5; *AJ Sunday Magazine* 28 August 1927, and 11 September 1932.

2. For a local study that treats many of the themes covered in this chapter in a different geographical context, see Waller, *Main Street Amusements*.

3. For the history of the vitascope, see Musser, *Emergence of Cinema*, 109–32; Nasaw, *Going Out*, 135–42.

4. *AJ* 17 November 1896, 18 November 1896; *AC* 18 November 1896; and Musser, *Emergence of Cinema*, 118–19. For other vitascope appearances in Atlanta, see *AJ* 21 November 1896 and 21 December 1896.

5. *AC* 18 November 1896; Musser, *Emergence of Cinema*, 134. An ad for the show appears in *AC* 23 November 1896.

6. *AJ* 30 December 1896, 8 December 1897, 17 December 1897, and 30 July 1898. The Spanish-American War proved something of a watershed for the young film industry. See Musser, *Emergence of Cinema*, 261; Nasaw, *Going Out*, 149–51.

7. See, for example, *AJ* 22 January 1901, 1 November 1904, 8 November 1904; and *AJ Sunday Magazine* 11 September 1932.

8. On the rise of nickelodeons, see Nasaw, *Going Out*, chap. 12; Musser, *Emergence of Cinema*, 417–29.

9. Gue, "Nickel Madness," 36.

10. *AJ Sunday Magazine* 11 September 1932. The 1907 *City Directory* lists the Electric as being at 127 Whitehall Street and as being managed by Ezekiel Wall (who shared a residence with Robert Wall, listed as a ticket seller at the Electric; and with Walter Wall, listed as picture operator at 91 Peachtree, the address of the Dreamland Theater). For other claims regarding Atlanta's first movie house, see this *Sunday Magazine* article.

11. As with other types of amusement, it has been difficult for historians to

determine precisely who made up the audiences for early motion pictures. One wave of film scholars, focusing primarily on New York City, argued that the earliest film audiences were made up predominantly of workers and immigrants, and that this aroused suspicions among middle-class guardians of morality and social order. See, for example, Sklar, *Movie-Made America,* especially 18–19, 30–32; May, *Screening Out the Past,* 55, 66. More recent scholarship, however, has shown that in other parts of the country the movies attracted a much broader audience and did not always provoke the middle-class hostility documented by Sklar. See Allen and Gomery, *Film History,* 202–7; Bowser, *Transformation of Cinema,* chap. 1; Merrit, "Nickelodeon Theaters," 83–102; Mann, "Movies Come to Middletown, 1, 74, 97–98; Fuller, "Shadowland," especially 128–37, 144–56, 302–7; and Waller, *Main Street Amusements.*

12. *AJ* 10 April 1907; Gue, "Nickel Madness," 38. Small advertisements appeared in the *Journal* during the first four months of 1907 for the Nickel Theater at 118 Marietta Street; the Little Grand, "opposite the Candler building"; the Amuse U. at 7 Viaduct Place; the Vee (no address given); the Paris Electric Theater at 100 Whitehall Street; the Twin Theater at 46 Whitehall (featuring a northside and a southside show); the Columbia at 132 Peachtree Street; the Crescent Theatre at 123 Whitehall; the Crystal (no address given); and Roll's Electric Theater at 127 Whitehall. See *AJ* 3 March 1907, 13 March 1907, 14 March 1907, 18 March 1907, 26 March 1907, 29 March 1907, 2 April 1907, 4 April 1907, 9 April 1907, and 10 April 1907. The 1907 Atlanta *City Directory* also lists, under the heading "Amusements," the Dreamland at 91 Peachtree and the Wonderland at 77 Peachtree.

13. Fuller, "Shadowland," 18–21.

14. The Chicago Projecting Company catalog is quoted in Nasaw, *Going Out,* 160–61; the Sears, Roebuck catalog is cited in Fuller, "Shadowland," 21, 111–12.

15. Fuller, "Shadowland," 18–32, 38, 41. Fuller notes (p. 19) that "As in the retail goods industry, movie theater owners were a diverse lot that included both newcomers and native-born Americans, part-time farmers, sign-painters, soda fountain and candy shop owners, families, and women."

16. Information on these men, as well as on other early theater owners such as Robert Walter, J. A. Rebb, and Alpha Fowler (who later became a Georgia state representative from Douglas County), can be found in the Atlanta city directories of 1903, 1904, 1905, 1907, 1908, 1909, 1910, 1912, 1916, and 1918; and in *AJ Sunday Magazine* 28 August 1927 and 11 September 1932. The reference to Oldknow being an ex-councilman and poolroom owner is from Deaton, "James G. Woodward," 16. For the information cited on Posey's amusement company, see *AG* 5 March 1909. At one point the son of Atlanta's chief of police ran a movie house, the Crystal Theater on Viaduct Way. *AG* 5 March 1909.

17. *The Moving Picture World*, 7 August 1915; *AC* 26 February 1911. The *Constitution* claimed that the Vaudette's capacity made it not only the largest movie house in Atlanta aside from the Bijou (which also staged vaudeville), but that it was the largest in the South as well. For an interior photo of the new theater, see *AC* 24 September 1911. The Vaudette was closed in 1924 and became a part of J. M. High's department store. *AJ* 11 January 1924. Another businessman who entered movie exhibition as a sideline was Leonidas J. Daniel, who ran the Daniel Brothers Clothing Company. He was elected first president of the Atlanta Amusement Association, an apparently short-lived organization founded in 1907 to promote the interests of the city's electric theater owners. See *AJ* 10 April 1907; and the 1907 Atlanta *City Directory*.

18. *AJ* 10 April 1907; *AJ* 5 September 1909 and 4 April 1909. See also *AG* 1 September 1908. Later, in an effort to attract a more upscale audience, Atlanta's larger theaters employed "orchestras" to play classical and operatic music. See *AC* 25 July 1915. Other movie houses sought a wider appeal. Thus, the Alpha Theater featured Mrs. Frank Pearson, "Atlanta's most popular singer," who performed a mixture of "popular and classic songs." *AC* 5 September 1915. In 1922 the editor of the *Journal* praised the movie theaters for giving "incalculable thousands . . . their first taste of real music." *AJ* 6 January 1922.

19. *AJ Sunday Magazine* 11 September 1932 and 28 August 1927.

20. *AJ* 1 May 1907; *AG* 1 May 1907. See also *AG* 28 March 1907. In 1909, Atlanta's movie projector operators took advantage of such an ordinance requiring that all projectionists be licensed by the city. The operators went on strike, counting on the fact that under this law they could not easily be replaced. See *AJ* 20 September 1909 and 21 September 1909. Perhaps due to the city council's efforts, there were no major movie theater conflagrations during the 1910s and 1920s, although there were occasional small fires. See *AJ* 6 February 1910; *AC* 25 October 1911.

21. *AJ* 19 August 1909. The dangers of fire and disease associated with the nickelodeons were national concerns. See Nasaw, *Going Out*, 178–83, 185.

22. *AJ* 1 May 1907; *AG* 1 May 1907.

23. *AG* 23 May 1907.

24. *AC* 9 February 1911. For another noise controversy, this time arising on Decatur Street, see *AG* 3 April 1912. For complaints about noisy nickelodeons in other cities, see Nasaw, *Going Out*, 162.

25. *AJ* 4 April 1909.

26. *AG* 19 September 1907 and 23 September 1907.

27. *AG* 7 May 1909. For other examples of the public-spirited use of movie houses and films, see *AG* 4 December 1911, 5 December 1911, 13 March 1912, 13 May 1912, 13 September 1912, and 5 November 1912.

28. On the bid for a more "respectable" audience, see Merrit, "Nickelodeon Theaters"; Nasaw, *Going Out,* chap. 14; and Gue, "Nickel Madness," 39–40.

29. *AG* 3 March 1911 and 4 February 1910.

30. *AJ* 17 February 1909, 18 April 1909, 22 April 1909; Gue, "Nickel Madness," 40–41.

31. *AJ Sunday Magazine* 28 August 1927. The author of this article claims that the Alcazar had the first movie-house pipe organ in the country. A New York representative of the Pathé Frère film company praised the Alcazar's equipment as equal "to the finest motion picture palaces on Broadway, in New York, or in the Champs Elysees." *AG* 24 February 1911.

32. *AJ* 2 May 1909 and 7 September 1909. The Howard Amusement Company later bought the Posey Theater, built by O. D. Posey in 1908, and changed the name to the Savoy, making it a five-cent counterpart to the ten-cent Alcazar. *AJ* 3 January 1908 and 4 February 1910. For a description of the renovated theater, see *AC* 26 February 1911.

33. *AJ* 11 February 1910 and 14 February 1910.

34. *AJ* 25 February 1910; *AG* 11 February 1910, 16 February 1910, and 17 February 1910. Oldknow argued that he needed to sell two thousand tickets a day at five cents apiece to meet expenses and that 75 percent of his customers were women and children. Despite complaints, the hat amendment stood.

35. This was not an unusual stance at the time among middle-class reformers, many of whom hoped to harness the power of the moving picture to reinstill waning Victorian values in the viewing public. See May, *Screening Out the Past,* 52–53 and chap. 4.

36. This account is drawn from *AC* 13 November 1910. The women also reported that poor ventilation was a problem in almost all Atlanta movie theaters. Another committee, drawn from the College Women's Association, conducted a survey of the Gate City's movie houses at about the same time and drew similar conclusions regarding both theater ventilation and the quality of the films being shown, which the committee found "on the whole to be excellent." *AJ* 21 November 1910. For a euphoric view of the educational potential of movies, see *AG* 13 February 1913.

37. On the Men and Religion Forward Movement, see *AG* 25 September 1911. On the EMA, see *AG* 2 December 1912.

38. For example, see *AG* 26 September 1912 and 7 October 1912.

39. *AC* 24 September 1912. See also *AC* 24 September 1912, 26 September 1912, 23 November 1912; and *AJ* 19 November 1909.

40. *AG* 23 September 1912.

41. *AG* 24 September 1912 and 25 September 1912.

42. For more on this issue of class and gender in Progressive Era Atlanta, see Hickey, "Visibility, Politics, and Urban Development," especially chap. 5; as well as Hickey's articles "'Meet Me at the Arcade,'" 5-15; and "Waging War," 775-880. See also Judson, "Cultivating Citizenship," 17-30; MacLean, "Leo Frank Case Reconsidered," 917-45.

43. Sabbatarian battles were common at this time. In 1911, for example, the mayor of New York City vetoed an ordinance that would have closed movie theaters on Sundays. See Nasaw, *Going Out,* 179-80. Closer to Atlanta, the question of Sunday movies in Birmingham represented "the most controversial public issue in the city during the first few decades of the twentieth century." Brownell, "Urban South Comes of Age," 148. See also Brownell, *Urban Ethos in the South,* 113-14.

44. *AG* 14 May 1912 and 15 May 1912.

45. *AG* 28 October 1912, 11 December 1912, and 10 January 1913.

46. *AG* 8 March 1913; *AC* 22 March 1913. On Wesley Memorial's use of movies, see *AJ Sunday Magazine* 11 January 1914. In May of 1914, the International Bible Students Association held free screenings of biblical films, with "phonograph accompaniment," at the Atlanta Theater. *AJ Sunday Magazine* 3 May 1914. For more on the use of movies by churches across the country during this period, see Fuller, "Shadowland," 181-89.

47. *AC* 10 March 1913. For a local review of the film, see *AC* 6 March 1913.

48. *AC* 16 March 1913. The donations received on this Sunday were to go to the families of two local firemen killed in action.

49. *AG* 17 March 1913. See also the letter to the editor in *AG* 24 March 1913. Atlanta's 1913 population was reportedly 173,713. See *AC* 18 January 1915, cited in Dinnerstein, *Leo Frank Case,* 180 n.

50. *AC* 17 March 1913.

51. *AC* 22 March 1913, 23 March 1913, 24 March 1913; *AG* 24 March 1913.

52. *AG* 14 March 1913 and 18 March 1913.

53. *AC* 16 March 1913.

54. *AC* 13 March 1913; *AG* 15 March 1913. For letters to the editor echoing Woodward's sentiments, see *AG* 24 March 1913, 12 April 1913, and 21 April 1913.

55. *AC* 17 March 1913 and 18 March 1913. See also *AC* 19 March 1913.

56. *AC* 18 March 1913; *AG* 17 March 1913. See also the editorial in the same issue of *AG,* and the letter to the editor in 24 March 1913.

57. *AC* 17 March 1913 and 19 March 1913. See also *AC* 19 March 1913 for a reference to a supposed appeal to the theater managers by "laboring people" for charitable contributions for the construction of a church.

58. *The Journal of Labor,* 21 March 1913; *AG* 21 March 1913.

59. *AC* 16 March 1913, 17 March 1913, 18 March 1913, 22 March 1913, 23 March

1913, and 24 March 1913. There were a few exceptions to clerical opposition to Sunday films. See *AG* 14 March 1913, 21 March 1913, and 22 March 1913. Atlanta merchant Frederic Paxon argued that the churches themselves should do more to provide wholesome entertainment on Sundays. *AG* 20 March 1913.

60. Here again there were exceptions. Methodist bishop Warren Candler blasted movies as "the sorriest of diversions." *AG* 18 March 1913. For letters to the editor supporting the clergy's position, see *AG* 17 March 1913, 27 March 1913, and 1 April 1913.

61. *AG* 19 March 1913 and 24 March 1913.

62. *AC* 22 March 1913. See also EMA Minutes, Atlanta History Center/Archives, box 3, folder 8, p. 120. For similar statements of clerical position, see *AC* 17 March 1913 and 24 March 1913. For threats of a boycott of movie houses by churchgoers, see *AC* 17 March 1913, 18 March 1913, and 22 March 1913.

63. *AC* 22 March 1913; *AG* 20 March 1913, and 22 March 1913. See also *AC* 1 April 1913. For a repudiation by Jewish leaders of the claim that Jews supported the EMA position, see *AC* 25 March 1913; *AG* 25 March 1913. For other references to the "southern" Sabbath, see *AG* 24 March 1913 and 6 April 1913.

64. *AG* 29 March 1913 and 31 March 1913.

65. *AC* 28 March 1913, 29 March 1913, 2 April 1913; *AG* 17 March 1913, 18 March 1913, 19 March 1913, 20 March 1913, 26 March 1913, 1 April 1913, 2 April 1913, 3 April 1913; *AJ* 22 April 1913; and Atlanta History Center/Archives, *Council Minutes, City of Atlanta,* vol. 24, 2. Some Atlanta theaters continued to open sporadically on Sundays, to the great chagrin of local religious leaders but with the apparent tacit approval of the city attorney so long as the proceeds went to charity. See, for example, the investigative report filed by John Manget in the Men and Religion Forward Movement Ledger, Atlanta History Center Library/Archives, MS 686, box 7, 18 January 1915. For other references to Sunday movie openings and efforts to halt them, see EMA Minutes, Atlanta History Center Library/Archives, MS 686, box 3, folder 9, pp. 5, 55–56; *AC* 21 May 1915, 22 September 1915, 4 February 1916, 8 February 1916, 18 February 1916, 21 February 1916, 29 February 1916, 17 October 1916, 14 January 1917, 16 March 1917, 3 April 1917, 17 March 1918, 18 March 1918, 20 March 1918; *AJ* 21 December 1920, and 28 February 1927.

66. There were exceptions: movie theaters were occasionally allowed to open on Sundays for explicitly charitable purposes. See *AG* 19 December 1915. Vaudeville houses also sometimes gave Sunday performances for charity. Ibid. On the opening of theaters during the Depression, see Kuhn, Joye, and West, eds., *Living Atlanta,* 325. For an account of a battle over Sunday movies that played out differently, see Waller, *Main Street Amusements,* 128–35. In Lexington, Kentucky, the movies won the day, and the conflict was pitched more as a battle over middle-

class women and children in the Sunday audiences than over working-class movie patrons.

67. Such investigations included the one by elite women described above. In another example, the recorder went to a movie house in 1911 to judge the fitness of a prize-fight movie but determined that the film was legal. *AG* 16 September 1911. The Georgia Federation of Women's Clubs boasted in 1912 of having used informal means to persuade Georgia theater owners to show more uplifting movies. *AG* 23 October 1912.

68. Bowser, *Transformation of Cinema*, 49–52; *AG* 25 March 1913.

69. Ibid., 51–52. For fears in Atlanta that the national board's efforts were not adequate to protect the city from immoral films, see *AC* 17 September 1911.

70. *AG* 15 March 1913; *AG* 19 March 1913.

71. *AG* 19 March 1913. Laing refers in this article to an incident that is reported in *AG* 12 October 1912. For another call for censorship, see the letter to the editor in *AG* 21 April 1913.

72. *AJ* 6 May 1913. The trustees were also empowered to visit vaudeville theaters and demand the removal of unacceptable acts. See also *AJ* 3 September 1913. Elsewhere in the South, Ft. Worth established a board of censorship in 1911, Nashville in 1914, and Memphis began censoring pictures in 1921. Brownell, "Urban South Comes of Age," 148–49.

73. Of the censorship board members whose names appear in the local newspapers, two—W. L. Percy and J. W. Mason—were business executives; two others—J. W. Peacock and E. L. Harling—were in real estate; and four—Harrison Jones, Arthur Heyman, Willis M. Everett, and W. W. Gaines—were lawyers. One—A. W. Farlinger—was a city councilman. See the city directories of 1913 and 1916. For the board members' view of themselves and of their mission, see *AJ Sunday Magazine* 31 May 1914, 31 October 1915, and 13 August 1916.

74. Bowser, *Transformation of Cinema*, 51.

75. The previous four paragraphs are based on *AJ Sunday Magazine* 31 May 1914, 31 October 1915, and 13 August 1916.

76. *AC* 21 January 1917.

77. *AC* 1 August 1915; Dittmer, *Black Georgia*, 183–84. Dittmer notes that numerous unsuspecting white Augustans appeared in this film, which they were told would be an innocuous picture entitled *The New Governor*. This synopsis of the picture is based on those in *The Moving Picture World*, 24 July 1915; Hanson, ed., *American Film Institute*, vol. f1, 658. On the portrayal of blacks during this period, see Bowser, *Transformation of Cinema*, 10. It is unclear from newspaper coverage whether or not the board successfully prevented a private screening of the film, but apparently *The Nigger* did not show in any local theater for public view. Many

blacks, convinced that the film's message was a racist one, opposed screening of *The Nigger* in northern cities. But others, including W. E. B. Du Bois, felt that the film indicted white racism. See Cripps, *Slow Fade to Black,* 65–66.

78. *AC* 17 October 1913. The manager's claim that the local censorship board had already cleared *The Vampire Dance* may indicate that the board had approved the film without seeing it, perhaps because it had received the approval of the national board.

79. Wade, *Fiery Cross,* 140–48. The reborn KKK received a charter from the state of Georgia just as *The Birth of a Nation* arrived in Atlanta. According to Wade, William J. Simmons, a local organizer of fraternal societies and a fraternal insurance salesman—as well as a former minister, Spanish-American War veteran, and onetime history teacher—had dreamed of a revived Klan since 1913. See also Jackson, *Ku Klux Klan in the City,* chap. 1. The Leo Frank–Mary Phagan murder case, along with the release of *The Birth of a Nation,* helped Simmons to achieve his goal. He viewed the movie over and over again during its Atlanta run, perhaps while intoxicated. See ibid., 4, 257 n. Regarding the opening-night parade outside the Atlanta Theater, Wade notes, "It was an enormously effective stunt, and Simmons would repeat it at other premiers, making 'The Birth of a Nation' a hapless gimmick in Klan publicity." For the ceremony atop Stone Mountain at which Simmons initiated the new Klan, see ibid., 4; *AJ* 28 November 1915. For a local advertisement for the new Klan, see *AC* 9 December 1915. For an admission by an Atlanta reviewer that the film aroused racial prejudice among its viewers, see *AC* 28 November 1916.

80. *AC* 4 October 1915; *AC* 24 October 1915. On response to the film elsewhere, see Cripps, *Slow Fade to Black,* chap. 2; Campbell, *Celluloid South,* 59–60; and Waller, *Main Street Amusements,* 151–60. *The Birth of a Nation* premiered in Los Angeles on February 8, 1915; in New York City on March 3; in Boston on April 9; and in Chicago on June 4. Ibid., 50. The film also showed in other southern cities en route to Atlanta. See the *AC* article cited above.

81. Men and Religion Forward Movement Ledger, Atlanta History Center Library/Archives, MS 686, box 7, p. 112. Representatives of EMA and the Men and Religion Forward Movement visited local newspaper editors to seek their aid in suppressing the film. Ibid., 113.

82. *AC* 2 December 1915. In late November a large advertisement, taking up almost two pages, appeared in the *Journal* extolling Griffith's film. The ad was made up of excerpts from positive reviews of *The Birth of a Nation* that had appeared in other southern newspapers. See *AJ* 28 November 1915. That same day a similar ad appeared in the *Georgian,* but this time it included a copy of a telegram sent to Homer George by Mayor Wyndham Mayo of Norfolk, Virginia, in which

the mayor stated that in his city the film had caused "No disturbance of any kind" and that "it would have been a mistake" for him to interfere with what had been described to him as a "most wonderful product." *AG* 28 November 1915.

83. *AC* 8 February 1914; *AJ Sunday Magazine* 7 March 1915. By the mid teens Atlanta had close to twenty theaters presenting motion pictures for whites. See the advertisements in *AC* 30 November 1915 and 2 July 1916. For attendance information for other years, see *AC* 7 November 1912, "Georgia Compendium" supplement; *AJ* 20 April 1913; *AJ Sunday Magazine* 31 August 1919, and 7 October 1923.

84. The ticket prices are in an advertisement in *AC* 25 December 1915. On Griffith's aiming the film at the socially elite, see Campbell, *Celluloid South,* 58. As a filmmaker, Griffith believed he had a mission to elevate humankind. See Lary May's discussion of Griffith in *Screening Out the Past,* chap. 4.

85. *AG* 10 December 1915, 12 December 1915, 19 December 1915; *AC* 13 December 1915, and 19 December 1915. The *Constitution* article of December 13 claims that people were coming to Atlanta from up to two hundred miles away to see the film. When *The Birth of a Nation* returned to Atlanta a year later, luckless patrons were once more turned away from the packed theater, and management again held over the film. See *AC* 26 November 1916, 28 November 1916, and 7 December 1916. *The Birth of a Nation* went on to make dozens of appearances in the Gate City. Nationally, the film grossed thirteen million dollars, more than any film prior to 1934. May, *Screening Out the Past,* 67.

86. Reviews are quoted from *AG* 7 December 1915; *AC* 7 December 1915; and *AJ* 7 December 1915. In exuberantly positive terms, the *Georgian* took the unusual step of editorially urging its readers to see the film. *AG* 7 December 1915. Also see McIntosh's review of the picture upon its return to Atlanta in 1916. *AC* 28 November 1916.

87. *AC* 14 December 1915. See also *AG* 14 December 1915. A special "Confederate Matinee" was also given by manager Homer George to honor the United Daughters of the Confederacy. See *AG* 17 December 1915 and 19 December 1915.

88. *AC* 18 December 1915.

89. Indeed, newspaper advertisements played to and promised just this sort of pride. One ad promised Atlantans that "YOU WILL FEEL the hot surging patriotism that drove your grandfather to don a suit of gray" as well as experience "a glow of undying pride that they're YOUR stars and YOUR bars." *AG* 12 December 1915.

90. For more on the intimate relationship between Atlanta and the Klan, see Jackson, *Ku Klux Klan in the City,* chap. 3.

91. *AC* 9 May 1915. See also James B. Nevin's "Saturday Evening" column in *AG* 11 December 1915. By early 1914 DeGive's Grand Theater had given up the cause

of legitimate drama and begun to screen motion pictures. *AC* 9 August 1914, 1 November 1914, and 6 December 1914. The Atlanta Theater, the Grand's successor as Atlanta's premier showcase for the legitimate drama, had also begun showing first-run films in addition to the normal stage fare by the summer of 1914, more than a year before *The Birth of a Nation* arrived. *AC* 30 August 1914.

92. *AJ Sunday Magazine* 12 September 1920, 20 March 1921, 21 January 1923, and 25 November 1923. For responses to Candler, see *AJ* 8 April 1921 and 16 April 1921. For more on Candler's views, see Bauman, *Warren Akin Candler,* 203–4.

93. For information on the financial transactions that ultimately centered control of Atlanta's movie theaters in New York City, see *AC* 5 November 1919, 17 November 1919; *AJ* 2 January 1923, 3 January 1923, 7 January 1923, and 16 March 1924. To give one example, the Vaudette Theater, built by the Evins brothers and discussed above, eventually came under the control of the Famous-Players-Lasky Corporation. See *AJ* 11 January 1924.

94. For coverage of Atlanta's moving picture "palaces," see *AJ* 14 November 1920, 14 December 1920, 3 July 1921, 5 July 1921, and 26 June 1927. For the improbable history of Atlanta's Fox Theatre, which opened on Christmas Day of 1929, see Bryant, "Yaarab Temple and the Fox Theatre," 5–22. For a broader perspective on the picture-palace phenomenon, see May, *Screening Out the Past,* chap. 6; Nasaw, *Going Out,* chap. 16.

95. For an example of white Atlanta's continued preoccupation with race, see coverage of the controversy over presentation of the film *Uncle Tom's Cabin* in *AJ* 13 August 1928 and 15 August 1928. Lynn Watson-Powers discusses the "branch-office town" moniker in "Atlanta Spirit," 86–87.

4. MUSIC AND THE WHITE ATLANTA ELITE

1. Doyle, *New Men,* 19, 38, 87–103, 144, 189–223. An important part of what historian Richard J. Hopkins has referred to as the "status race" in Atlanta involved the continual movement of better-off residents to newer neighborhoods ever more distant from downtown. See Hopkins, "Status, Mobility, and the Dimensions of Change," 227. For more on suburbanization in the Gate City, see Preston, *Automobile Age Atlanta,* 47, 76–89, 92–94. For more on the postwar rise of a new southern ruling class, see Woodward, *Origins of the New South;* Carlton, *Mill and Town in South Carolina.*

2. Inman, *Inman Diary,* 1:36.

3. Many contemporaries and historians have commented on Atlanta's unparalleled boosterism. Blaine A. Brownell refers to the "pervasive braggadocio" of the 'Atlanta Spirit'" and observes, "Of all the forms of southern urban boosterism, the

'Atlanta Spirit' reigned supreme, 'inextinguishable and all-pervading,' the envy of smaller towns and cities throughout the region, the prototype of intense civic patriotism." Brownell, *Urban Ethos in the South,* 13, 137. See also p. 94. See also Roth, *Matronage,* 18–19; Preston, *Automobile Age Atlanta,* chap. 1; Brownell and Goldfield, "City in Southern History," 10–11; and Rabinowitz, "Continuity and Change," 97. For more on the Atlanta spirit, see Garofalo, "Atlanta Spirit," 34–44; Watson-Powers, "Atlanta Spirit," 83–93. For other examples of potshots taken at Atlanta by her rivals, see *Urban Ethos in the South,* 82, 150; Davis, *Henry Grady's New South,* 43.

4. For a testy response to a northerner's remark about the South's needing "civilizing," see the editorial in *AG* 21 February 1907.

5. Cited in *AC* 28 January 1900.

6. Levine, *Highbrow/Lowbrow,* especially chap. 2; Broyles, *Music of the Highest Class.*

7. Dizikes, *Opera in America,* 214–222. The quote is on p. 284.

8. Doyle, *New Men,* 90–94, 220–23.

9. *AC* 4 October 1891, 11 March 1894; *AJ* 15 March 1886; and *AG* 30 March 1907. See also *AJ* 31 March 1904; *AJ* 30 November 1901.

10. For Atlanta's musical history before 1880, see Orr, *Alfredo Barili,* chap. 2.

11. The entire "Committee of Patronage" is listed in an advertisement in *AJ* 9 October 1883.

12. Orr, *Alfredo Barili,* 117. For more on the festival, see pp. 114–18. For a full program, see *AC* 15 November 1883.

13. *AC* 14 November 1883 and 11 November 1883. See the former for boldface sentences scattered across a page encouraging potential ticket buyers. One line reads, "A revelation in music will be the great Musical Festival on Thursday night. Secure your seats at once." Characteristically, the Atlanta press had a long history of exaggerating the Gate City's love for music. See Gough, "Entertainment in Atlanta," 74–75, 77, 81.

14. *AJ* 1 November 1883; *AC* 17 November 1883. Tickets remained relatively expensive, however, with the parquet and dress circle seats selling for $2.00, and balcony seats for $1.50 and $1.00. For references to the size of the festival's audiences, see the coverage in *AC* 17 November 1883.

15. *AC* 10 March 1888. Critics blamed the festival's financial problems on Doepp's extravagance and on high ticket prices. See ibid.; *AC* 8 March 1888.

16. The chorus members apparently reconsidered their decision later. *AC* 13 November 1883, 14 November 1883, and 15 November 1883.

17. *AC* 16 November 1883.

18. *AC* 17 November 1883.

19. *AJ* 19 November 1883. The satirical review is in *AJ* 17 November 1883.

20. *AC* 16 November 1883 (see also *AC* 17 November 1883); *AJ* 16 November 1883.

21. *AC* 17 November 1883.

22. *AJ* 19 November 1883; *AJ* 16 November 1883; *AC* 17 November 1883. This enthusiastic response for popular music presented at classical performances was an Atlanta tradition. See Gough, "Entertainment in Atlanta," 7.

23. *AC* 6 March 1888. Sternberg's invitation stated, "All ladies and gentlemen in possession of voices and able to read music (if only fairly) are welcome." The description of Sternberg is from *AC* 24 May 1888.

24. *AC* 6 March 1888 and 24 May 1888.

25. *AC* 24 May 1888 and 8 March 1888; *AC* 25 May 1888. For Sternberg's reply to the letter, see *AC* 9 March 1888. For another letter questioning the viability of the festival, see *AC* 10 March 1888.

26. *AC* 25 May 1888.

27. *AC* 24 May 1888.

28. *AC* 25 May 1888.

29. *AC* 26 May 1888.

30. *AJ* 17 November 1883.

31. *AJ* 12 May 1893; *NYDM* 20 May 1893, 27 January 1900, and 28 January 1905.

32. *AJ* 11 March 1902 and 12 March 1902. Years after the fact, *Constitution* music critic Louise Dooly blamed the poor showing on an earlier experience that Atlanta had had with the French company, but the reviewer quoted here gave no indication of such an explanation. *AC* 4 February 1912.

33. *AJ* 18 February 1903. Only about three hundred people attended Kocian's performance. *AJ* 19 February 1903. For another example of a disappointing audience turnout, see coverage of the 1907 May-June Music Festival in *AG* 3 June 1907. Ticket prices for classical and operatic concerts in Atlanta were often relatively high, and this likely played a role in holding down attendance for some shows. For the Metropolitan Opera Company's poorly attended 1905 performance of *Parsifal,* for example, ticket prices ranged from two to ten dollars. *AC* 19 March 1905. Referring to the prices charged for classical productions in Atlanta, local musician J. Lewis Browne wrote, "For the most part concerts, even when participated in by artists of the first rank, are too expensive by far." *AJ* 28 March 1905.

34. *AJ* 15 May 1885. A *Constitution* correspondent lamented six years later, "While it is true that Atlanta has a number of music-loving people, the proportion is not as large as it should be in a city of our size." *AC* 30 March 1891. A small group of prominent Atlantans and local musicians periodically formed organizations during this period with the aim of presenting classical music performed by

local or imported talent. The Atlanta Musical Association, for example, was created in 1885 to produce classical concerts. But such organizations were frequently riven by competing factions, and in any event their productions attracted small audiences. For information on and references to such local associations, see *AC* 18 October 1885, 12 November 1887, 4 February 1912; *AJ* 6 January 1886, 11 March 1886, 12 March 1886, 14 May 1886, 2 July 1886, 30 November 1886, 13 February 1899, 24 February 1899, 4 March 1899, 15 April 1899, 18 November 1901, 15 November 1903, 1 March 1904; and Orr, *Alfredo Barili,* 155, 165, 202, 207.

35. *AC* 30 April 1905; *AC* 11 November 1900; *AC* 19 February 1905. For more Dooly diatribes, see Orr, *Alfredo Barili,* 190–92.

36. *NYDM* 23 February 1889; Dizikes, *Opera in America,* 264–68. The quote is from p. 264. Atlantans supported "light" opera as well. See, for example, *AC* 24 April 1892 and 3 July 1892.

37. *AJ* 14 February 1902. See also 18 April 1895, 20 April 1895, 2 December 1895, and 3 February 1899. Other bandleaders who offered similarly mixed programs were also warmly received in Atlanta. See the review of the appearance by the Patrick Gilmore band in *AC* 20 April 1888, and that of the Frederick Innes band in *AJ* 21 February 1898. On the other hand, the *Georgian* reported that a 1908 concert by Ignace Paderewski created great excitement but was only "enjoyed throughout by a few," the reason being that "Quite a little that he played was so cruelly classical that it shot over the heads of common people." *AG* 24 March 1908.

38. *AC* 15 January 1905; *AC* 5 March 1905; *AJ* 16 February 1899; *AJ* 30 October 1901. For an earlier expression of similar attitudes, see George Leonard Chaney's letter to the editor in *AC* 2 November 1888.

39. *AC* 12 February 1891; *AJ* 20 April 1899; *AJ* 12 March 1898. The second article notes that when a reporter asked Thomas, upon his arrival in Atlanta, whether he would play any popular music, the bandmaster replied, "We couldn't play 'Dixie' if we tried. We play orchestral music only. Our training has all been to playing artistic orchestral music." The article also claimed that the local guarantors for Thomas's performances sought to distance themselves from Burke's comments. See also *AJ* 15 April 1899. Earlier in 1899, an Atlantan had suggested that the audience for a Moriz Rosenthal concert had been small because the Polish pianist "would not give a selection from 'Hot Time In The Old Town.'" *AJ* 24 February 1899.

40. *AC* 4 March 1900.

41. *AJ* 14 December 1903.

42. For allusions to this criticism of Atlanta and to the role that culture might play in negating it, see *AC* 30 September 1900; *AJ* 7 December 1903, and 31 March 1904.

43. *AC* 16 September 1900. For another reference to businessmen's support of classical music, see *AJ* 18 February 1907.

44. *AC* 4 February 1912; *AJ Sunday Magazine* 18 March 1928, p.11. For articles treating the Met's 1901 appearance, see *AJ* 5 October 1901, 15 October 1901, 18 October 1901, 25 October 1901, 26 October 1901, 29 October 1901, and 30 October 1901.

45. The race riot of 1906 inspired city leaders to construct the new armory. See *AJ* 7 October 1906. The building was located in downtown Atlanta at the corner of Courtland and Gilmer Streets. For a map showing its location, see *AJ* 1 February 1907. The cost of the auditorium-armory is cited in T. Eldrin Burton, "Music Festival of 1909," 199.

46. *AJ* 2 May 1909.

47. The executive committee of the festival was made up of the auditorium building committee and the music committee. The former was composed of John E. Murphy, chairman; Colonel W. L. Peel; James R. Gray; General Clifford L. Anderson; and R. S. Wessels. The members of the music committee were Victor Lamar Smith, chairman; George W. Wilkins; Ben Lee Crew; C. B. Bidwell; R. S. Wessels; V. H. Kreigshaber; W. Woods White; and H. W. Barnes, who served as the festival's musical director. *AJ* 2 May 1909.

48. Burton, "Music Festival of 1909," 199–201; *AJ* 15 February 1909. On the pursuit and signing of Caruso, see *AJ* 28 February 1909 and 1 March 1909.

49. *AJ* 14 February 1909 and 1 March 1909; *AJ* 28 February 1909; *AJ* 23 February 1909.

50. *AJ* 14 February 1909 and 28 February 1909. For an example of criticism of Atlanta from other cities, see the reprint of an editorial from the *Americus Times-Recorder* in *AJ* 1 May 1909. This editorial lauds the festival and allows that Atlanta is a "great city," but nevertheless notes with understatement, "We all feel inclined at times to criticize some phases of its spirit."

51. *AJ* 15 February 1909; *AJ* 2 May 1909; *AJ* 16 February 1909. To promote interest in the festival and to ease the fears of potential guarantors, the *Journal* ran a series of articles from towns across Georgia, in which locally prominent citizens spoke of their excitement regarding the festival and their determination to attend. See, for example, *AJ* 18 February 1909 and 19 February 1909.

52. *AJ* 23 February 1909; *AJ* 28 February 1909.

53. For a list of guarantors, see *AJ* 4 May 1909.

54. Tickets sold for $2.00 and $3.00 for individual evening performances, and for $1.00 and $2.00 for the two matinees. *AJ* 28 March 1909. Season tickets for all five performances sold for $5.00 and $7.50, with season tickets for four-seat boxes going for $40.00, and six-seat boxes for $60.00. *AJ* 15 March 1909. Thus the *Jour-*

nal was clearly targeting an affluent audience when it made statements such as that appearing in a mid-March editorial: "The low price at which season tickets are being sold makes it possible for every music-lover to enjoy this form of music. . . . The box seats are also cheap." 16 March 1909. For pleas that Atlantans take advantage of these "low" prices and purchase tickets—pleas that continued up until the eve of the festival—see *AJ* 17 February 1909, 10 March 1909, 28 March 1909, 31 March 1909, 9 April 1909, and 2 May 1909. In what would become familiar practice over the years, the *Journal* couched its worried call for ticket buying in terms of concern for the beleaguered patron: "People who are aware of what the rush will be during the days immediately [preceding] the festival . . . are seizing the opportunity now and supplying themselves with seats." 28 March 1909.

55. *AJ* 2 May 1909; *AJ* 4 May 1909; *AJ* 15 April 1909. For a reference to Chicago, see *AJ* 2 May 1909.

56. As the *Journal* dramatically described it, Atlanta found itself following Caruso's withdrawal "standing on the verge of a critical moment, reaching into the greatest opera houses of the world, steeled with determination, careless of money, stirred to an ambition the like of which she has never known before, reaching forth to secure as added attractions to the Southern Music festival the greatest vocal artists on the continent. And she succeeded; succeeded more brilliantly than the most hopeful could have dreamed." 11 April 1909. See also *AJ* 14 April 1909.

57. *AJ* 5 May 1909.

58. On the audience's enthusiastic reception of Geraldine Farrar's rendition of "Annie Laurie," see *AJ* 5 May 1909. For the reception of "Suwanee River" and "The Last Rose of Summer," see *AJ* 7 May 1909. For more applauding of popular favorites, see *AJ* 7 May 1909.

59. *AJ* 5 May 1909; *AJ* 24 February 1909. Elsewhere the *Journal* noted in a typical observation that the festival would "bring together . . . the most highly representative people of the section, those who appreciate music and the finer things of life." 4 May 1909.

60. See *AJ* 5 May 1909, 6 May 1909, and 7 May 1909.

61. *AJ* 5 May 1909. Another reception was held at the Capital City Club following the festival's conclusion. See *AJ* 7 May 1909.

62. *AJ* 5 May 1909; *AJ* 7 May 1909; *AJ* 30 May 1909. The *Constitution* claimed that twenty-five thousand people paid a total of $32,500 to attend the festival. *AC* 7 May 1909 and 8 May 1909; cited in Burton, "Music Festival of 1909," 200. The Macon correspondent is Leila Richardson Legg. As she puts it elsewhere in her column, "What remedy for low thoughts and unholy desires? Give the lofty and pure. How take away the taste for the 'yellow-backed novel,' obscene and degrading songs and plays? By giving only what is grandest, purest and best."

63. Burton, "Music Festival of 1909," 201–2; Eaton, *Opera Caravan,* 145–46.

64. The New York Metropolitan Opera Company visited Atlanta annually from 1910 through 1930 (with the exception of 1918, when the visit was canceled due to the war). The Met also came to Atlanta in 1939, 1940, 1941, and 1942, and in 1947 resumed annual visits that continued until 1986. For several years from the mid teens through the early 1920s, Atlanta was the only American city in which the Met played outside of Brooklyn and the company's outpost in Philadelphia. For complete programs and appearance dates for Met performances from 1883 through 1956, including the company's stops in Atlanta, see Eaton, *Opera Caravan,* 188– 388. The *AJ Sunday Magazine* of 18 March 1928 also lists every Met performance in Atlanta from 1910 through 1927. Newspaper coverage of Atlanta's Opera Week was generally quite extensive, so complete listing of relevant citations is impracticable. But for examples of newspapers imploring Atlantans to buy tickets or underwrite guarantees, see *AC* 17 January 1915, 19 March 1915, 25 April 1915, 16 April 1916, 20 April 1919; and *AJ* 12 October 1909. For comparisons of Atlanta with northern cities and assertions that Atlanta was the cultural center of the South, see *AC* 27 March 1910, 1 May 1910, 30 April 1911, 21 April 1912, 1 May 1914, 3 May 1914, 7 March 1915, 19 March 1915, 2 May 1915, 27 April 1919; *AG* 29 March 1910, 7 May 1910; *AJ* 28 March 1910, 29 March 1910, 3 May 1910, 4 May 1910, 5 May 1910, and 1 May 1920. See newspaper coverage for just about any year for evidence of the disproportionate attention given to society as compared to aesthetics. Eldin Burton notes that during the Met's appearances in Atlanta, "many columns—even pages— were devoted to minute descriptions of the costumes worn by the ladies, the number of these mentioned growing so numerous as to warrant, in some editions, an alphabetical index by last name." Burton, "Metropolitan Opera in Atlanta," 49– 50. For just such a listing, see *AG* 25 April 1912. As for each year surpassing the year before, as late as 1928 the *Journal* editorialized, "Trite as it is to say that the season which opens tomorrow evening promises to excel all others, truth requires that it be said again." 22 April 1928. See also *AJ* 23 April 1922 and 29 April 1923.

65. *AC* 24 April 1916; *AC* 24 April 1919; *AJ* 2 May 1920.

66. For attendance figures, see Burton, "Metropolitan Opera in Atlanta," 37– 61; Burton, "Metropolitan in Atlanta," Part 2, 146–69. By 1922 the Metropolitan Company demanded a guarantee of $110,000, a figure that receipts for Opera Week of that year failed to match; thus the guarantors were called upon to make up the deficit. *AJ* 30 April 1922. On the broad popular appeal of Caruso and Farrar, see Dizikes, *Opera in America,* 397–404. On the large crowds drawn by these two stars, see Burton, "Metropolitan Opera in Atlanta," Parts 1 and 2; *AC* 23 April 1913, 27 April 1913, 2 May 1914, 25 April 1916, 29 April 1916; and *AJ* 5 May 1910. Ticket prices alone would have severely restricted the number of Atlantans who could

afford to attend Metropolitan productions. In 1911, for example, prices ranged from $1.00 for a single performance and $4.00 for a season ticket for the last two rows of the gallery, to $5.00 for a single performance and $16.00 for a season ticket for the first twenty-four rows on the floor. *AC* 6 February 1911. For 1913 and 1914, single-seat prices still ran from $1.00 to $5.00, with season tickets ranging from $7.00 to $21.00. Boxes sold for $30.00 to $45.00 for a single performance, and $126.00 to $189.00 for a season. *AC* 8 March 1914. By 1920, single-performance tickets ranged from $3.50 to $6.00; season tickets cost $17.50 to $30.00; and boxes cost $34.00 to $51.00 for a single show, and $190.00 to $285.00 for a season. *AJ* 22 February 1920.

67. *AC* 1 May 1911 and 30 April 1916; Burton, "Metropolitan Opera in Atlanta," Part 2, pp. 167–9. Total attendance for the Opera Week of 1916 was reported to be 36,850. When the near-record crowd that came to see Enrico Caruso in *Martha* is subtracted, that leaves 30,050 patrons for six operas.

68. *AC* 22 December 1895; *The Concert Goer* is quoted in *AC* 17 June 1900; Candler is quoted in Bauman, *Warren Akin Candler,* 172.

69. *AC* 29 March 1916; *AG* 30 April 1916, cited in Burton, "Metropolitan Opera in Atlanta," Part 2, p. 166.

70. *AC* 1 April 1917; *AG* 26 April 1912, cited in Burton, "Metropolitan Opera in Atlanta," 50. For other references to audience behavior during this period, see *AC* 30 April 1911, 18 April 1912, 23 April 1912, 3 May 1914, 30 April 1916, 25 March 1917, and 25 April 1919. See also the cartoons in *AC* 23 April 1913; *AJ* 24 April 1923. For more complaints, see *AG* 28 April 1911.

71. Local newspaperman Frank Daniel once discussed the reputation of the Metropolitan stars: "That singers drank too much was a superstition here. Matter of fact, all the drinking was in the audience." Quoted in Eaton, *Opera Caravan,* 147.

72. *AC* 15 June 1913; *AC* 4 February 1912 (Ben Lee Crew makes the same point in *AC* 28 February 1913); *AC* 12 February 1914; *AC* 6 October 1916.

73. *AJ* 10 December 1910; *NYDM* 21 December 1910. An advertisement for the Abbott company appears in *AC* 30 November 1910.

74. *AC* 24 October 1913. N. Lee Orr perceptively points out that the once-a-year nature of the Metropolitan's appearances may have been essential to its success in Atlanta. "Opera performances, limited to a few weeks a year, comfortably fit into the busy business schedule of the city. . . . When the opera troupes finally arrived everyone could dress up, endure the opera, enjoy the glittering parties, and thus discharge their 'artistic' obligations for the rest of the year. Having done so, the city was spared the financial expense of constructing houses for operas, symphonies, and ballet companies, as well as the enormous costs involved with supporting

them." *Alfredo Barili,* 182. For other references to Atlanta's failure to support higher music, see *AC* 4 September 1910, 21 March 1912, 13 December 1913, 15 December 1913, 28 March 1915, 11 June 1916; *AG* 4 November 1910, 5 November 1910, 6 March 1912, and 7 December 1912. For a few exceptions, see *AC* 29 April 1919; *AJ Sunday Magazine* 7 March 1920; and *AJ* 10 March 1928.

75. *AC* 31 July 1910. The quote is from *AC* 7 August 1910.

76. *AC* 28 August 1910.

77. *AJ* 28 October 1910; *AC* 30 September 1912, 3 October 1912, 7 October 1912, 21 October 1912, 28 February 1918, 7 March 1918, 8 March 1918, and 9 March 1918. Starnes at one point gamely insisted that there was "more natural desire for real music in Atlanta, relatively speaking, than in any other city of the nation." Unfortunately, he confessed, this musical passion was, for the time being, "latent." *AG* 12 February 1913.

78. *AC* 23 February 1914.

79. *AC* 16 December 1916, 30 November 1917, 28 November 1919; *AJ* 28 September 1919; and *AJ Sunday Magazine* 7 March 1920. The *Constitution* noted that McCormack's 1919 Atlanta audience was "composed of people from every walk of life," because the tenor appealed to everyone, from "the musician wont to scoff at the singing of so-called popular ballads to the newsboys on the streets." The article went on, "A minstrel he is of a kind, a sweet singer of the folk songs of his own race." *AC* 28 November 1919.

80. *AJ* 21 February 1922. It was perhaps recognition of such audience preferences that led the *Georgian* to warn in a 1912 editorial promoting a concert by the Atlanta Philharmonic Orchestra, "The Philharmonic will not play rag-time, for there is plenty of rag-time at any five-cent theater." *AG* 11 December 1912.

81. *AJ Sunday Magazine* 7 March 1920; Street, *American Adventures,* 364–65.

82. *AC* 29 March 1916. Atlanta routinely boasted of the Met's visits in its promotional literature. See, for example, Industrial Bureau, Atlanta Chamber of Commerce, *Key to Atlanta* (n.p., [1928?]).

83. For complaint about Atlanta's exaltation of money over culture, see the comments of Emma Boyd in *AJ Sunday Magazine* 5 December 1915.

84. *AJ* 9 May 1909. A photograph of "Society Beauties" arriving at the auditorium, aided by a liveried but anonymous African American chauffeur, appears on page 134. The need for such display is suggested in the fact that, as late as the 1920s, after decades of elite self-promotion, an Atlantan disconsolately noted of the Gate City's social leaders that "you can go down the list and find dozens of houses now prominent in social life, the family trees of which sprouted out of a whitewash bucket, a second-hand furniture shop, or a grist mill, and in one well-known case, out of a peddler's pack." Quoted in Brownell, "Urban South Comes of Age," 137.

5. THE BLACK ELITE IN A JIM CROW CITY

1. Dittmer, *Black Georgia*, 26-27.

2. Porter, "Black Atlanta," 106-7, 111-15; Bolden, "Political Structure," 75-76, 177; and James Michael Russell, *Atlanta, 1847-1890*, 156, 215-31. For deplorable black school conditions in Atlanta, see Rouse, *Lugenia Burns Hope*, 74-79; Neverdon-Morton, *Afro-American Women*, 158; Leroy Davis, *Clashing of the Soul*, 218-20; and Dittmer, *Black Georgia*, 146-48. For segregated hospital conditions, which may have contributed to the death of W. E. B. Du Bois's young son, see Leroy Davis, *Clashing of the Soul*, 123-24. For protest over the lack of a black public library, see ibid., 145-47. For black poverty and slum conditions, see Neverdon-Morton, *Afro-American Women*, 139; Rouse, *Lugenia Burns Hope*, 57-64; Preston, *Automobile Age Atlanta*, 106; and Brownell, *Urban Ethos in the South*, 114-15. Beginning in 1913, the Atlanta city government employed residential segregation ordinances to keep blacks out of white neighborhoods. See Dittmer, *Black Georgia*, 13-14; Preston, *Automobile Age Atlanta*, 96, 102, 111-12, 157; Brownell, *Urban Ethos in the South*, 183-84; and Neverdon-Morton, *Afro-American Women*, 140. The 1920s witnessed an increase in home ownership by middle-class blacks on Atlanta's West Side, an area officially designated for African Americans by the city in 1922. Preston, *Automobile Age Atlanta*, 103-11. On Atlanta's high arrest rate and the disproportionate arrests of black Atlantans, see Dittmer, *Black Georgia*, 13.

3. More than twenty thousand arrests of blacks for idleness took place in the 1920s alone. Brownell, *Urban Ethos in the South*, 165-66. See also Watts, "Police in Atlanta," 171-72; Dorsey, "'To Build Our Lives Together,'" 204. In 1911 Atlanta's police commissioner advocated hunger as a useful means of combating black vagrancy. *AG* 13 October 1911. Even ostensibly race-neutral laws such as prohibition were frequently seen by their proponents as being aimed at curbing black behavior. Brownell, "Urban South Comes of Age," 149-50. As for the behavior of the police themselves, in 1881 a black journalist offered, "We have lived in Atlanta twenty-seven years, and we have heard the lash sounding from the cabins of the slaves, poured on by their masters; but we have never seen a meaner set of low down cut throats, scrapes and murderers than the city of Atlanta has to protect the peace." Quoted in Watts, "Police in Atlanta," 172.

4. Dittmer, *Black Georgia*, chap. 1, especially pp. 20-21; Porter, "Black Atlanta," 8, 15, 24-25; and Jerry John Thornberry, "Development of Black Atlanta," 279-80. Atlanta's black population did not always take police oppression lying down. See *AG* 27 January 1913.

5. *AG* 20 October 1910.

6. *AG* 4 January 1911.

7. For the sickening conditions of the city stockade to which Broyles routinely

sent most of those he convicted, see the exposés in *AG* December 1909–January 1910. Though perfectly willing to imprison black children in the stockade, Broyles showed more mercy to younger whites, noting that to incarcerate white children in this facility "would mean their complete ruin." Quoted in Dittmer, *Black Georgia,* 89.

8. *AG* 20 April 1913.

9. This account is drawn from Benjamin J. Davis, *Communist Councilman From Harlem,* 40–42. For photographs taken inside the recorder's court, see *AJ Sunday Magazine* 16 February 1913.

10. *AC* 1 April 1900.

11. *AC* 18 February 1900. For other examples of matinee columns, see *AC* 1 July 1900, 28 March 1915; *AJ* 29 March 1900; *AJ Sunday Magazine* 9 May 1915, 13 June 1915, 14 January 1917, 18 March 1917, and 22 April 1917. A white minister heavily fined by Broyles for an automobile infraction claimed in a heated sermon that such newspaper columns had gone to the judge's head. As reported by the *Georgian,* "Another feature of his attack on the recorder was to the effect that the latter has been spoiled by a certain newspaper reporter who has ascribed all kinds of witty sayings and remarks to him, which he could never have made, but which he has taken as a mark to be lived up to." *AG* 20 March 1911.

12. *AC* 8 May 1910. For another long editorial and the ministers' response, see *AC* 29 May 1910. For a typical use of the Bible in justification of white notions of black inferiority, see *AG* 10 April 1909.

13. Leroy Davis, *Clashing of the Soul,* 292.

14. Kuhn, Joye, and West, *Living Atlanta,* 12. Many whites viewed blacks as "natural" criminals. A "humorous" *Georgian* account of a razor fight at a supposedly "select" black social event concluded that "blood will tell and habit and instinct are stronger than ethical codes." *AG* 22 May 1909.

15. For the idea that Reconstruction had ruined southern race relations, see Rev. John White's column in *AG* 30 March 1907.

16. *AC* 30 December 1900; Baker, *Following the Color Line,* 44, 28. *Constitution* columnist Bill Arp (the pen name of Charles Henry Smith) likewise declaimed against what he termed "the alarming degeneracy of the negro." According to his biographer, Arp attributed this decline to "education, the corrupting influence of cities, northern agitation, decreased dependence upon the white race, and, above all else, the rejection of what Arp saw as the proper race relations." Parker, "Bill Arp," 228.

17. *AG* 4 April 1907. The supply of "old-time mammies" had supposedly dwindled so by 1915 that one white Atlantan developed an impersonation through which she "educated" local youth. See *AG* 2 December 1915.

18. *AG* 16 September 1912. At least one prominent white Atlantan believed that changing times and racial conditions had diminished the white race as well. Rev. John White wrote, "If you were to ask me what loss of the Southern white man through the past forty years was the sorest, I would without doubt say that it was the loss of [a] consciousness of supremacy conceived in moral obligation." *AG* 30 March 1907.

19. *AC* 9 February 1890. Sarge Plunkett was the pen name of A. M. Wier. See *AC* 15 May 1890.

20. *AG* 30 March 1910 and 16 April 1910.

21. *AG* 3 March 1909.

22. *AC* 4 April 1890 and 22 March 1891. The quote is from *AC* 21 November 1891.

23. *AJ Sunday Magazine* 3 April 1921.

24. *AC* 29 November 1894.

25. *AJ* 22 July 1923. For a characteristic appraisal of jazz, see the review of the Paul Whiteman concert in *AJ* 16 January 1925, in which the white bandleader is credited with making "an honest woman of jazz." In 1922 the Savannah, Georgia, city council went so far as to ban "All forms of jazz dancing, as well as all forms of dancing to jazz music or syncopated music." *AC* 18 April 1922.

26. For a preview of one of the Grand's cakewalks, see *AC* 6 May 1894.

27. Thornberry, "Development of Black Atlanta," 283–84; *AC* 28 September 1883.

28. Thornberry, "Development of Black Atlanta," 284; *AC* 27 September 1881, and 28 September 1881. Thornberry speculates that the initial failure of the *Constitution* to mention Burke's attempt to enter the white section of the Opera House may indicate that the police simply fabricated the charge "to justify the beating they gave him." Pp. 284–85 n.

29. This account is based on Thornberry, "Development of Black Atlanta," 285; *AC* 24 February 1883, 28 September 1883, and 16 October 1883. The *New York Dramatic Mirror* also carried reports of the Moore-DeGive controversy. See 3 March 1883, 6 October 1883, and 27 October 1883.

30. *AJ* 12 March 1885.

31. *Voice of the Negro* 2, no. 2 (Nov. 1905): 836–37, 871–72; and 3, no. 11 (Nov. 1906): 465, 471–79.

32. *AI* 4 November 1905.

33. *AI* 11 November 1905.

34. *AI* 4 November 1905. This article was apparently supplied to the *Independent* by the *Atlanta Daily News,* a white newspaper. This account is also cited, and slightly exaggerated, in Dittmer, *Black Georgia,* 66–67. Tera W. Hunter takes the

embellishment a step further by having blacks in the gallery hurl soda bottles on whites seated downstairs. *To Joy My Freedom,* 161.

35. This paragraph is based on Leroy Davis, *Clashing of the Soul,* especially 180–82, 293–94, 295–96; Rouse, *Lugenia Burns Hope,* 7–8, 132; Dorsey, "'To Build Our Lives Together,'" especially 120–21, 230–44; Gatewood, *Aristocrats of Color,* especially x, 23, 28, 92, 285, 290–92, 348, chap. 7; Higginbotham, *Righteous Discontent,* 20–21, 42–46, 204–11; Gaines, *Uplifting the Race,* especially 1–17; Judson, "Cultivating Citizenship," 17–28; and Rolinson, "Community and Leadership," 7, 12–14. Some scholars note a shifting of black leadership, particularly following World War I, to a rising entrepreneurial class. See Meier and Lewis, "History of the Negro Upper Class," 128–39; Rolinson, "Community and Leadership," 8; Gatewood, *Aristocrats of Color,* epilogue; and Brownell, *Urban Ethos in the South,* 14, 37. Such changes, however, did not significantly alter the overall black social and cultural strategy described here. The groups designated by the notoriously imprecise terms "elite" and "middle class" are roughly equivalent in the local black population, given that the middle class was relatively small and that there were so few African Americans who could be remotely termed "upper class." So I will generally use the terms interchangeably, though "elite" will tend to describe those African Americans who self-consciously saw themselves as social and political leaders. See Dittmer, *Black Georgia,* 15 n., 59.

36. Gaines, *Uplifting the Race,* 4.

37. For a biography of a onetime Atlantan whose life was immersed in the cultural and class tensions present in the black community at this time, see Harris, *Rise of Gospel Blues.* See also Bastin, *Red River Blues,* 209–11.

38. *AI* 8 May 1909. For a statement of Davis's Washingtonian principles, see *AG* 2 January 1907. He appears to have altered his stance by 1928, when he editorially denounced segregation as "wrong as a principle and unwise in policy." *AI* 17 May 1928.

39. For more on Davis and his aversion to what he saw as a light-skinned elite, see Davis, *Clashing of the Soul,* 157–58; Gatewood, *Aristocrats of Color,* 158, 292; and Dittmer, *Black Georgia,* 61–62.

40. *AI* 29 November 1919; *AI* 21 February 1924; *AI* 31 March 1921. Davis could be extremely critical of white behavior as well, when he felt the case warranted. See, for example, his scathing denunciation of the exclusion of blacks from the Great Southern Music Festival of 1909. *AI* 8 May 1909.

41. See, for example, *AI* 10 February 1906 and 9 August 1923.

42. *AI* 3 February 1921. See also 13 December 1919. John Dittmer notes that many leading black Atlantans would not allow the *Independent* into their homes. *Black Georgia,* 164.

43. Porter, "Black Atlanta," 131.

44. *AI* 16 May 1914; 23 May 1914; and Dittmer, *Black Georgia*, 57–58. The Odd Fellows Auditorium also offered some live entertainment. See, for example, *AI* 24 October 1914, 5 December 1914, 13 November 1915, and 4 May 1922. For more on the Odd Fellows and Auburn Avenue, see Grant, *Way It Was in the South*, 249, 262; Dittmer, *Black Georgia*, 57–58.

45. For Black Patti's appearances at Turner's Tabernacle, see *AJ* 8 October 1902, 22 September 1903, 12 December 1909; *AI* 19 March 1904; and *AC* 5 November 1905. For Billy Kersands, see *AI* 20 February 1904; *AJ* 20 March 1909. For the Whitman Sisters, see *AI* 6 February 1909, 11 September 1909, 18 September 1909, and 15 October 1910. For the Fisk Jubilee Singers, see *AI* 20 August 1904. The appearance at the Tabernacle of Richard's and Pringle's Famous Georgia Minstrels in 1910 featured a noon street parade and an evening concert in front of the theater. *AI* 12 March 1910. Whites sometimes attended performances at the Tabernacle. See *AJ* 22 September 1903; Sampson, *Ghost Walks*, 261–62.

46. *AC* 23 April 1905. See also *AI* 5 May 1906 and 15 March 1919.

47. Randy Gue notes that "the first verifiable motion picture theater catering exclusively to African Americans" opened on Decatur Street in 1907. "Nickel Madness," 37–38. The Luna Park Theater advertised itself in 1910 as "The only house in the city under colored management," listing Walter Holmes as manager. *AI* 5 November 1910. P. A. Thomas had been listed as manager the previous April. *AI* 9 April 1910. Another black proprietor was William H. Estes, co-owner of the Moving Picture Theater at 219 Auburn Avenue. *AI* 7 December 1912. Charles S. Cox, a black undertaker, purchased the Princess Theater in 1913. *AI* 13 December 1913, p. 5. The first black theater listed in an Atlanta *City Directory* was the Gayoso, at 14 Central Avenue, in 1908. In a "partial list" of U.S. theaters "owned and managed by Blacks," the *Indianapolis Freeman* of 16 July 1910 listed five Atlanta venues: the Arcade, at 81 Decatur Street; the Luna Park, at 99 Decatur Street; the Airdome, on Central Avenue near Union Station; the Paradise, at 170 Peters Street; the Famous, at 124 Decatur Street (J. B. Kelley, manager); and the Palm Garden, at 43 Glenwood Avenue (W. G. Gray, manager). Cited in Sampson, *Ghost Walks*, 519–21. The Atlanta *City Directory* of 1910 lists only two black theaters: the Luna Park, and the Peekin, at 86 Decatur Street. Other theaters advertised in Atlanta newspapers over the years that catered to black audiences, while not necessarily being owned by blacks, include the Central, at 16 Central Avenue (*AC* 22 January 1911); the Washington, at 127 Decatur Street (*AI* 2 December 1911); the Majestic, on Auburn Avenue between Butler Street and Piedmont Avenue (*AI* 16 May 1914); the Dixie, at 127 Decatur Street between Piedmont Avenue and Crandal Street (1913 *City Directory; AI* 16 May 1914); the Herndon (*AI* 14 August 1915); the Standard, at 162 Auburn Avenue (*AI* 13 May 1916); the Universal, on Houston Street (*AI* 4 September 1914); the Crystal (*AI* 16 October 1924); and the Royal (later the 91) at

91 Decatur Street (*AI* 4 December 1915). In addition, the *Journal* in 1929 reported a melee involving blacks that broke out at the Strand Theater, on Decatur Street. *AJ* 25 January 1929.

48. See, for example, the advertisements in *AI* 25 April 1914, 14 August 1915, 5 August 1916, 15 July 1916, 30 September 1916, and 16 October 1924. For an exception, see the 1916 ad for the Standard Theater, which promised a "5-Reel Drama acted and produced by colored people." *AI* 7 October 1916.

49. In fact, the case remained a source of potential turmoil through the 1950s and beyond. See Dinnerstein, *Leo Frank Case*, 157–58, 220 n; Wiggins, *Fiddlin' Georgia Crazy*, 33. The police force might have been particularly sensitive about its reputation at this time, given recent allegations of corruption and collusion with criminals. See Brownell, *Urban Ethos in the South*, 108–9.

50. *AJ* 2 February 1923 and 4 February 1923. *The Gunsaulus Mystery*, originally titled *Within Our Gates*, was produced by black filmmaker Oscar Micheaux and debuted in January 1920. In Chicago, blacks as well as whites opposed the film on the grounds that it might spark a race riot. See Cripps, *Slow Fade to Black*, 183–91.

51. *AI* 26 July 1923. See also *AI* 19 July 1923.

52. Some black Atlantans defended their patronage of white theaters by pointing out that these venues could provide vaudeville while the auditorium (later the Paramount) could not. See *AI* 18 January 1923 and 14 February 1924.

53. *AC* 31 July 1910; *AI* 4 February 1911; Gatewood, *Aristocrats of Color*, 291.

54. In addition to Proctor, who served as secretary, the Atlanta Colored Music Festival Association included A. F. Herndon, president; J. B. Greenwood, vice president; C. C. Cater, treasurer; and L. G. Watts, auditor. *AI* 6 August 1910 and 4 February 1911.

55. Proctor, *Between Black and White*, 107–8; *AC* 31 July 1910. An advertisement for the 1911 festival promised that through their examples the performers and audiences would "vindicate" the "honor" of black "womanhood," which, the ad claimed, was then under attack in Atlanta, presumably from racist whites. *AI* 29 July 1911.

56. *AC* 31 July 1910. The festivals were held in the Municipal Auditorium-Armory through 1913, then moved to the Congregational Church in 1914, after which they were apparently discontinued. *AC* 5 July 1914.

57. *AC* 11 August 1912, 16 August 1912, and 29 June 1913.

58. *AI* 23 July 1910 and 30 July 1910 (see also 22 July 1911); *AC* 31 July 1910. Similarities between the black and white festivals did not extend to ticket prices, which ranged from twenty-five cents to one dollar for the black festival.

59. *AC* 6 August 1911; *AC* 29 June 1913.

60. Cited in *AI* 13 August 1910. See also *AC* 23 July 1911. The *Independent* was less consistent in its praise. A 1911 editorial lauded the festival, arguing, "This

entertainment is proving a great developer of the possibilities of the race along the lines of music, art and song." *AI* 5 August 1911. Just a year later, however, the *Independent*'s support of the festival had become a casualty of Ben Davis's growing rivalry with H. H. Proctor. Davis asserted in an editorial that Proctor was really interested only in benefiting himself and his own church. Specifically, Davis charged that Proctor robbed other congregations of talent to use in the Colored Festival chorus, but that all of the festival proceeds went to Proctor's church, thus sowing division within the black community. *AI* 31 August 1912.

61. *AI* 4 February 1911 (see also *AC* 11 February 1911); *AC* 1 December 1917; *AC* 2 July 1918.

62. Benjamin J. Davis, *Communist Councilman from Harlem*, 35.

6. ATLANTA AS A REGIONAL MUSIC CENTER

1. Hitchcock and Sadie, eds., *Dictionary of American Music*, 88–89.

2. *AJ* 18 November 1886. For DeGive's condescendingly noncommittal response, see *AJ* 27 December 1886.

3. For an extended discussion of elite interaction with southern mountaineers and of the type of elite cultural ambivalence I discuss here, see Whisnant, *All That Is Native and Fine*, especially 43–44, 55, 110.

4. *AC* 26 January 1919; *AC* 12 November 1911; *AC* 15 November 1905. To aid the mountain folk at Rabun Gap, the Daughters of the Confederacy built a school that was supported by the Georgia Federation of Women's Clubs until the Federation constructed its own school at Tallulah. Isma Dooly describes the efforts in *AC* 25 June 1911. For more mountaineer stereotypes, see *AJ* 24 May 1902.

5. Whisnant discusses such views of culture—and the utter confidence with which they were held—in *All That Is Native and Fine*, especially 48, 172, 228–29, 233.

6. A 1909 *Journal* editorial entitled "Educate the Mountain Folk" claimed that the mountaineers were "the purest strain of the sturdy colonists who sought freedom on this side of the ocean," but went on to lament that "in their ignorance and isolation they present a situation which is nothing short of pathetic." *AJ* 20 April 1909.

7. *AJ Sunday Magazine* 25 December 1927. The nation as a whole harbored similarly dichotomous views of white southerners. See Malone, *Singing Cowboys*, 3, 71-74, 76-77.

8. For fuller treatment of Atlanta's fiddling conventions, see Burrison, "Fiddlers in the Alley," 59–87; Daniel, *Pickin' on Peachtree*, chap. 1. See also Wiggins, *Fiddlin' Georgia Crazy*, especially 46–60.

9. *AC* 30 March 1913; Daniel, *Pickin' on Peachtree*, 17–19.

10. For representative articles on the conventions that stress these themes, see *AC* 15 February 1914, 18 February 1914, 24 January 1916, 27 January 1916, 26 February 1918, 2 March 1918, and 20 November 1919. The quotes are from *AC* 2 April 1913 and 2 February 1915. For more on the nature of the newspaper coverage, see Wiggins, *Fiddlin' Georgia Crazy,* 46–47, 51–52.

11. *AC* 16 November 1919. For other references to the breadth of the conventions' appeal in general and their attraction to high society in particular, see *AC* 15 February 1914, 19 February 1914, 23 January 1916, 27 January 1916, 1 March 1918, 2 March 1918, 7 March 1919; *AJ Sunday Magazine* 21 June 1914, and 14 November 1920. Convention audiences could sometimes rival in size the crowds that turned out for the Metropolitan Opera Company. See *AC* 29 January 1916, 2 March 1918, and 20 April 1920.

12. The description of early-twentieth-century Atlanta as "largely a town of rural refugees" is from Burrison, "Fiddlers in the Alley," cited in Daniel, *Pickin' on Peachtree,* 4. Leonard Dinnerstein writes, "In 1913 the people of Atlanta, many of whom had been coaxed from the countryside with the promise of a better life, rose up and attacked a symbol of the new industrial culture which had reneged on its promise. Leo Frank was chosen to stand trial for the tribulations of a changing society." *Leo Frank Case,* viii–ix.

13. *AC* 7 March 1919.

14. *AC* 1 April 1913; cited in Burrison, "Fiddlers in the Alley," 65. See also *AG* 14 March 1913.

15. Quoted in Burrison, "Fiddlers in the Alley," 65. See also Wiggins, *Fiddlin' Georgia Crazy,* 58–59.

16. *AC* 1 March 1918.

17. *AJ Sunday Magazine* 14 November 1920.

18. On the "civil religion" of the New South, see Wilson, *Baptized in Blood.* See also Woodward, *Origins of the New South,* especially chap. 6.

19. "City of Atlanta," 43; *AC* 12 May 1895. The latter article goes on to note about the accordionist, "It is a fact peculiar, but true, that this blind darky is supported more generously than other beggars in more fashionable centers."

20. Porter, "Black Atlanta," 268–69; Kuhn, Joye, and West, *Living Atlanta,* 177; and Harris, *Rise of Gospel Blues,* 39–45. As a teenager, William "Piano Red" Perryman got his professional start playing at these affairs. He recalled, "You couldn't make a livin' playin' them rent parties, but you could have a good time. You could make a little something extra, eat and drink all you want, and hang around with the other musicians." Quoted in Barlow, *"Looking Up at Down,"* 194.

21. Hunter, *To 'Joy My Freedom,* chap. 8.

22. Quoted in Wiggins, *Fiddlin' Georgia Crazy,* 24. See also Porter, "Black At-

lanta," 257–59. For white condemnation of Decatur Street, see *AG* 17 April 1909 and 28 April 1909.

23. The comparison to Beale Street and the song lyrics are from Barlow, *"Looking Up at Down,"* 192–93.

24. For more on the TOBA, see Barlow, *"Looking Up at Down,"* 120–22.

25. Albertson, *Bessie,* 27–28.

26. Barlow, *"Looking Up at Down,"* 164–79; Harris, *Rise of Gospel Blues,* 42, 83–84; Levine, *Black Culture,* 226; Spottswood, "Country Girls," 90–91, 99–100.

27. Interview with Rev. S. C. Usher, quoted in Porter, "Black Atlanta," 259.

28. Homer E. Eichlenberger told Michael Leroy Porter in a 1973 interview that the 81 "was a place where the high and the low, the saint and the sinner went." Porter, "Black Atlanta," 260. By 1923, the 81 had begun offering "Midnight Frolics" at which the black performers played to all-white audiences. See, for example, *AJ* 23 November 1923.

29. Quoted in Kuhn, *Living Atlanta,* 37.

30. Ibid., 260.

31. *AC* 9 September 1915 and 27 September 1915. See also 4 October 1915. Ben Davis had in 1905 opposed a proposed reopening of the dance halls following their original closing in 1903, referring to them as "hovels of immorality and dens of crime." *AI* 25 February 1905. But he found Proctor's 1915 statements to be too much, arguing angrily that they justified the riot and confirmed white racist stereotypes. *AI* 2 October 1915.

32. *AI* 15 October 1925 (see also Levine, *Black Culture,* 293–94); *AI* 25 August 1927. For praise of black spirituals by Hall, see *AI* 11 August 1927. For more on the class division among blacks so far as it involved music, see Harris, *Rise of Gospel Blues,* introduction and chaps. 1 and 2; Dittmer, *Black Georgia,* 67–68.

33. *AC* 20 July 1881. The author of this article was touring the city, looking specifically for blacks who had no association with whites. While finding these men and women to be predictably degenerate, he did encounter at the same time many blacks and black business establishments that, being not so isolated from white influence, appeared to him to be moral and respectable.

34. *AJ* 25 November 1899. The Atlanta police often allowed black dance halls and "dives" to remain open just so they could round up criminals there. Watts, "Police in Atlanta," 173. For examples of newspaper campaigning against dance halls, see *AC* 21 February 1905, 9 September 1915, 27 September 1915, and 4 October 1915. It was not just the alleged propensity for crime among dance hall patrons that troubled Atlanta whites; exaggerated stereotypes of sexually predatory black males filled whites with dread as well. Like H. H. Proctor, whites feared that

blacks lusted after white women and that this lust was further fueled in the licentious atmosphere of Decatur Street.

35. For advertisements for these Midnight Frolics, see *AJ* 23 November 1923, 5 February 1924, 5 December 1924, 26 March 1925, and 29 March 1925.

36. *AC* 1 November 1916.

37. Daniel, *Pickin' on Peachtree*, 56–57, 102; Green, "Hillbilly Music," 209; *AJ* 8 October 1922. For typical *Journal* boasting about WSB's range, see 5 September 1922.

38. Daniel, *Pickin' on Peachtree*, 92–93.

39. Wiggins, *Fiddlin' Georgia Crazy*, 69, 80–81; Daniel, *Pickin' on Peachtree*, 48–89. For examples of this early mixing of performers and styles, see *AJ* 31 December 1924 and 12 July 1925.

40. *AJ* 5 February 1924, 6 February 1924, 19 December 1928, 9 March 1923, and 13 March 1923. The Cornfield Chorus had been previously known to Atlantans as the Royal American Glee Club. *AJ* 10 March 1923. Through the mid 1920s, the *Journal* contains numerous references to blacks performing on WSB.

41. Burrison, "Fiddlers in the Alley," 59; Daniel, *Pickin' on Peachtree*, 4, 18, 82–83.

42. Daniel, *Pickin' on Peachtree*, 10–12.

43. Malone, *Singing Cowboys*, 64; Wiggins, *Fiddlin' Georgia Crazy*, 74–76; Daniel, *Pickin' on Peachtree*, 93; Green, "Hillbilly Music," 208; and Cohen, "Early Pioneers," 11–21. Daniel gives the recording date as June 14, but Wiggins in his discography claims that the session took place on June 19. Wiggins also states that despite subsequent interpretations of his famous "pluperfect awful" comment, Peer was likely more dissatisfied with technical aspects of the recordings than with Carson's performance. See p. 75. The flip side of the record was "The Old Hen Cackled and the Rooster's Going to Crow."

44. This paragraph is based on Wiggins, *Fiddlin' Georgia Crazy*, xii, chap. 2, 128–29; Burrison, "Fiddlers in the Alley," 70; Cohen, "Early Pioneers," 16–17; and Daniel, *Pickin' on Peachtree*, 87–96.

45. Burrison, "Fiddlers in the Alley," 70. See also Green, "Hillbilly Music," 209; Daniel, *Pickin' on Peachtree*, 50, 93.

46. Green, "Hillbilly Music," 208; Wiggins, *Fiddlin' Georgia Crazy*, 74–75; Burrison, "Fiddlers in the Alley," 70–72. Polk Brockman became one of the most important talent scouts in the South. See Barlow, *"Looking Up At Down,"* 132–33, 194–95; Bastin, *Red River Blues*, 36–37.

47. Daniel, *Pickin' on Peachtree*, 69. The quote, cited in Daniel, is from Charles K. Wolfe, *Tennessee Strings* (Knoxville: University of Tennessee Press, 1977), 43. For more on local Atlanta artists, see Daniel, especially chap. 4; Cohen, "Early Pioneers," 27–34.

48. The ideas in this paragraph are derived from Levine, *Black Culture,* chap. 4; Bastin, *Red River Blues,* 19-24; and Harris, *Rise of Gospel Blues,* 26-30, 59-60.

49. Bastin, *Red River Blues,* 102; Barlow, *"Looking Up at Down,"* 194.

50. Bastin, *Red River Blues,* 38-43, chaps. 7 and 8; Barlow, *"Looking Up at Down,"* 128-32; Lowry, "Atlanta Black Sound," 88-113. This description of the blues and its sometimes therapeutic role should not be taken to imply that working-class blacks and the blues singers they heard made up a unified, happy family. There was stratification within the Atlanta blues scene as there is among any complex group of people. City musicians, especially those who could read music, often saw themselves as a cut above musicians from the hinterland, and there were divisions and factions even among these rural artists themselves. See Harris, *Rise of Gospel Blues,* 39-40, 42-43; Bastin, *Red River Blues,* 88, 209-11. See also Higginbotham, *Righteous Discontent,* 204.

51. Barlow, *"Looking Up at Down,"* 114-15, 123-24; Charters, "Workin' on the Building," 25; Levine, *Black Culture,* 228, 230-32. Pete Lowry credits Atlanta with having "fixed" the blues as the dominant black musical form of the period. See "Atlanta Black Sound," 89-90.

52. This paragraph is based on biographical information in Bastin, *Red River Blues,* 128-40; Lowry, "Atlanta Black Sound," 97-98; and Barlow, *"Looking Up at Down,"* 92-94.

53. Quoted in Levine, *Black Culture,* 251.

54. Both songs are quoted in Bastin, *Red River Blues,* 66.

55. William Barlow describes the blues as "the oral literature of the black masses" in *"Looking Up at Down,"* 117-18.

56. Cohen, "Skillet Lickers," 229-44; Cohen, "Early Pioneers," 27-34; and Burrison, "Fiddlers in the Alley," 73-80.

57. On the realism of black and white working-class music, see Levine, *Black Culture,* 270-74.

58. Ivey, "Border Crossing"; Perry, "Digging Country's Roots."

59. This account is drawn from Wolfe, "A Whiter Shade of Blue," 233-37.

60. Daniel, *Pickin' on Peachtree,* 65-66.

61. Ibid., 66.

62. Barlow, *"Looking Up at Down,"* 133. Barlow also points out that the Depression swamped the "thriving night-life subculture along Decatur Street" and that by the 1930s the "Atlanta blues community had lost too much talent" through deaths, imprisonment, and abandonment of blues careers. See p. 198.

63. For a book-length treatment of the influence of southern musical forms, see Malone, *Southern Music, American Music.*

⊰ BIBLIOGRAPHY ⊱

MANUSCRIPT SOURCES

Evangelical Ministers' Association Minutes. Atlanta History Center Library/Archives. Atlanta, Georgia.

Men and Religion Forward Movement Ledger. Atlanta History Center Library/Archives. Atlanta, Georgia.

Council Minutes, City of Atlanta. Atlanta History Center Library/Archives. Atlanta, Georgia.

NEWSPAPERS

Atlanta Constitution, 1880–1930
Atlanta Georgian, 1906–15
Atlanta Independent, 1903–30
Atlanta Journal, 1883–1930
Journal of Labor, 1913
Moving Picture World, 1907–15
New York Dramatic Mirror, 1880–1911
New York Times, 1887, 1910

OTHER SOURCES

Albertson, Chris. *Bessie.* New York: Stein and Day, 1972.

Allen, Robert C. *Horrible Prettiness: Burlesque and American Culture.* Chapel Hill: University of North Carolina Press, 1991.

Allen, Robert C., and Douglas Gomery. *Film History: Theory and Practice.* New York: McGraw-Hill, 1985.

Ayers, Edward L. *The Promise of the New South: Life after Reconstruction.* New York: Oxford University Press, 1992.

Baker, Ray Stannard. *Following the Color Line: American Negro Citizenship in the Progressive Era.* 1908. Reprint, New York: Harper and Row, 1964.

Barber, Max J. "The Atlanta Tragedy." *Voice of the Negro* 3 (November 1906): 471–79.

Barlow, William. *"Looking Up at Down": The Emergence of Blues Culture.* Philadelphia: Temple University Press, 1989.

Bastin, Bruce. *Red River Blues: The Blues Tradition in the Southeast.* Urbana: University of Illinois Press, 1986.

Bauman, Mark K. *Warren Akin Candler: The Conservative as Idealist.* Metuchen, N.J.: Scarecrow Press, 1981.

Bernheim, Alfred L. *The Business of the Theatre: An Economic History of the American Theatre, 1750–1932.* 1932. Reprint, New York: Benjamin Blom, 1964.

Bolden, Willie Miller. "The Political Structure of Charter Revision Movements in Atlanta during the Progressive Era." Ph.D. diss., Emory University, 1978.

Bowser, Eileen. *The Transformation of Cinema, 1907–1915.* Vol. 2 of *A History of the American Cinema,* edited by Charles Harpole. New York: Scribner's, 1990.

Brownell, Blaine A. *The Urban Ethos in the South, 1920–1930.* Baton Rouge: Louisiana State University Press, 1975.

———. "The Urban South Comes of Age, 1900–1940." In *The City in Southern History: The Growth of Urban Civilization in the South,* edited by Blaine A. Brownell and David R. Goldfield. Port Washington, N.Y.: Kennikat Press, 1977.

Brownell, Blaine A., and David R. Goldfield. "Southern Urban History." In *The City in Southern History: The Growth of Urban Civilization in the South,* edited by Blaine A. Brownell and David R. Goldfield. Port Washington, N.Y.: Kennikat Press, 1977.

Broyles, Michael. *"Music of the Highest Class": Elitism and Populism in Antebellum Boston.* New Haven, Conn.: Yale University Press, 1992.

Bryant, James C. "Yaraab Temple and the Fox Theatre: Survival of a Dream." *Atlanta History* 39, no. 2 (summer 1995): 5–22.

Budke, Timothy Daniel. "Assessing the 'Offense of Public Decency': The Advent of Censoring Particular Dramas on the New York Stage, 1890–1905." Ph.D. diss., University of Missouri–Columbia, 1989.

Burrison, John A. "Fiddlers in the Alley: Atlanta as an Early Country Music Center." *Atlanta Historical Bulletin* 21, no. 2 (summer 1977): 59–87.

Burton, Eldin. "The First Season of Metropolitan Opera Presentations (Music Festival of 1910)." *Atlanta Historical Bulletin* 4 (October 1930): 270–74.

———. "The Metropolitan Opera in Atlanta." *Atlanta Historical Bulletin* 5 (January 1940): 37–61.

———. "The Metropolitan Opera in Atlanta, Part 2." *Atlanta Historical Bulletin* 5 (April 1940): 146–69.

———. "The Metropolitan Opera in Atlanta, Part 3." *Atlanta Historical Bulletin* 5 (October 1940): 285–95.

———. "Music Festival of 1909." *Atlanta Historical Bulletin* 4 (July 1939): 199–202.

Campbell, Edward D. C., Jr. *The Celluloid South: Hollywood and the Southern Myth.* Knoxville: University of Tennessee Press, 1981.

Carlton, David L. *Mill and Town in South Carolina, 1880–1920.* Baton Rouge: Louisiana State University Press, 1982.

Charters, Samuel. "Workin' on the Building: Roots and Influences." In *Nothing but the Blues: The Music and the Musicians,* edited by Lawrence Cohn. New York: Abbeville Press, 1993.

"The City of Atlanta." *Harper's New Monthly Magazine* (December 1879–May 1880): 30–43.

Click, Patricia C. *The Spirit of the Times: Amusement in Nineteenth-Century Baltimore, Norfolk, and Richmond.* Charlottesville: University Press of Virginia, 1989.

Cohen, Norm. "Early Pioneers." In *Stars of Country Music: Uncle Dave Macon to Johnny Rodriguez,* edited by Bill C. Malone and Judith McCulloh. Urbana: University of Illinois Press, 1975.

———. "The Skillet Lickers: A Study of a Hillbilly String Band and Its Repertoire." *Journal of American Folklore* 78, no. 309 (July-September 1965): 229–44.

Cripps, Thomas. *Slow Fade to Black: The Negro in American Film.* New York: Oxford University Press, 1977.

Daniel, Wayne W. *Pickin' on Peachtree: A History of Country Music in Atlanta, Georgia.* Urbana: University of Illinois Press, 1990.

Davis, Benjamin J. *Communist Councilman from Harlem: Autobiographical Notes Written in a Federal Penitentiary.* New York: International Publishers, 1969.

Davis, Harold E. *Henry Grady's New South: A Brave and Beautiful City.* Tuscaloosa: University of Alabama Press, 1990.

Davis, Leroy. *A Clashing of the Soul: John Hope and the Dilemma of African American Leadership and Black Higher Education in the Early Twentieth Century.* Athens: University of Georgia Press, 1998.

Davis, Mary Roberts. "The Atlanta Industrial Exhibitions of 1881 and 1895: Expressions of the Philosophy of the New South." Master's thesis, Emory University, 1952.

Deaton, Thomas M. "Atlanta during the Progressive Era." Ph.D. diss., University of Georgia, 1969.

———. "James G. Woodward: The Working Man's Mayor." *Atlanta History* 31 (fall 1987): 11–23.

Dennett, Andrea Stulman. *Weird and Wonderful: The Dime Museum in America.* New York: New York University Press, 1997.

DiMeglio, John E. *Vaudeville, U.S.A.* Bowling Green, Ohio: Bowling Green University Press, 1973.

Dinnerstein, Leonard. *The Leo Frank Case.* New York: Columbia University Press, 1968.

Dittmer, John. *Black Georgia in the Progressive Era, 1900–1920.* Urbana: University of Illinois Press, 1977.

Dizikes, John. *Opera in America: A Cultural History.* New Haven, Conn.: Yale University Press, 1993.

Dorsey, Allison G. " 'To Build Our Lives Together': African American Community Formation in the Redeemed South, Atlanta, 1875–1906." Ph.D. diss., University of California, Irvine, 1995.

Doyle, Don H. *New Men, New Cities, New South: Atlanta, Nashville, Charleston, Mobile, 1860–1910.* Chapel Hill: University of North Carolina Press, 1990.

Eaton, Quaintance. *Opera Caravan: Adventures of the Metropolitan on Tour, 1883–1956.* New York: Da Capo, 1978.

Erenberg, Lewis A. *Steppin' Out: New York Nightlife and the Transformation of American Culture, 1890–1930.* Chicago: University of Chicago Press, 1981.

"The Fate of the Clansman." *Voice of the Negro* 3 (November 1906): 465.

Fort, Randolph L. "History of the *Atlanta Journal.*" Master's thesis, Emory University, 1930.

Fuller, Kathryn Helgeson. "Shadowland: American Audiences and the Movie-Going Experience in the Silent Film Era." Ph.D. diss., Johns Hopkins University, 1992.

Gaines, Kevin K. *Uplifting the Race: Black Leadership, Politics, and Culture in the Twentieth Century.* Chapel Hill: University of North Carolina Press, 1996.

Garofalo, Charles. "The Atlanta Spirit: A Study in Urban Ideology." *South Atlantic Quarterly* 74, no. 1 (winter 1975): 34–44.

Garrett, Franklin M. *Atlanta and Its Environs: A Chronicle of Its People and Events.* 3 vols. New York: Lewis Historical Publishing, 1954.

Gatewood, Willard B. *Aristocrats of Color: The Black Elite, 1880–1920.* Bloomington: Indiana University Press, 1990.

Godshalk, David Fort. "In the Wake of Riot: Atlanta's Struggle for Order, 1899–1919." Ph.D. diss., Yale University, 1992.

Golson, Graham. "The Accuracy of Atlanta Newspapers." Master's thesis, Emory University, 1938.

Gorn, Elliot J., and Warren Goldstein. *A Brief History of American Sports.* New York: Hill and Wang, 1993.

Gossett, Thomas F. *Uncle Tom's Cabin and American Culture.* Dallas: Southern Methodist University Press, 1985.

Gough, Peggy Malott. "Entertainment in Atlanta, Georgia, 1860–1870." Master's thesis, University of California, Santa Barbara, 1977.

Grant, Donald L. *The Way It Was in the South: The Black Experience in Georgia.* New York: Birch Lane Press, 1993.

Green, Archie. "Hillbilly Music: Source and Symbol." *Journal of American Folklore* 78, no. 309 (July-September 1965): 204–28.

Gue, Randy. "Nickel Madness: Atlanta's Storefront Theaters, 1906–1911." *Atlanta History* 43, no. 2 (summer 1999): 34–44.

Hanson, Patricia King, ed. *The American Film Institute Catalog of Motion Pictures Produced in the United States.* Vol. F1. Berkeley: University of California Press, 1988.

Harris, Michael W. *The Rise of Gospel Blues: The Music of Thomas Andrew Dorsey and the Urban Church.* New York: Oxford University Press, 1992.

Hickey, Georgina Susan. "'Meet Me at the Arcade': Women, Business, and Consumerism in Downtown Atlanta, 1917–1964." *Atlanta History* 40, nos. 3–4 (fall-winter 1996–1997): 5–15.

———. "Visibility, Politics, and Urban Development: Working-Class Women in Early-Twentieth-Century Atlanta." Ph.D. diss., University of Michigan, 1995.

———. "Waging War on 'Loose Living Hotels' and 'Cheap Soda Water Joints': The Criminalization of Working-Class Women in Atlanta's Public Space." *Georgia Historical Quarterly* 82, no. 4 (winter 1998): 775–800.

Higginbotham, Evelyn Brooks. *Righteous Discontent: The Women's Movement in the Black Baptist Church, 1880–1920.* Cambridge: Harvard University Press, 1993.

Hitchcock, W. Wiley, and Stanley Sadie, eds. *The New Grove Dictionary of American Music.* Vol. 1. London: MacMillan Press, 1986.

Hoggart, Richard. *The Uses of Literacy: Changing Patterns in English Mass Culture.* Fair Lawn, N.J.: Essential Books, 1957.

Hopkins, Richard J. "Status, Mobility, and the Dimensions of Change in a Southern City: Atlanta, 1870–1910." In *Cities in American History,* edited by Kenneth T. Jackson and Stanley K. Schultz. New York: Knopf, 1972.

Hunter, Tera W. *To 'Joy My Freedom: Southern Black Women's Lives and Labors after the Civil War.* Cambridge: Harvard University Press, 1997.

Inman, Arthur Crew. *The Inman Diary: A Public and Private Confession.* Edited by Daniel Aaron. 2 vols. Cambridge: Harvard University Press, 1985.

Ivey, Bill. "Border Crossing: A Different Way of Listening to American Music." In *From Where I Stand: The Black Experience in Country Music.* Country Music Foundation compact discs 9 46428–2.

Jackson, Kenneth T. *The Ku Klux Klan in the City, 1915–1930.* New York: Oxford University Press, 1967.

Judson, Sarah. "Cultivating Citizenship in the Kindergartens of Atlanta, 1890s–1920s." *Atlanta History* 41, no. 4 (winter 1998): 17–30.

Kasson, John F. *Rudeness and Civility: Manners in Nineteenth-Century Urban America.* New York: Hill and Wang, 1990.

Kelkres, Gene G. "A Forgotten First: The Armat-Jenkins Partnership and the Atlanta Projection." *Quarterly Review of Film Studies* 9 (winter 1984): 45–58.

Kuhn, Clifford, Harlon E. Joye, and E. Bernard West. *Living Atlanta: An Oral History of the City, 1914–1948.* Athens: University of Georgia Press, 1990.

Kuszarski, Richard. *An Evening's Entertainment: The Age of the Silent Feature Picture, 1915–1928.* Vol. 3 of *A History of the American Cinema,* edited by Charles Harpole. New York: Scribner's, 1990.

Levine, Lawrence W. *Black Culture and Black Consciousness: Afro-American Folk Thought from Slavery to Freedom.* New York: Oxford University Press, 1977.

———. *Highbrow/Lowbrow: The Emergence of Cultural Hierarchy in America.* Cambridge: Harvard University Press, 1988.

Lowry, Pete. "Atlanta Black Sound: A Survey of Black Music from Atlanta during the Twentieth Century." *Atlanta Historical Bulletin* 21, no. 2 (summer 1977): 88–113.

Lynes, Russell. *The Lively Audience: A Social History of the Visual and Performing Arts in America, 1890–1950.* New York: Harper and Row, 1985.

Maclachlan, Gretchen Ehrmann. "Atlanta's Industrial Women, 1879–1920." *Atlanta History* 36, no. 4 (winter 1993): 16–23.

———. "Women's Work: Atlanta's Industrialization and Urbanization, 1879–1929." Ph.D. diss., Emory University, 1992.

Maclean, Nancy. "The Leo Frank Case Reconsidered: Gender and Sexual Politics in the Making of Reactionary Populism." *Journal of American History* 78, no. 3 (December 1991): 917–45.

Malone, Bill C. *Singing Cowboys and Musical Mountaineers: Southern Culture and the Roots of Country Music.* Athens: University of Georgia Press, 1993.

———. *Southern Music, American Music.* Lexington: University Press of Kentucky, 1979.

Mann, William J. "The Movies Come to Middletown: The Cinematic Experience of a Small Town, 1897–1917." Master's thesis, Wesleyan University, 1987.

Martin, Harold H. "The Biggest Event Since Sherman's March." *Georgia Trend* 1, no. 3 (November 1985): 91–94.

May, Lary. *Screening Out the Past: The Birth of Mass Culture and the Motion Picture Industry.* New York: Oxford University Press, 1980.

McArthur, Benjamin. *Actors and American Culture, 1880–1920.* Philadelphia: Temple University Press, 1984.

McElreath, Walter. *Walter McElreath: An Autobiography.* Edited by Albert B. Saye. Macon, Ga.: Mercer University Press, 1984.

——. "When Atlanta Was Just a Big Town." *Atlanta Historical Bulletin* 8 (October 1948): 82–88.

McLean, Albert F. *American Vaudeville as Ritual.* Lexington: University Press of Kentucky, 1965.

McNamara, Brooks. "'A Congress of Wonders'": The Rise and Fall of the Dime Museum." *ESQ* 20 (1974): 216–32.

Meier, August, and David Lewis. "History of the Negro Upper Class in Atlanta, Georgia, 1890–1958." *Journal of Negro Education* 28 (spring 1959): 128–39.

Merrit, Russel. "Nickelodeon Theaters, 1905–1914: Building an Audience for the Movies." In *The American Film Industry,* edited by Tino Balio. Madison: University of Wisconsin Press, 1985.

Minnix, Kathleen. "The Atlanta Revivals of Sam Jones: Evangelist of the New South." *Atlanta History* 33 (spring 1989): 5–34.

——. *Laughter in the Amen Corner: The Life of Evangelist Sam Jones.* Athens: University of Georgia Press, 1993.

Mixon, Gregory L. "The Atlanta Riot of 1906." Ph.D. diss., University of Cincinnati, 1989.

Moore, John Hammond. "The Negro and Prohibition in Atlanta, 1885–1887." *South Atlantic Quarterly* 69 (winter 1970): 38–57.

Musser, Charles. *The Emergence of Cinema: The American Screen to 1907.* Vol. 1 of *A History of the American Cinema,* edited by Charles Harpole. New York: Scribner's, 1990.

Nasaw, David. *Going Out: The Rise and Fall of Public Amusements.* New York: Basic Books, 1993.

Neverdon-Morton, Cynthia. *Afro-American Women and the Advancement of the Race.* Knoxville: University of Tennessee Press, 1989.

Newman, Harvey Knupp. *Southern Hospitality: Tourism and the Growth of Atlanta.* Tuscaloosa: University of Alabama Press, 1999.

——. "The Vision of Order: White Protestant Christianity in Atlanta, 1865–1906." Ph.D. diss., Emory University, 1977.

Orr, N. Lee. *Alfredo Barili and the Rise of Classical Music in Atlanta.* Atlanta: Scholars Press, 1996.

Parker, David Bryce, Jr. "Bill Arp: Homely Philosophy and the New South." Ph.D. diss., University of North Carolina, Chapel Hill, 1988.

Perry, Claudia. "Digging Country's Roots." In *From Where I Stand: The Black*

Experience in Country Music. Country Music Foundation compact discs 9 46428-2.

Poggi, Jack. *Theater in America: The Impact of Economic Forces, 1870–1967.* Ithaca, N.Y.: Cornell University Press, 1968.

Porter, Michael Leroy. "Black Atlanta: An Interdisciplinary Study of Blacks on the East Side of Atlanta, 1890–1930." Ph.D. diss., Emory University, 1974.

Preston, Howard L. *Automobile Age Atlanta: The Making of a Southern Metropolis, 1900–1935.* Athens: University of Georgia Press, 1979.

———. "A New Kind of Horizontal City: Automobility in Atlanta, 1900–1930." Ph.D. diss., Emory University, 1974.

Proctor, Henry Hugh. *Between Black and White: Autobiographical Sketches.* 1925. Reprint, Freeport, N.Y.: Books for Libraries Press, 1971.

Rabinowitz, Howard N. "Continuity and Change: Southern Urban Development, 1860–1900." In *The City in Southern History: The Growth of Urban Civilization in the South,* edited by Blaine A. Brownell and David R. Goldfield. Port Washington, N.Y.: Kennikat Press, 1977.

Reardon, William R. "The American Drama and Theatre in the Nineteenth Century: A Retreat from Meaning." *ESQ* 20 (1970): 170–86.

"Rev. Dr. Broughton Versus Stage Manager Dixon." *Voice of the Negro* 2 (November 1905): 871–72.

Riess, Steven A. *Sport in Industrial America, 1850–1920.* Wheeling, Ill.: Harlan Davidson, 1995.

Rolinson, Mary Gambrell. "Community and Leadership in the First Twenty Years of the Atlanta NAACP, 1917–1937." *Atlanta History* 42, no. 3 (fall 1998): 5–21.

Roth, Darlene R. *Matronage: Patterns of Women's Organizations, Atlanta, Georgia, 1890–1940.* Brooklyn: Carlson Publishing, 1994.

Rouse, Jacqueline Anne. *Lugenia Burns Hope: Black Southern Reformer.* Athens: University of Georgia Press, 1989.

Russell, James Michael. *Atlanta, 1847–1890: City Building in the Old South and the New.* Baton Rouge: Louisiana State University Press, 1988.

Rydell, Robert W. *All the World's a Fair: Visions of Empire at American International Expositions, 1876–1916.* Chicago: University of Chicago Press, 1984.

Sampson, Henry T. *The Ghost Walks: A Chronological History of Blacks in Show Business, 1865–1910.* Metuchen, N.J.: Scarecrow Press, 1988.

Sklar, Robert. *Movie-Made America: A Cultural History of American Movies.* New York: Vintage Books, 1975.

Snyder, Robert W. *The Voice of the City: Vaudeville and Popular Culture in New York.* New York: Oxford University Press, 1989.

Spottswood, Richard K. "Country Girls, Classic Blues, and Vaudeville Voices:

Women and the Blues." In *Nothing but the Blues: The Music and the Musicians,* edited by Lawrence Cohn. New York: Abbeville Press, 1993.

"The Staging of the Clansman." *Voice of the Negro* 2 (November 1905): 836–37.

Street, Julian. *American Adventures: A Second Trip "Abroad at Home."* New York: The Century Company, 1917.

Taylor, Arthur Reed. "From the Ashes: Atlanta during Reconstruction, 1865–1876." Ph.D. diss., Emory University, 1973.

Thornberry, Jerry John. "The Development of Black Atlanta, 1865–1885." Ph.D. diss., University of Maryland, 1977.

Toll, Robert C. *Blacking Up: The Minstrel Show in Nineteenth-Century America.* New York: Oxford University Press, 1974.

———. *On with the Show: The First Century of Show Business in America.* New York: Oxford University Press, 1976.

Wade, Wyn Craig. *The Fiery Cross: The Ku Klux Klan in America.* New York: Simon and Schuster, 1987.

Waller, Gregory A. *Main Street Amusements: Movies and Commercial Entertainment in a Southern City, 1896–1930.* Washington, D.C.: Smithsonian Institution Press, 1995.

Watson-Powers, Lynn. "The Atlanta Spirit: What Is It?" *Atlanta History* 37, no. 3 (fall 1993): 83–93.

Watts, Eugene J. "The Police in Atlanta, 1890–1905." *Journal of Southern History* 39, no. 2 (May 1973): 165–82.

Whisnant, David E. *All That Is Native and Fine: The Politics of Culture in an American Region.* Chapel Hill: University of North Carolina Press, 1983.

White, Walter. *A Man Called White.* New York: Arno Press; the *New York Times,* 1969.

Wiggins, Gene. *Fiddlin' Georgia Crazy: Fiddlin' John Carson, His Real World, and the World of His Songs.* Urbana: University of Illinois Press, 1987.

Wilson, Charles Reagan. *Baptized in Blood: The Religion of the Lost Cause, 1865–1920.* Athens: University of Georgia Press, 1980.

Wolfe, Charles. "A Lighter Shade of Blue: White Country Blues." In *Nothing but the Blues: The Music and the Musicians,* edited by Lawrence Cohen. New York: Abbeville Press, 1993.

Woodward, C. Vann. *Origins of the New South, 1877–1913.* Baton Rouge: Louisiana State University Press, 1971.

Index